To Tirion,

With best wishes,

Janet Sully.

9th. July, 2010.

HOWELL'S SCHOOL, LLANDAFF 1860-2010

A Legacy Fulfilled

HOWELL'S SCHOOL, LLANDAFF 1860-2010

A Legacy Fulfilled

JANET SULLY

Howell's School, Llandaff (GDST)

© Howell's School, Llandaff (GDST)
First published 2010
ISBN 978 0 9565686 0 1

Published by Howell's School, Llandaff (GDST)

Author: Janet Sully
Designer: Andrew Griffiths

Printed in Europe by Xpedient Print Services

Picture Acknowledgements
The school is grateful to those listed below for granting permission to use images from their collections:
Glamorgan Archives 22 (bottom right, ref.DL52/4), 23 (both, ref.DL52/4), 37 (top and centre right, ref DHOW1);
Media Wales Ltd 104, 106 (top and centre), 109 (top), 158 (centre and bottom right), 166.

CONTENTS

FOREWORD

The first history of the school, *Thomas Howell and the School at Llandaff, 1860-1890*, written by Jean McCann, provided an invaluable record of the school's development during a formative period of its history. Janet Sully, who has taught for many years at Howell's in the History and Classics departments, has extended Jean McCann's research to produce this new and exciting record which documents the school's history to the present day. An experienced and talented historian, Mrs Sully has compiled an illuminating insight into the life of Howell's and its community; for this we, and future generations, are in her debt.

Mrs Sully's book is a fascinating social history and details what was achieved by previous Headmistresses in times when education for women was not universally valued; she has managed to capture the individuality and spirit of Howell's through a wealth of illustrated material.

I should like to take this opportunity to extend our grateful thanks to the Drapers' Company, with whom we have always had very strong links and who still support the school in many ways today. Thomas Howell's legacy has been amply fulfilled, as this book so fully documents.

Howell's School faces the future and the next 150 years with optimism. We look forward to meeting the challenges that educating young people in the 21st Century and beyond will bring.

Sally Davis
Principal
March 2010

ACKNOWLEDGEMENTS

The idea of writing this book derived from the approach of the one hundred and fiftieth anniversary of Howell's School, Llandaff, and I am grateful to the former and current Principals, Mrs Jane Fitz and Mrs Sally Davis, for encouraging me to undertake the task. It is not the first publication on the history of the school. A booklet was written for the Centenary Year in 1960 and a detailed account of its origins and the first thirty years, *Thomas Howell and the School at Llandaff, 1860-1890*, written by Dr Jean Redfearn, was published under her maiden name of Jean McCann in 1972. The school is fortunate to possess extensive archives, including a complete set of Governors' Minutes from the first meeting in November 1859 to the present, which are, as the Headmistress Miss Trotter wrote in 1930, "the history of the school". In order to be able to locate the materials readily it has been necessary to undertake the massive task of organising the archives and I owe a great debt to those who have given me assistance in doing this, especially Jean Ballinger and Sue Rayner (née Davies).

The interviewing of some fascinating Hywelians, ranging in age from eighteen to five months short of one hundred, gave me enormous pleasure, and I am most grateful to Marguerite Desmond (Milner), Catherine Powell (Morgan), Patricia Kernick, Elizabeth Jones (Kernick), Barbara Forte (Meeling), Beryl Lowman (Box), Mary Lister (Williams), Sharon Spackman (Pritchard) and Claire Spackman. My thanks go to Anne Bryan, Siân Griffiths and Liz Jenkins for arranging some of these meetings. Christine Grint kindly agreed to interview her mother, Dorothy Wickett, in Cornwall on my behalf. Fortunately, the recollections of other pupils from the early days of the school have survived in old school and Hywelian magazines and surviving letters. These all provide a flavour of different periods in a way that formal written accounts are unable to do. The possible errors in such kinds of evidence are well known but I have endeavoured to check the accuracy of the factual information as far as possible, and the testimony provided unwittingly is itself also of value and interest. My main challenge has been to condense a huge amount of information into a manageable length and structure for inclusion in one book. This has posed difficult problems of selection and inevitably much material has had to be omitted or greatly abbreviated.

I greatly appreciate the time and effort taken by Hywelians who have recorded their reminiscences in writing: Ruth Campbell (Sully), Katy Chantrey (Webster), Nicola Davies (Salter), Sheila Hinton (Sharman), Rosemary Lee (Day), Lydia Lewis, Karen Plambeck (Millar), Sue Rayner, Joyce Shields (Bingham), Eira Smith (Jones) and Debbie Ward (Buss). At the Hywelian summer lunch in 2009, a number of boarders from the 1980s were also willing to put some jottings on paper, and Lydia Phillips, Bronwen Warner and Priyantha Kulatilake have offered their thoughts on life at Howell's in 2010. Sadly, a former pupil who was keen to share her memories, Joyce Davey (Hoffman), died in 2009 aged 97, just before I was due to interview her. Fortunately, Joyce Shields had visited her in 2005 and written an account of her recollections. Another sad loss, in June 2009, was that of my former colleague, Dorothy Bowen; she had shown interest in this project and, as a Hywelian, member of staff and historian, had a tremendous store of useful knowledge. I am pleased that we have her recollections of life at school during the Second World War, recorded in 2006 for the Centenary of the Hywelian Guild, and I am grateful to Daisy Gibbs for sending me a copy of the recording.

The majority of the photographs, diagrams and plans come from the school archives. Other photographs were kindly supplied by Jane Bryant, Katy Chantrey, Julia Davage (Full), Liz Jenkins, Elizabeth Jones, Rosemary Lee, Catherine Powell, Sue Rayner, Joyce Shields and Daphne West (Moore), or were taken by me. I am grateful to the Glamorgan Archivist, Susan Edwards, for giving me permission to print copies of photographs of mid-nineteenth century Llandaff and of a Cathedral seating plan of 1860, which are held in the Glamorgan Record Office. Tony Woolway, the Chief Librarian at Media Wales, kindly sent scans of photographs of the fire of 1932 and of girls on the front driveway in 1964 and on The Green in 1973. Penny Fussell, the Archivist at Drapers' Hall, willingly produced the documents I required, allowed me to take photographs and answered questions. Ruth Price sent the letters written to her grandmother in 1908 and her school report of 1909. Others who have helped in a variety of ways include Ian Beckett, Carol Davies, Maggie Fletcher, Gaynor Howard, Miyuki Nagayama, Carol Phillips and Margaret Seager. All these, and others who have responded to queries, I thank wholeheartedly.

Finally, I am indebted to Alex Christ, Anne Eddy and Sue Rayner for their proof-reading and helpful comments on the text, and to Andrew Griffiths, who has given useful advice and worked with great dedication on the design. Joyce Shields has responded promptly to all sorts of requests for help and given words of encouragement; she also provided me with the idea for the subtitle of the book. Thanks to their efforts, a number of errors and ambiguities have been eliminated, but any which remain are my responsibility. For me, the whole experience has been pleasurable and rewarding, and I hope that everyone with an interest in the school will gain as much enjoyment from reading it as I have from producing it.

Janet Sully
March 2010

HEADMISTRESSES 1860-2010

Miss Emily Baldwin
1860-1872

Miss Letitia Ewing
1872-1880

Miss Maria Kendall
1880-1920

Miss Eleanor Trotter
1920-1937

Miss Edith Knight
1937-1941

Miss Margaret Lewis
1941-1977

Miss Jill Turner
1978-1991

Mrs Jane Fitz*
1991-2007

Mrs Sally Davis**
2007-

*designated Principal 2005

**Principal

HEAD GIRLS

1888-9	Hester Bellamy	1942-43	Alison Rees	1976-77	Elizabeth Mullins
1893-4	Gertrude Kathleen Robertson	1943-44	Alison Rees	1977-78	Hilary Prescott
1909-10	Alice Dorothy Harris	1944-45	Marianne Phillips	1978-79	Jane Stevens
1910-11	Margaret Herbert	1945-46	Lynette Jones	1979-80	Lisa Williams
1911-12	Dorothy Hopkin	1946-47	Dorothy Rees	1980-81	Siân Roberts
1912-13	Gwladys Randall	1947-48	Dorothy Evans	1981-82	Louise Rees
1913-14	Gwladys Randall	1948-49	Zoe Richards	1982-83	Jayne Watkins
1914-15	Gwladys Randall	1949-50	Rosemary Morris	1983-84	Ceri Godwin
1915-16	Gwyneth David	1950-51	Ann Rudge	1984-85	Cathryn McGahey
1916-17	Margaret John	1951-52	Adrienne Timothy	1985-86	Ceri Williams
1917-18	Hannah Reynolds	1952-53	Tessa Willan	1986-87	Suzanne Bruton
1918-19	Dilys Cussans	1953-54	Janie Moon	1987-88	Carolyn Hurcom
1919-20	Eluned Saunders	1954-55	Kathleen Helliwell	1988-89	Madeleine Pill
1920-21	Dorothy Harrison	1955-56	Anna Sinclair	1989-90	Joanna Smith
1921-22	Mary Hewart Jones	1956-57	Judith Beynon	1990-91	Julia Haworth
1922-23	Joyce West	1957-58	Vivienne Jones	1991-92	Anna Bicarregui
	Ruth Frewer	1958-59	Elaine Marshall	1992-93	Sapna Shah
1924-25	Verna Reynolds	1959-60	Eira Shapcott	1993-94	Abigail Underwood
1925-26	Hilda Thomas	1960-61	Janice Couzens	1994-95	Shona Power
1926-27	Margaret Charters	1961-62	Gillian Lewis	1995-96	Sarah Finlay
1928-29	Edwina Harrison	1962-63	Madeline Hayward	1996-97	Geeta Iyer
	Elizabeth Jones	1963-64	Lynne Bailey	1997-98	Eira Jones
1929-30	Nest Phillips		Margaret Price	1998-99	Cristina Crunelli
	Grace Harris	1964-6	Glenys James	1999-2000	Dionne Antrobus
1930-31	Elizabeth Jones	1965-66	Ester Williams	2000-01	Kate Beresford
1931-32	Kathleen Cossens	1966-67	Janet Elizabeth Jermine	2001-02	Catherine Penny
1932-33	Audrey Turner	1967-68	Mary Foreman	2002-03	Danielle Trcharne
1933-34	Megan Anthony	1968-69	Megan Emery	2003-04	Charlotte Bendon
1934-35	Doreen King	1969-70	Janet Hay	2004-05	Khushboo Sinha
	Mary David	1970-71	Jane Chubb	2005-06	Furat Ashraf
1935-36	Margaret Roberts	1971-72	Jane Rosser	2006-07	Lucy Allanby
1936-37	Patricia Green		Anne Rees	2007-08	Lydia Lewis
1937-38	Dorothy Eyre Evans	1972-73	Helen Beeson	2008-09	Eleri Davies
1938-39	Mary Gwynne Jones	1973-74	Frances Gray	2009-10	Bronwen Warner
1939-40	Dulcie King	1974-75	Linda Mitchell		
1940-41	Dorette Gould	1975-76	Beatrice Trotman-Dickenson		
1941-42	Dorette Gould				

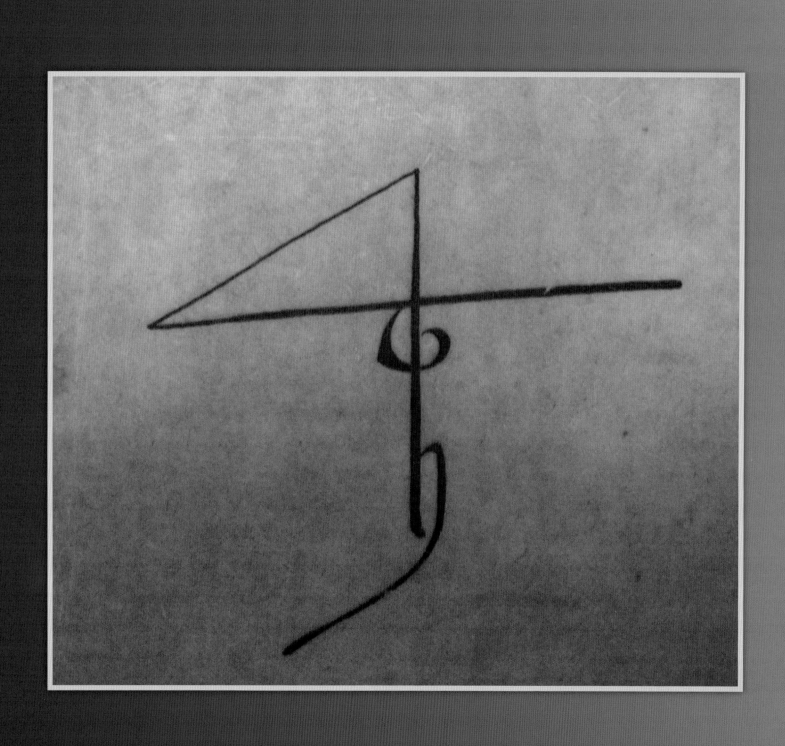

1

THOMAS HOWELL AND THE ORIGINS OF THE SCHOOL

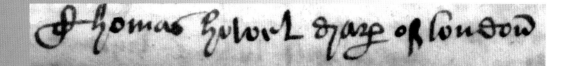

Facing page
*Thomas Howell's merchant's mark,
from the front of his ledger.*

Above: Thomas Howell's signature.

'I command my executors that . . . after my death, they do send to the city of London 12,000 ducats of gold . . . to deliver to the House called Drapers' Hall – to deliver them to the Wardens thereof; and the said Wardens, as soon as they have received the same 12,000 ducats to buy therewith 400 ducats of rent yearly for evermore – in possession for evermore. And it is my will, that the said 400 ducats be disposed of unto four maidens, being orphans – next of my kin and of blood – to their marriage – if they can be found – every one of them to have 100 ducats – and if they cannot be found of my lineage, then to be given to four other maidens . . . honest of good fame, and every of them 100 ducats – and so every year, to marry four maidens for ever. And if the same 12,000 ducats will buy more land then the said 12,000 ducats to be spent to the marriage of maidens, being orphans, increasing the four maidens aforesaid as shall seem by the discretion aforesaid of the Master and Wardens of the said House of Drapers' Hall.'

From the third will of Thomas Howell, 1536.

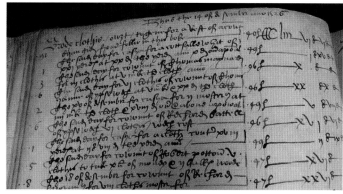

This school for the board clothing and education of orphan girls was erected in the year 1859 by the Drapers' Company of the City of London out of funds bequeathed to them by Thomas Howell one of their members who died at Seville in Spain Anno Domini 1537.

There can be few current or former members of Howell's School, Llandaff, who are unaware that it was a bequest of 12,000 ducats in the last will of Thomas Howell, a Tudor merchant, which led, more than three hundred years after his death, to the founding of the school which bears his name. It may, however, come as a surprise to learn that he never lived in Wales. He was almost certainly born in Bristol in 1485, coincidentally the year of the accession of the first Tudor monarch, Henry VII, whose promotion of Anglo-Spanish trade links made his wealth possible. Nevertheless, Thomas's family links with Wales were strong, his paternal grandfather being Hywel ap Rhys ap Hywel Grono. His father John, a merchant, died when he and his brother Clement were young, and his mother Alice subsequently formed a relationship with Sir Thomas Morgan, Knight, who owned three small estates in Monmouthshire. Whether or not Thomas and Alice married is uncertain but it is known that Alice had two more sons before she died in 1505.

Thomas Howell began his many years of sailing between England and Spain as an apprentice to a wealthy Bristol merchant, Hugh Elyot. By the time he was in his mid-twenties, he had moved to London in search of greater opportunities. He became a Freeman of the Drapers' Company, partly through his association with the powerful Sir William Roche, who was its Master on six occasions. Thomas joined the Company, which had been granted its first royal charter in 1364, at a time when its fortunes were running very high, as a result of the expansion of the woollen cloth trade in the later Middle Ages. Its wealth is denoted by the ram with the golden fleece on the Company's Coat of Arms, which is sculpted above the door of the wing to the side of the school's main entrance.

An ambitious and resourceful young man, Thomas built up trade with places as diverse as Seville, Bordeaux, Calais, Danzig and the Indies. He imported raisins, alum, soap, iron, oil, grain powder, satin, damask and wine. However, his chief business was with Spain and Portugal, exporting cloth, both dyed and undyed, which was made mainly by clothiers in the south and east of England. His business links with Spain developed at a most opportune time. England had not then been affected by the great inflation which had hit Spain, so he was able to make great profits by buying goods at pre-inflationary prices in England and then selling them at the higher Spanish prices. He amassed property in London, Hampshire and Essex. In 1521 he became a Liveryman of the Company and in 1527 Junior Warden. He married during the 1520s; his wife, Joanna, probably came from the family named Christian, which had links with the Drapers' Company.

Top: Inscription above main entrance door.
Above: Broadcloth entry in Thomas Howell's ledger, 1520s.
Left: Drapers' Company crest over door of wing by main entrance.

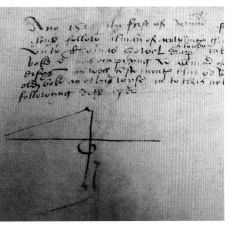

Left: Thomas Howell's ledger.
Above: First entry in the ledger, 1522.
Below right: Seville, c.1510.

Above: Page in the ledger showing debts owed to Thomas Howell.
This begins: The detts that both unto me Thomas Howel in Yngland takyn owzt of the balans in the side per contra

Thomas Owen Jentillman of Pembrocke	£10	0	0
Hewgh Elliot merchant of Bristow	£4	0	0
Thomas Barkar of Collchester broker	£1	12	0

Thomas Howell's ledger, which recorded his transactions from 1517 to 1528 in minute detail, is a most valuable document. Apart from providing the earliest example of double entry book-keeping in English, to economic historians it is the most useful source for the study of Anglo-Spanish trade as it is one of only two surviving examples of account books for trade between England, Spain and the New World. The main entries begin in 1522 but Thomas recorded earlier transactions retrospectively. As time went on, it became more than a mere ledger, recording, for example, information about other people and a list of his wife's jewellery. It therefore serves also as a social document and provides detailed evidence of the life and work of a merchant draper in the 1520s.

By 1528 the deteriorating relationship between England and Spain, caused largely by Henry VIII's desire to annul his marriage to his Spanish wife Catherine of Aragon, was having an adverse effect on trade. Since by then almost all Thomas Howell's business was with Spain, he made the decision to move there permanently, leaving Joanna to look after their London home and to supervise his English interests. Sadly she died, childless, only two years after his move.

In Seville, where he lived in a rented house near the port, he began a new ledger, while his agents continued to be busy buying and selling at the great European fairs. As well as being wealthy and ambitious, he appears to have undertaken all his duties conscientiously and to have been generous, pious and scrupulously honest. His wills also show him to have been a great philanthropist and, of course, without his legacy, Howell's School would not have come into being.

Thomas Howell is known to have made three wills, in 1520, 1528 and 1536. The first two, written in English, show his charitable concerns. In his second will he expressed a desire to have his London house in Tower Street enlarged to provide accommodation for forty fatherless or motherless children who were to wear bills on their back and chest labelled *Howell*. His last will, which was extremely lengthy and written in Castilian Spanish, was made when he realised that his health was failing; he died a few months later, in 1537. The lion's share of his estate was left to charity as he had no close family, his only full brother, Clement, having drowned. The will included a bequest of 2,000 ducats for the poor of Bristol. Most importantly, he left 12,000 ducats to be held in trust by the Drapers' Company to provide dowries, the equivalent of £21 each, to four orphan maidens every year, of his lineage if they could be found and, if not, to four other maidens of good name. His intention was to protect the orphans against destitution. If the investment of the 12,000 ducats produced more than 400 ducats a year, then the Draper Wardens were to decide how best to deal with the surplus in providing the dowries. This charitable endowment for marriage subsidies was by far the largest in the sixteenth century.

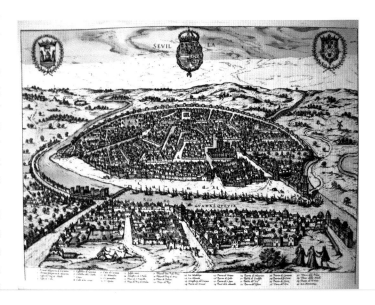

Above left: Reference to orphan children ("children that be fatherless and motherless") in Howell's will of 1527.
Left: Request in the 1527 will that orphans' clothing should be marked Howel.

Above: Information panel on Drapers' Hall.
Below: Company's Coat of Arms over main door of Drapers' Hall.

The Masters and Wardens of the Drapers' Company managed many trusts and benefactions during this period but the worry and expense relating to Thomas Howell's Trust was by far the greatest, largely because of the difficulty in finding maidens of his kin. Numerous problems arose in carrying out the terms of the will, ranging from the Spanish authorities being unwilling to send any part of the legacy to England (as they refused to recognise any power of attorney which referred to Henry VIII as Supreme Head of the Church in England) to fraudulent claims, which once led to the perpetrators being put in the pillory. Describing the complications, the Reverend A H Johnson was moved to write in 1915, "In short, the history of Howell's legacy is a warning to would-be benefactors never to leave portions to marriageable maidens, especially if they be Welsh." Most of the legacy did eventually reach England, the first instalment being shipped in the form of oil and wine. It was invested in the purchase of valuable land and houses, including Thomas Cromwell's former home in Throgmorton Street, which Henry VIII had confiscated from him and then sold to the Drapers' Company for their Hall. The building has been completely destroyed twice since then, once in the Great Fire of London in 1666 and again in a serious fire in 1772.

The first orphan dowries were granted in March 1544 to Margaret and Joan Christian. Details of the legacy were advertised in Bristol but it was subsequently claimed that the pedigree sent by its Mayor in support of some recipients was erroneous, they being "neither maidens nor orphans". Rivalry arose between two families of claimants, those of a Bristol brewer also named Thomas Howell, and a Monmouthshire farmer, Howell ap Thomas, who was supported by the county gentry. Deputations supporting the two sides presented themselves at Drapers' Hall but the brewer died before the case came to court, leaving Monmouthshire the winner by default. Consequently, almost all the orphans (over 1,200) who received dowries during the next three hundred years came from

Monmouthshire, the last being Elizabeth Odam from Michaelston-y-Fedw, who claimed her £21 in 1849 at the age of. thirty-three.

The first mention of Llandaff came in 1559. After four female orphans alleged that the Drapers' Company had not acted properly, the Court of Chancery decreed that the Bishop of Llandaff (or the Dean and Chapter) – in whose diocese Monmouthshire lay – should make out a certificate of a certain pedigree or "herbal" and deliver it to the Master and Wardens of the Drapers' Company, in order to prove that they were the next of kin of Thomas Howell. Another order in 1593 directed that the certificate should be made by two, three or four Justices of the Peace in Monmouthshire as well as the Bishop.

By the mid-nineteenth century, questions were being raised. The annual income from the Trust's estates had risen from about £105 to over £2,000 and yet it was still only providing four dowries of £21 a year. In addition, by the 1840s it was considered that a good education rather than a marriage was the best protection against

Left: Alfred Ollivant, Bishop of Llandaff 1849-82.
Above: Letter of Herbert Williams to William Sawyer, Clerk to the Drapers' Company, 8th December, 1858.

Facing page
Herbert Williams' drawing, 1859.

destitution. A court case in 1845 led to the judgement that all the income from the Trust must be used to carry out the purposes of the charity, at least in spirit, and in 1852 an Act was passed to establish two boarding schools in Wales "for the Education and Advancement of deserving Orphan Maidens". The Drapers' Company was directed to purchase ten acres of land in both North and South Wales. The diocese of Llandaff was to have priority in terms of location and size of the Foundation, and the two dioceses in which the schools were built were to have their Bishop as Chairman of the Governors. Since Thomas Howell's first two wills provided for orphan children to be cared for and educated in his London home, he would undoubtedly have been satisfied that his intentions were being carried out. In addition, the existence of a Portion and Endowment Fund, set up to provide marriage portions of £100 for orphans educated at the Howell's Schools, fulfilled his desire in his final will to provide dowries. The idea was also to have pay boarders and day pupils, who would make the schools economically viable and ensure that they would not simply be seen as other orphanages.

In the autumn of 1852, John Fearon, the Solicitor to the Attorney General, set off with his friend, the architect Decimus Burton, to inspect six possible sites. In South Wales, Llandaff was deemed to have more to recommend it than Abergavenny, Usk or Swansea. To a large extent it was the influence of Alfred Ollivant, the Bishop of Llandaff, supported by Sir Thomas Phillips, a former Mayor of Newport and landed proprietor in Herefordshire and Monmouthshire, which swayed that decision. Denbigh was chosen in preference to Ruthin in North Wales. Finally, on 23rd March 1853, the Scheme for the Extension of Howell's Charity

received Chancery approval. The first Governors, in both Llandaff and Denbigh, were to be appointed by the Court of Chancery and subsequently, as vacancies arose, by the Drapers' Company.

Even then, proceedings did not advance smoothly. The Llandaff site consisted of seven fields, of which four were leased for pasture, two were under the plough and the seventh was a garden attached to the estate of Bishop's Court. There were delays in purchasing it from the Ecclesiastical Commissioners, who had bought it to prevent it from falling into speculative builders' hands. The Drapers were aggrieved: they had been consulted over neither the choice of site nor the architect. They considered Burton's designs far too lavish and he, having sent them a bill and three sets of plans, declared that he would have nothing more to do with the project. Certain modifications were subsequently made by the Company's surveyor, Herbert Williams. In April 1857, the contract for building was signed by a representative of the successful contractors, John Barnsley and Sons of Birmingham, and the building work at last began on 1st May 1858. Further delays were caused by a strike of Barnsley's employees, complications over drainage and lack of a water supply. The last unfortunate incident occurred when a mason, Stephen Thomas, fell forty feet to his death from a loose scaffold plank. The building and furnishings at Llandaff cost altogether £22,653, compared with £18,980 for the school at Denbigh. At last, more than three hundred years after the death of Thomas Howell, ten newly-appointed Governors arrived at the new school at Llandaff on 29th November 1859 for their very first meeting and the formal transfer of the building to their hands. It was to open its doors to sixty pupils eight months later, on 1st August 1860.

2

CARDIFF, LLANDAFF AND EDUCATION IN THE MID-NINETEENTH CENTURY

Facing page
Map showing part of Cardiff, 1851, before the development of the 19th century castle.

Right: John Speed's map of Llandaff, 1610.

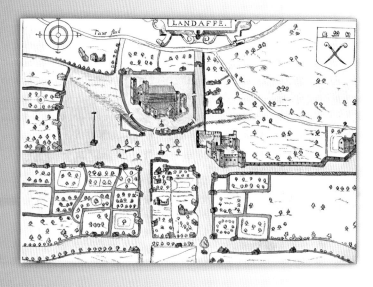

Left: Llandaff Cathedral in 1778, before restoration.
Below left: Llandaff Cathedral in about 1860, after restoration.
Below: Bridge Street, Llandaff, looking towards Llandaff Green, mid-19th century.

Facing page
Top: Llandaff High Street in the mid-19th century. The building with the rose window is the old Junior School, with the Butcher's Arms beyond.
Below: The Castle from Llandaff Green, mid-19th century.

At the time Howell's School was founded, Cardiff's population had been expanding rapidly, from a mere 4,600 in 1801 to 32,431 by the time of the 1861 census. The export of coal and the growth of the docks and railways had led to a huge influx of labourers looking for work. Inevitably, in the heart of the town there were attendant problems of overcrowding, poverty and disease, notably typhus and cholera in the 1840s. By 1860, however, it was a much more pleasant place to live, with cleaner streets, a public water scheme and an infirmary, largely because the terms of the Public Health Act of 1848 been applied. Llandaff was not part of Cardiff at that time, being separated from it by the undeveloped Cathedral fields. In the early nineteenth century, it too had its problems, being described in 1849 as "a primitive insanitary village of 113 houses". Almost all the cottages were straw thatched, often with pig-sties adjoining. Slops were disgorged on to the roads, which were rutted by carts, and the cobbled pavements. Twenty-five deaths were recorded from cholera as late as 1854.

The arrival of Bishop Alfred Ollivant at Llandaff in 1849 heralded the beginning of a transformation. He was the first bishop to live in the diocese for over one hundred and fifty years. After centuries of neglect, the Cathedral was restored in the mid-nineteenth century under the supervision of the Diocesan Architect, John Prichard.

In 1860, the year of the opening of Howell's School, it acquired a new roof, and a new burial ground on the far side of the mill stream was completed and consecrated. By 1861 the new building was almost complete and in April 1869 local resident Ebenezer Moses recorded the completion of the Cathedral's new tower and spire, noting, "At five o'clock the Bishop laid the last finial stone on the spire. He did not carry his episcopal gaiters to the top of the spire but pulled a rope from below which lowered the stone into its place." It was the firm of William Clarke and Son which restored the Cathedral, and William's great-grandchildren Dorothy, Joan and Isabel Clarke all attended Howell's, Dorothy (whose married name was Wickett) having the distinction of becoming the first Hywelian Guild representative on the Board of Governors.

Llandaff village remained small in the 1860s, consisting of the Cathedral, the Deanery, the Bishop's Palace, nine inns, two mills and a handful of thatched cottages and farms as well as a few gentlemen's residences. Although Moses commented in 1861 that the Old House, which later became one of the school's boarding houses, was partly patched up and that most of the houses in St Mary Street were hovels in bad repair, two years later Clement Waldron wrote that "the old buildings in Llandaff are fast disappearing and many new houses springing up". The improvements to the Cathedral came to be reflected in the development of the village, which became a desirable residential area for wealthy citizens. Waldron was a solicitor and future Clerk to the Governors,

whose move to the White House on the Cathedral Green in 1860 coincided with the opening of the school, which was an aspect of Llandaff's growth at that time. Its location on the outskirts of the village, on fields adjoining the turnpike road from Cardiff, seemed ideal. Its merits were argued by Bishop Ollivant: elevated and cheaper than the rival site proposed in Swansea, it commanded "a fair and considerable prospect both to the front and to the back"; it was accessible by rail; and it was near both to the Cathedral, enabling the girls to walk there easily, and to the homes of well-to-do merchants in Canton who would be likely to want to send their daughters to the school. With an eye to recruitment, he also pointed out, "The Spot not being more than a mile and a half from Cardiff, the Institution will be conveniently placed for marketing".

Howell's became the first endowed school for girls in South Wales; indeed, with its sister school in Denbigh, it was the first in the Principality. Girls had attended Llanwrst Grammar School following its re-opening in 1828 but by the 1840s the only endowed grammar schools were for boys. Welsh girls in general were portrayed as immoral and ignorant in the notorious "Blue Books" of 1847, and the first edition of the short-lived Y Gymrais in January 1850 stressed the lack of educational opportunities for women.

There was no national system of education in Wales or England at the time. Both had elementary schools, under the auspices of two voluntary religious societies. In Cardiff these included the National School in Llandaff and the Cardiff Ragged Industrial School, established in 1855 on the old ship *Havannah*. In the 1850s, most children in Wales who attended the voluntary schools would have been likely to acquire only basic skills of literacy and numeracy, and most attended for no more than two years. Girls who attended were taught domestic subjects to prepare them for lives as servants or poor men's wives. The Registrar General's figures of 1864 show that in South Wales only 43% of girls (as opposed to 64% of boys) could write their names.

There were also private schools for the middle classes in all towns which, for girls, varied from cheap to expensive finishing schools. They had a distinctly English ethos: most of the parents whose daughters attended saw the Welsh language as a barrier to progress, so no Welsh was taught or spoken. No experience or training was needed to open private schools, which were often opened by widows wanting to make ends meet, so it is hardly surprising that standards were usually poor. It is estimated that less than a third of the children in Cardiff were receiving any

Facing page
School run by Mrs Ellen Woods at her home in Sully, 1849.

Left: Thomas Howell's crest on the façade of the school. Note that the mason carved Rowell *rather than* Howell.

education at all when Howell's School opened, with girls faring worse than boys. By 1863, there were fourteen Academies and Ladies' Seminaries in Cardiff. The quality of instruction varied but the girls' institutions seem to have concentrated more on social accomplishments and a basic education than on providing a rigorous academic experience. Middle class families of sufficient wealth sent their daughters to boarding schools in such places as Chester, Bristol, Bath and London.

A variety of factors – political, social, economic, religious and cultural – explain widely-held attitudes towards the education of girls at the time Howell's was built. The dearth of educational opportunities was one aspect of their general inferior place in society, which included being disenfranchised and suffering from professional and trade disabilities. The traditional notion that "a woman's place is in the home" and that motherhood was her noblest function was firmly rooted in Victorian society, so education for women was often seen as useful only in terms of improving their effectiveness as wives and mothers. In debates in the 1860s, the inherent inferiority of women's intellectual capacity was argued, on the grounds that their brains were smaller in cubic content.

Despite such ideas, in the 1850s and 1860s the case for the education of middle class girls built up in England by pioneers like Miss Frances Buss, who opened the North London Collegiate School for Ladies in 1850, Miss Dorothea Beale, Headmistress of Cheltenham Ladies' College from 1858, and Miss Emily Davies (herself of Welsh ancestry), who campaigned for gender equality in education. The demand for improved educational opportunities for

girls in England came largely from the middle classes but in Wales these formed only a small section of society, though their number increased in the 1860s. Welsh activists and Victorian liberals, who advocated educational improvements as part of the general drive for female emancipation and to promote moral reform, gradually made an impact. Of course, increased educational opportunity for the majority of girls in Wales would have been limited to elementary education; they would not have considered attending a school such as Howell's.

The two Howell's Schools were among a number of charity schools set up for middle class orphan children. What made them different was the fact that they had ancient endowments behind them and they were built on a lavish scale, whereas almost all the rest had a precarious existence, being dependent on fund-raising and financial support from their subscribers. They were also unusual in that that they did not specify orphans from a particular occupational background. Their founding was arguably the most significant educational landmark in Wales in the mid-Victorian period. But even at the Howell's Schools in the early days, the Governors – all male – saw the purpose of the education of the pupils in limited terms: to enable them to become good governesses or wives. Most upper and middle class parents would have concurred; their aspirations for their daughters would have been, for the most part, for them to marry at a social level commensurate with their education. It was in the later Victorian period that a higher premium was placed on academic work with a view to girls taking examinations, entering universities and embarking on careers in a range of professions.

3

PREPARATIONS FOR THE OPENING

Facing page
Earliest photographs of the school,
probably taken early in 1860.
Above: The front façade.
Below: The south wing. Notice the
horses in the foreground.

Left: The first entry in Governors'
Minutes' book, 1859.

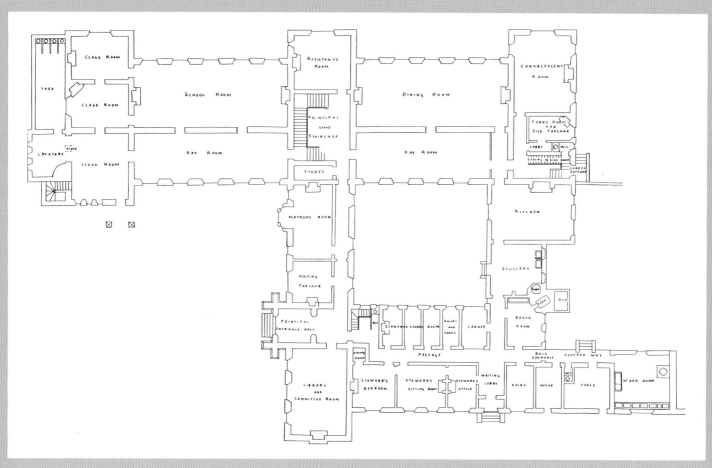

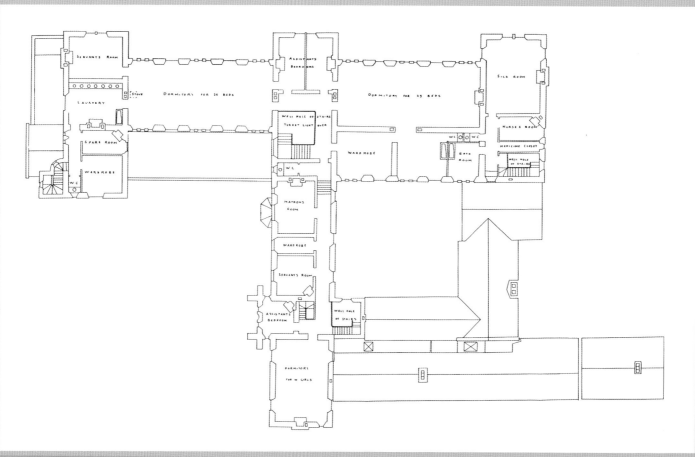

The exterior of the new school building was striking. Built of a light grey stone, it was a mixture of medieval ecclesiastical, Tudor, Gothic, Rhineland castle and French château. *The Building News* of October 29th 1858 described it in this way: *The architectural style adopted is the Domestic Gothic; one of the most prominent features in the design being a tower, 88 feet in height from the ground level. . . . Externally, the walling is of limestone, and Forest of Dean stone has been adopted for the various quoins, copings and the dressings of the various doors and windows.* The original building consisted of rooms on the ground floor on all four wings around the quadrangle, and an extra wing to the side of the main entrance. The main rooms on this floor were a Schoolroom and Dining Room, two Day Rooms, a Committee Room, rooms for the Chief Matron and her assistants, an office for the House Steward, a kitchen and laundry. Upstairs were to be found the sleeping accommodation and washrooms on the east and south wings, including the extension.

The day on which the first Governors' meeting took place, on 29th November 1859, was far from ideal. In accordance with the terms of the Chancery Scheme, sixteen Governors, all of whom were male and of considerable standing in the area, had been appointed. On this day six of them, including Bishop Ollivant, were unable to be present, and one of them, the Honourable Robert Windsor Clive of St Fagans Castle, was actually on his deathbed. The ten who arrived were all elderly and had to endure journeys in the rain, cold and wind. Six had made the journey on horseback and there was no accommodation for horses, carriages, grooms or coachmen. As for the interior of the building itself, it was far from ready, being described by one Governor as "a draughty and uncomfortable building". It was only semi-furnished and the fire lit in the Committee or Board Room exuded so much smoke and soot that eventually the door had to be opened, creating a smoky smell in the building. Outside, there was no boundary wall, and no gardens had been laid out.

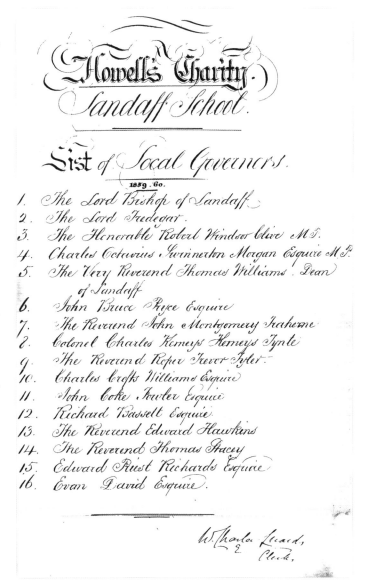

Howell's Charity.
Landaff School.

List of Local Governors.

1859. 60.

1. The Lord Bishop of Landaff.
2. The Lord Tredegar.
3. The Honorable Robert Windsor Clive M.P.
4. Charles Octavius Swinnerton Morgan Esquire M.P.
5. The Very Reverend Thomas Williams, Dean of Landaff
6. John Bruce Pryce Esquire
7. The Reverend John Montgomery Traherne
8. Colonel Charles Kemeys Kemeys Tynte
9. The Reverend Roger Trevor Tyler.
10. Charles Crofts Williams Esquire
11. John Coke Fowler Esquire
12. Richard Bassett Esquire
13. The Reverend Edward Hawkins
14. The Reverend Thomas Stacey
15. Edward Priest Richards Esquire
16. Evan David Esquire.

W. Charles Luard,
Clerk,

The first part of the meeting, chaired by Lord Tredegar, which was opened by William Sawyer, Clerk to the Drapers' Company, was not particularly informative. He told the Governors that it was their first meeting and the reason why they were there, both points being rather obvious. He then proceeded to read through and comment on all fifty-nine points of the Chancery Scheme, a copy of which all the Governors had already received. A more interesting interlude ensued, when they were taken by the architect on a thorough tour of the building. Every room was inspected and its exact dimensions, purpose and attributes explained. The workmanship was impressive and the kitchens were equipped with "the best and latest improvements". Following the tour, the Governors re-assembled in the Board Room for more business, including the official transfer of the building. They agreed to hold the second meeting two weeks later, by which time there had been five applicants for the House Steward's post. One of these was Bishop Ollivant's butler, George White, who was duly appointed. His wife was to act as under-housekeeper, and they were to live in some of the rooms on the ground floor of the north wing. At this second meeting the weather was again very poor, prompting a request for the new Clerk to the Governors, Mr Charles Luard, to write to the Drapers' Company requesting accommodation for the horses, carriages, coachmen and grooms.

The third meeting, on 7th January 1860, consisted largely of drawing up documents relating to the admission of the pupils, and the fourth, exactly one month later, of considering the applications received. By this time, the House Steward had taken up residence; a gardener was living in the lodge with his wife, who was the gatekeeper; stables were being constructed near the Steward's quarters, along with a hayloft which provided a waiting-room for the coachmen and grooms, so that they would not mix with the servants of the school; and there were pigsties nearby to provide home cured bacon. The building was still intolerably cold and draughty and the Governors asked for the architect to come from London as soon as possible. They were at pains to check genuine financial need and the respectability of the homes from which the applicants came. There were numerous deserving cases and each application had to be accompanied by a letter of support from at least one person of standing in the community. By the end of the meeting the Governors had decided to offer places to fifteen orphans and three pay boarders.

Although originally it had been planned to take day girls from the outset, it was decided to wait until the school was established. Thirty orphans (interpreted as meaning girls who had lost one parent, but not necessarily both) and thirty pay boarders were to be admitted. The orphans were to have their schooling, clothing, board and lodging paid for ten months of each year until the age of seventeen. Not surprisingly, therefore, the places were in great demand, especially as admission was not restricted to those from any particular background. By contrast, the pay boarders were to pay £20 per annum for board and lodging but were to be given free tuition and outer clothing.

While all these preparations were being made, a major attack was launched on the whole idea of opening the Howell's Schools. In his pamphlet *The Mystery of Improvidence*, published early in 1860, Thomas Falconer, Judge of the Glamorganshire and Breconshire County Courts, asserted that the money should not have been spent on two "gigantic and costly buildings" and he disliked the fact that there was not a single non-conformist among the Governors. While he acknowledged the need for girls' schooling in the Llandaff diocese, he would have preferred to see the money spent on working class orphans in the mining districts. He recommended that the Llandaff school be converted into a County Hospital or an Institution for the Deaf and Dumb. While there was a considerable amount of support for his views in the Welsh press, the Governors naturally rejected them.

Meanwhile, in London, Howell's first Headmistress, or Chief Matron as she was to be known, had been appointed. On 7th February, the Governors heard that Miss Emily Baldwin, a Londoner aged fifty-three, who had run a successful school for fourteen years in Notting Hill, had been appointed by the Drapers' Company, and she arrived at Howell's for the first time early in March. A short, energetic and self-confident woman wearing voluminous petticoats and with curly hair partly covered by a be-ribboned cap profusely trimmed with pink roses, she came from a wealthy family of publishers. Not surprisingly, therefore, she was very well-read and concerned that the new school should be generously equipped with books and periodicals. On her first visit, apart from meeting the Governors (wearing a pair of lavender kid gloves for propriety's sake, as she always did when she entered the Committee Room), Miss Baldwin undertook a thorough tour of the school, which led to her producing a lengthy inventory of further requirements. She was not entirely impressed: three rooms had no furniture whatsoever; there were no carpets or mats in the dormitories, and no pillowcases; the Schoolrooms lacked blackboards and easels; and she had no feather bed. Miss Baldwin was also introduced to the newly-formed "Sub-committee to assist the Chief Matron". This small body, headed by Bishop Ollivant, was to work extremely effectively with Miss Baldwin during the next twelve years.

The following few months witnessed a great deal of activity to prepare for the opening. Miss Baldwin's requests included bookcases, crockery, glass, pianos, a music stand for her Sitting Room, a wheelbarrow, sixty black alpaca umbrellas for the pupils and a feather bed for herself. The Governors sifted through the many applications made on behalf of prospective pupils. The Drapers had sanctioned £50 for laying out "Pleasure Gardens", which resulted in a south-facing gravelled playground with a swing and two chestnut trees for shade, a circular drive at the front around a lawn, and a garden at the side with a lawn, shrubberies, roses and two garden seats for the staff. The local newspaper reported that "... the gardens and pleasure grounds would not be better laid out were they attached to a gentleman's residence." The House Steward compiled a list of the items needed for his department's work. Mr Sawyer had seen to sending vast rolls of cloth including calico,

twill, brown holland and merino, silk and flannel, together with one thousand needles, with the intention that the orphans should make their own clothes and bed linen. Since the youngest pupil was merely seven years old, Miss Baldwin recognised immediately that this was an unrealistic proposal, and demanded that a seamstress be engaged to make up the material.

Even as late as May, there were no school books, blackboards, sheets of music or globes. Miss Baldwin produced a list of books which she considered essential and ordered *The Times*. The books, all of which had to be approved by the Bishop or the Dean, the Governors and the Drapers before they could be ordered, included standard Victorian schoolbooks, some light reading, simple illustrated stories for younger children and some scholarly books to stretch the older girls. Miss Baldwin prevailed upon members of her family to donate some of their books, and the very first book in the school library was *The Topography and History of Italy*, presented by her younger sister Agnes Jane.

Another major urgent task was to select assistant governesses. By May only two had been appointed, Miss Fenton and Miss Powell, and neither of these was to last beyond the first term; both had previously been governesses but had no school experience. The reason for the dearth of satisfactory applicants may in part have been the salary of £40 a year offered, as an experienced governess could expect to be paid more than this. Miss Baldwin wisely and successfully resisted the exhortations of the Drapers' Company to open the school in May, before the necessary staff and equipment had been obtained. At Denbigh, the newly appointed Chief Matron, the widowed Mrs Elizabeth Charlotte Booth, succumbed to this pressure and the results were unsatisfactory, leading to her departure under a cloud five years later.

By the end of July, with three of the original Governors already dead, the school was ready to admit its first pupils. The essential furniture and equipment were in place. Two more assistant governesses had been appointed, Miss Emmeline Horsey and a niece of Mrs Booth at Denbigh, Miss Letitia Ewing, who was destined to become Miss Baldwin's successor. At long last, the legacy of Thomas Howell was to bear fruit in Llandaff, and the first endowed girls' school in South Wales was about to open.

MISS BALDWIN (1860-72) AND THE FIRST PUPILS

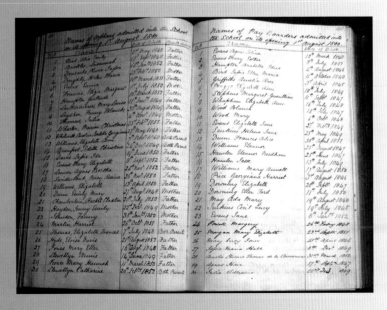

Facing page
Miss Emily Baldwin, 1860-72.

Left: *The first sixty pupils.*

The first thirty orphans, who arrived at the school on 1st August 1860, came from places as diverse as London, Brighton, Bath and the Welsh marches as well as from Cardiff and other parts of South Wales. The pay boarders were more local, Gwenllian Stephens from Swansea having the furthest to travel. These were accompanied by a guardian, who brought with them £5 to cover board and lodging for the first quarter. They were also instructed to bring a bonnet and a complete change of underclothes.

The orphans ranged from seven to twelve years of age and, apart from being Anglicans and from families who had aspirations for them, they had little in common. The majority were from tradesmen's backgrounds. Alice Emily Bird from Hereford was the first and oldest to be accepted. The youngest was the delicate Agnes Bertha Lemon, aged seven, from Bath. Annie Llewellyn from Cowbridge was one of the brightest. Probably the naughtiest was Helen Maria Doughty, whose widower father had described himself as a commercial traveller, so the Governors and Miss Baldwin strongly disapproved of his subsequently becoming innkeeper at the disorderly Patriot Inn in Merthyr Tydfil. Helen herself often arrived at school after the holidays looking unkempt and in 1863 Miss Baldwin complained to the Governors about "the extremely dirty state, both of person and linen, in which Miss Helen Doughty was sent back to school". All these young girls, and the other original orphans, stayed at Howell's for at least six years.

Ready to greet the first sixty pupils were Miss Baldwin's assistant governesses. Miss Baldwin lamented the fact that Miss Ewing was the only teacher with significant experience. Miss Horsey was tactless and aggressive, constantly referring to the problems at Denbigh, of which Miss Ewing, as Mrs Booth's niece, can hardly have been unaware. After Miss Fenton and Miss Powell left, unable to cope with the pressures, the conscientious Miss Mary Louisa Haynes was appointed at the beginning of 1861, but the other governesses of the early years were young and inexperienced. However, they were apparently less troublesome than Mrs Booth's at Denbigh, where the situation continued to be most unsatisfactory until her departure in 1865. Fortunately her successor, Miss Corner, was experienced and capable, and the school recovered from its unpromising start.

Each day, the rising bell went at 6.30am. The girls had an hour for piano practice and other tasks before they went to Prayers. They then had their appearance checked by the relevant governess before breakfast at eight. No talking was allowed in the Dining Room. Lessons began at nine o'clock and each lasted for an hour. Before they started, the monitress for the day had to open all the windows in the large Schoolroom and put out a Bible. The pupils sat on benches at long Victorian desks and wrote on slates. The school curriculum was laid down in the original Scheme as: "The principles of the Christian Religion, Reading, Writing, Arithmetic, English Grammar, Geography, Biography, History, the Elements of Astronomy, Garden Botany, Music, French and Drawing, together with such subjects as the Governors should decide." There was no Mathematics or Science. The pupils were to learn the Church of England catechism but they could be exempted if their parents made a written request to the Governors, as the school was open to children of all denominations. As there were only four assistant governesses at first, and one of these was fully occupied teaching Music, the sixty pupils were divided into three classes, each one necessarily consisting of girls of a wide range of both age and ability. Much of the learning was done by rote, including Lists of Popes and Tables of the Kings of Poland. The reading of the top class, known as the First Class, included leading articles in *The Times*, Gibbon's *Decline and Fall* and French literature.

At midday the girls had a piece of home-baked bread, before going on a daily walk to the first turnpike on the Llantrisant road. There were no organised games. Lunch followed, after which they spent the afternoon on "accomplishments" such as needlework

'I was one of the first to be elected as a pay boarder. I was small for my age, and therefore it was a surprise to find I was the eldest of all. The number given me was 5. My bed was at the upper end of the North Dormitory, under a window which looked out on the front of the lodge.

The governesses then were Miss Baldwin, the Matron, Miss Ewing (1st Class) and Miss Horsey and Miss Fenton for the other classes. Later on came Miss Haynes and Miss Powell, and, some time after, Miss Wingrave, who taught Music. Miss Baldwin took each class once a week. I remember she was very strong on Ancient History, and the date lists she drew up were a very great help. I have always been glad I learnt them. The Scripture class too on Sunday afternoons is a pleasant recollection, and the searching for answers to the Bible questions she gave. When the time came for me to leave, I was granted an extra year, and the following one I became a pupil teacher – the only one in the school.'

Amelia Rose Britten, née Griffiths (1860-64). Written 1913.

Above: The first orphans with Miss Baldwin and staff. The House Steward is at the top right.
Far left: The Schoolroom as it was in the 1860s.
Left: Quill pens and inkwells.

and drawing. Tea was followed by a Study Hour, with the older girls assisting the younger ones, and then they could all relax with skipping ropes, hoops and shuttlecocks or play piano duets, read or dance. There was a range of cooking equipment and the three daily meals appear to have been of very good quality, with large quantities of beef, veal, lamb and mutton. At eight o'clock the pupils assembled for Prayers in the Schoolroom and then, in pairs, they curtsied to Miss Baldwin before being escorted by the governesses to their dormitories where, according to a set of rules and in silence, they had to carry out their ablutions, simultaneous private prayers, hair-brushing and clothes-folding. Personal cleanliness was given

a high priority and the governesses were instructed to examine how much soap and water the girls used. Twice a week, they had what was described by Mr Sawyer, the Clerk, as "an extra washing" and a hair inspection. Each pupil had an admission number, which was painted on her iron bedstead – considered at the time to be the height of fashion and very hygienic – and on the adjacent dark brown varnished locker. All the beds were arranged in two long rows in each of the three dormitories – East, West and North – with a carpet down the middle, and a strip of matting by each bed. At the end of each dormitory was a huge fireplace. Every item, as far as possible, was decorated with the Drapers' coat of arms in blue and white.

The governesses also checked that the dormitories and lockers were tidy and every older girl was responsible for the good hygiene and tidiness of a younger one. These "mothers" helped the young boarders in both work and play, a practice which continued under the next two Headmistresses. The pupils, who wore their hair tightly plaited, dressed in a rather coarse brown dress, tight at the waist, with a very full skirt and a collar of white linen. On top of these, they wore brown pinafores. When they went outdoors, they donned black silk mantles and poke bonnets trimmed with green. They were all supplied with black boots and alpaca umbrellas.

Miss Baldwin soon introduced more fashionable and less voluminous skirts, with fewer layers of petticoats underneath. The black mantles were replaced by jackets of bronze serge coating. For summer there were brown straw bonnets with velvet ribbons and light print gowns, and for winter woollen garments trimmed with velvet and braid.

Taking an interest in the development of the school was a Ladies' Committee, consisting of wives of the Governors, and while declaring

'At first we were rather an undisciplined crew but our Head, Miss Baldwin, soon effected order. Being such a new building, it was visited by many of the County people. Mr Priest Richards was the most frequent. Upon one occasion he brought the young Marquis of Bute to see it; then to the young boy he said: "You have seen their home, now show them yours." So to our delight we were invited to the castle, where we were regaled with fruit and wine. . . . When the day pupils were first admitted, Miss Baldwin, who disliked it very much, warned us against being too familiar with them. . . . Some of the pleasures we had were a holiday on Miss Baldwin's birthday, another when Bishop Ollivant's daughter was married, and when the first organ was dedicated in the Cathedral.'

Annie Llewellyn (1860-7). Written 1942.

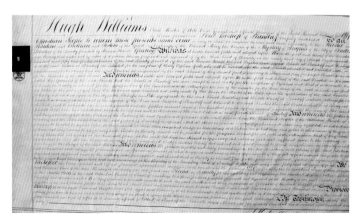

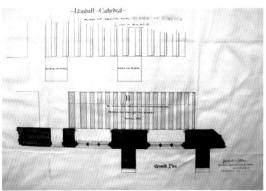

Orphans

Alice Bird	Beginning again; shows some little taste
Susan Buckler	Somewhat advanced, but wants industry & taste
Clara Denroche	Decided taste for Music
Emma Evans	A beginner, very dull and slow
E. M. Francis	Very little taste or industry, but had extra lessons in Holidays
G. Hampton	Just begun, seems very slow and dull
M L Leatherbarrow	Some taste, and improving
Fanny Leyshon	Taste and advancing
Julia Thomas	Taste and improving
Caroline Whitworth	No aptitude whatever, but rather more industrious
E A Williams	Industrious but no natural taste for Music
Edith Branfoot	Decided taste and industry
M R Swindenbank	A beginner, very attentive & shows some taste
Eliz'th Williams	A beginner, very slow, but industrious, has a Piano here
Emily Dunn	Advancing nicely
M C Chamberlain	Some taste, but wants industry
J E Hayden	Industrious, but not much taste
Fanny Johnson	Industrious no taste
Eliz F Thomas	No taste whatever, but anxious to learn
Eloisa Hyde	Just begun, absent from indisposition
Mary E Jones	Taste and industry
Annie Measly	Not the smallest aptitude, but Mama wishes her to learn
Mary H Price	Taste and industry

themselves "altogether pleased with the appearance of things" at their meeting on 26th March 1862, the four present made a few recommendations. They considered that the number of teachers was insufficient and suggested that "when a vacancy occurs amongst the younger teachers it might be possible in appointing one to tell her that she must provide herself with an assistant". This was accepted, as by 1865 six classes had been created. A junior assistant was appointed in 1864, and there was help with teaching from the senior orphan and a former pay boarder, Amelia Rose Griffiths. The Ladies' Committee also suggested that every girl intending to become a governess, not only those who had a piano at home, should learn Music.

At regular intervals from January 1862 the Governors appealed in vain to the Drapers' Court of Assistants to be allowed to appoint a male teacher to teach class music and singing. It was not until August 1871 that the Court agreed to the appointment of Mr T G Aylward, organist at Llandaff Cathedral, as Music Master, at a salary of £70 per year. However, one hundred copies of the Psalter, pointed for chanting, and five copies with music, were ordered in December 1863, so that the children could join in the services at the Cathedral, and the Reverend H B Bevan undertook to give them some instruction in chanting. Twice on Sundays and once on Wednesdays the pupils walked to the Cathedral, where places in the south aisle had been reserved for them on condition that the Drapers contributed towards the rebuilding. On Sunday afternoons, their "entertainment" consisted of Miss Baldwin asking them scriptural questions, to which they had to search in the Bible for the answers.

Miss Baldwin was frequently in correspondence with the Governors, asking for funds for improvements to the equipment and physical appearance of the grounds. Her very first requests were made the day after the school opened and began politely, as they always did: "Miss Baldwin begs to state to the Local Governors that she considers that three more Pianos will be required for the proper working of the school at Llandaff." She was also granted £5 for books for the girls' library and £5 for garden tools, hoops, skipping ropes and battledores. Almost every year, Miss Baldwin asked for money for plants for the gardens.

Great attention was also paid to the well-being and health of the children. Miss Baldwin was approachable enough for the girls to

Facing page
Top: Items marked with Drapers' Company crest – serving plate, jug and tray, soap dish, washing bowl.
Left: Candlestick holder.
Right: The earliest uniform.

Above: Piano reports, 1863.
Top right: 1860 Deed of Faculty confirming the reservation of seats in Llandaff Cathedral for Howell's pupils.
Centre right: Plan of seats in the south aisle of Llandaff Cathedral reserved for Howell's School, 1860.
Right: Miss Baldwin's request for bedding plants, 1864.

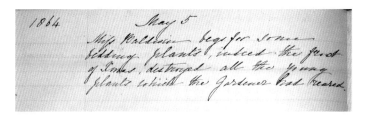

1864 May 5
Miss Baldwin begs for some bedding plants, indeed the frost of James, destroyed all the young plants which the Gardener had reared.

see her if they felt unwell; she herself nursed them and dispensed all the medicine. The school surgeon, Dr Thomas Evans, visited almost every day despite the fact that he had a very large practice which included all the county families. He was paid £20 a year for his school duties, which in times of serious illness involved attending several times a day. His book, in which he wrote comments on every patient, was read to the Governors at every meeting. On 3rd October 1861, they decreed that "every child be carefully examined on entrance into the school and on her return each half year" and "any child not found in a perfectly cleanly state be not received or allowed to return to the Institution". The building had a sick wing at the back of the building, with its own access stairs, and the school's water supply was very pure. All possible precautions were taken to prevent the introduction of infectious diseases.

Although Howell's had an excellent health record in the early years, there were of course outbreaks of illness, including gastric fever in May 1863. At about the same time, a young servant girl, Lettice Hughes, died at the school and was buried in the new graveyard at Llandaff Cathedral. The most serious health concern under Miss Baldwin was the scarlet fever epidemic which began in February 1864 and lasted for about a year. It claimed the life of nine-year-old Mary Elizabeth Cunnick, the only pupil to die in school during the 1860s. A number of children suffered from "general debility" and unfortunately two other girls succumbed at home after a long period of absence. There was just one case of smallpox, which affected a servant-girl – and she recovered – but no-one caught cholera. A death rate of only 0.1% amongst the pupils in the 1860s is a remarkable record for the time.

Discipline was strict but, unlike at Denbigh, corporal punishment was never used. The Schools Enquiry Commission of 1868, set up to investigate the state of secondary education, reported that: "Irregularity of attendance is punished by loss of marks. Other punishments are tasks of needlework and, very rarely, seclusion."

If the older girls did not ensure that the younger ones for whom they were responsible were clean and tidy, they would lose checks, or good marks. Sometimes pupils had to perform extra duties for minor offences. A dreaded punishment was to be made to sit alone at the side table in the Dining Room, which was there for that very purpose, and to be given only a piece of dry bread. Another sanction was to be sent to bed straight after supper. On 4th April 1861, Agnes Evans was reprimanded by the Bishop of Llandaff for "administering to one of her schoolfellows an Oath on the Bible not to tell of some trifling matter". In 1863, Julia Thomas and Mary Leatherbarrow, two orphans, were discovered to have been in regular secret correspondence with Cathedral choirboys who attended the National School in Llandaff. Their punishment was exclusion from school for three months.

In general, the behaviour of the orphans in the early years was better than that of the pay boarders, probably partly because the former were usually considerably younger than the latter and because they were so appreciative of the chance to be at the school. On 3rd November 1864, Miss Baldwin reported "a very painful circumstance" to the Governors: a number of edible items had disappeared and "on 21st October Edith Pugh was observed to take an apple from the stove in the [Stone] Hall". Her punishment is not recorded; the Governors decreed that Miss Baldwin should deal with the matter. The most serious punishment, expulsion, was applied to only one girl, Clara Frances Elliott from London. She was a pay boarder who had only been at the school for six weeks. Her exact crime was not documented but the decision to exclude her permanently in May 1863 was taken "both for her own sake . . . and also for the sake of other girls, into whose minds she might be the means of infusing evil thoughts, if she continued amongst them".

It is almost certainly the case that the governesses turned a blind eye to some misdemeanours such as dormitory feasts and the girls dancing quadrilles on top of the lockers. There were

also official times of relaxation and lighter occasions. On Miss Baldwin's birthday, 18th September, there was a day's holiday, on which the girls could choose what they wanted to do, and in the evening the older pupils provided entertainment for the younger ones. In December, Miss Baldwin held a little ceremony in which she distributed a few Good Conduct prizes in the big Schoolroom, which was usually divided in two by a curtain. On the same occasion, she issued marks of approbation.

Two major changes occurred in 1863. Charles Luard, the first Clerk to the Governors, resigned after taking over responsibility for the family law firm, which had been involved in the purchase of the land on which the school was built. He had taken the minutes conscientiously but when bored had drawn sketches of ecclesiastical architecture in his notebook. His connection with the school did not come to an end, however: he was associated with the business affairs of almost all the Governors, and he also drew up Miss Baldwin's will. His successor, who served until the 1890s, was Clement Waldron,

the solicitor who lived in the White House on the Cathedral Green. Mr Waldron became the leading Cardiff solicitor but he was totally unpretentious, kind and very patient.

The other key development in 1863 was the introduction of day girls. Miss Baldwin opposed the idea, writing on 23rd June, "Miss Baldwin will still hope that the school with which so much pains has been taken, may be spared the deterioration that will inevitably follow the admission of daily pupils." However, the Governors were insistent that more than sixty girls ought to be able to benefit from the education provided, and the extra income from fees could be used to pay the higher salaries demanded by the calibre of governesses they hoped to appoint. The Governors had set out their views for the Drapers' Company to consider as early as July 1861, stating that they envisaged the school having in future "a large class of Day Scholars of respectable position in life". The Scheme allowed fees of only sixpence a week to be charged at first, which attracted applicants from humble backgrounds. Five of the

'I left in 1869, after four years, and during that time not once late or absent one day, for which I received some well bound books for punctuality and good conduct. . . . Miss Baldwin was a strict disciplinarian, but kind and just. . . . I was a day scholar and walked from Ely if fine, every day, but if wet, was driven in a pony phaeton. . . .
The boarders in winter wore brown winsey frocks, trimmed with a band of velvet, and a tiny cape for outdoor wear in winter; and summer, brown lustre, a white bonnet with a band of green ribbon. The boarders had no games in those days, only croquet. If too wet to go for walks, well, they danced mid-day in the Day Rooms.'

Annie Pool, née Thomas (1865-9). Written 1941.
She was the last survivor of the pupils of the 1860s, living to the age of one hundred.

Howell's Charity Llandaff School
186

Sir,

I beg to inform you that

was on the   inst approved for admission into the School as a Pay Boarder subject to Confirmation at the next meeting of the Governors.

It will therefore be necessary that you attend with her at the School on Thursday the   next at one o'Clock.

Yours obediently,

Charles Luard.

Church Street, Cardiff,

186

Howell's Charity, Llandaff School.

Sir,

I beg to inform you that your application on behalf of

for admission into the School as a Pay Boarder was submitted to the Governors at their meeting on the   instant, but was not approved. Should you be desirous of renewing the application, a letter to that effect, addressed to me, will be all that is necessary, but additional recommendations may be furnished if thought advisable.

Yours obediently,

CLEMENT WALDRON,

Clerk to the Local Governors.

initial six were the daughters of local tradesmen from Canton and were barely literate, unpunctual and often absent. Miss Baldwin's worst fears seemed realised. The early day pupils rarely won prizes and did not wear uniform.

Bishop Ollivant soon recognised that the original Scheme had some major defects. In particular the low fees for day scholars and the low salaries of the staff meant that the school was unlikely to attract the desired calibre of pupils and governesses, but a series of frustrating delays meant that it was not until November 1865 that the New Scheme came into operation. This raised the fees to two guineas a quarter, which led to applicants from more respectable backgrounds. In consequence, the reputation of the school increased, as was indicated by the growing number of applications. Miss Baldwin's salary was increased immediately to £140 and that of the assistants was also raised, varying according to their experience.

The other great benefit of the New Scheme was that it made possible the expansion of the curriculum. The original Scheme stated that an Examiner was to be appointed to visit regularly and test progress but it was not until 1865 that this happened, largely because the Drapers did not want to incur the expense of paying an extra salary. The proposal to introduce a revised Scheme spurred on the Governors to feel that they must fulfil all the requirements of the original one. Bishop Ollivant immediately suggested the Reverend George Woods, who seemed eminently suited for the position, as an Oxford-educated classical scholar, father of seven girls, and a former Headmaster. Following his move to Sully he had also established a school in his Rectory for the village boys. For the next twenty-four years, until July 1889, he was associated with Howell's: he taught classes, wrote detailed and generally very favourable reports, prepared many girls for Confirmation and fulfilled his aim, as he expressed it, to "elevate the curriculum". He was responsible for introducing Geometry, Physical Science, Italian and Latin to the First Class and soon he was teaching Latin to three classes a week. When needed, he even volunteered his services to teach German after it replaced Italian in 1872. In the early 1870s younger pupils, too, were introduced to Geometry, Latin and Chemistry, and all but the youngest class studied French.

On the whole I have every reason to believe that the important objects for which the School was established are faithfully and efficiently carried out.

I am,
My Lords and Gentlemen,
Very respectfully yours
George Woods

The deputation consisting of the Master, John Jabez Esq and the Clerk having in obedience to the Orders of the Court proceeded into Wales to be present at the examination of the Children in the Schools at Llandaff and Denbigh Report that in the first instance they visited the School at Llandaff which they minutely examined, and found all the arrangements therein very complete and highly satisfactory — The examination of the Children on the 11th inst was by the Rev Stammers a Clergyman who had been appointed

Facing page
1: Letter offering a place as a boarder, 1860s.
2: Letter of rejection for a boarder, 1860s.

Above left: George Woods, Howell's Examiner from 1865 to 1889.
Above: Conclusion of George Woods' first report to the Governors, 1865.
Left: Report of Drapers' deputation and Rev Stammers' visit to school, 1863.

Before and after George Woods' appointment, the school was inspected by other visitors. From the earliest days, some of the Governors conducted their own small-scale examinations. There was also a Public Examiner, the Reverend Alexander Stammers, whose annual visits witnessed long viva voce examinations of the whole school in every subject. He wrote on 26th June 1865 that the written exercises of the sixty-seven pupils present were "superior to that of former years", and he made similarly favourable remarks the next two years. Another eminent visitor was the lawyer H M Bompas, who in 1865 produced a glowing report on the buildings, curriculum and effective utilisation of endowments. It was he who suggested that Latin and Geometry should be added to the curriculum. From 1869, Cambridge graduate the Reverend J Henry Thompson, who was Vicar of Datchet, near Windsor, provided detailed written reports based on oral and written examinations. In addition, representatives of the Drapers' Company conducted a triennial examination of the school. On June 19th 1869, *The Cardiff and Merthyr Guardian* reported that they toured the building and returned the next day to hear the oral examination of the Public Examiner. They also heard his comments on written papers which the girls had sat previously and distributed the prizes. The proceedings ended with the singing of the National Anthem, followed by a substantial meal. The newspaper's report began, "This school . . . is without exception the finest and best conducted school in the Principality." This occasion fortunately ran more smoothly than the 1867 prize-giving, when Bishop Ollivant, who always presented the prizes Miss Baldwin had chosen, refused to hand over a copy of Keble's *Christian Year* to its intended recipient as he was a staunch opponent of the Keble's High Church views. Apart from this embarrassing moment, relations between the Bishop and Miss Baldwin were excellent.

The report of the Taunton Commission (1864-8), published in 1870, which examined the secondary schools in England and Wales, also presented Howell's in a very favourable light. Among the comments were: "The proficiency of the pupils is decidedly above average. This does credit to the teaching as many of them on entry were deplorably ignorant" and "The moral tone of the school seemed to me to be very good." One strong criticism was made,

'Out of a large family I was the youngest and when I found myself for the first time in my life separated from my parents and amongst a host of strangers my little heart quailed, and during prayer time the first night this feeling of isolation amongst a crowd so overpowered me that I disgraced myself by howling. I was the youngest but one in the school, and as my junior bore the same name I was re-christened Bianca. It was rather disconcerting for a little child to lose her identity in this way, and I had so much difficulty in remembering my new name that I awoke my neighbour in the large dormitory that night and asked her to spell it to me. For two years before leaving I was under the tuition of Miss Ewing herself, in general subjects, in the highest class. The hours of study were long, there was very little variation in our routine, and in the playground we had to find our own amusements. But we enjoyed our country walks past Fairwater, when we were allowed to break the ranks and wander about in groups looking for wild flowers.

No Science lectures were given, and most of the lessons we learned by rote in the junior classes; in the two highest classes we were generally tested upon our preparations, and had greater scope for our reasoning and observing powers. English subjects including advanced Literature, Algebra, Latin, French, German, Italian, Drawing, Singing and Piano composed our curriculum. Our Annual Examinations were held in June, when the written papers occupied two days and the oral examination one. This, I always thought, was a most excellent test of the year's work, and the satisfactory reports we received were a high commendation of the thoroughness of the educational system adopted. During many years of private tuition and journalism I have had every reason to be grateful for the good grounding I received at Howell's School.'

Blanche Clark (1863-70). Written 1912.

Read a letter from the Clerk to the Local Governors of the Llandaff School with a letter from Miss Baldwin the Head Mistress of the School intimating her intention in consequence of failing health to resign that appointment at Midsummer next and appealing to the generosity of the Court with respect to a pension on her retirement

however. In the view of the Inspector, "The holding of the annual public examination is highly objectionable. It makes the boldest and most unfeminine of the girls most likely to succeed." On June 24th 1871, the *Pontypool Free Press* recorded: "Llandaff School is . . . excellently managed, and, in fact, is as rich in resources and extensive in accommodation, as any of the few such institutions to be met with in South Wales or the West of England." The star pupil was Margaret Hair, who won the First Class prizes for Conduct, English Studies, Arithmetic and Needlework, the prize for General Helpfulness and the Mother Prize, awarded for assisting with the younger children.

Miss Baldwin announced her decision to retire, aged sixty-five, in a letter to Bishop Ollivant in February 1872. For the next few months she worked as hard as ever, especially towards the end as she prepared for her final and most elaborate Prize Day. The assembly of dignitaries included four members of the Drapers' Company as it happened to be the year of their triennial visit. As soon as the event was over, Miss Baldwin took the train to London to begin retirement on a pension of a mere thirty pounds a year. She battled with the Drapers for an increase but to no avail. Her remaining years were spent in a variety of lodgings in the capital, sometimes with her sisters and sometimes alone. She died on 2nd December 1880. By then most of her savings had been used to supplement her pension; her three brothers had predeceased her and so were unable to support her financially.

By the time of Miss Baldwin's departure from Howell's, all the original pupils had left. The majority became governesses, as had been expected. Of the orphans, Emily Dunn stayed the longest as she became the first Junior Assistant at the age of eighteen and then, in 1869, a fully-fledged governess. She resigned to get married four years later. Julia Thomas, who had been in trouble for exchanging letters with local choirboys, lived to the age of one hundred, making her the longest surviving of the original orphans. The delicate schoolgirl Agnes Lemon developed into a strong and active woman who set up a successful private school for young boys in association with Clifton College in Bristol, receiving a grant of £50 from the Howell's Charity at the end of 1887 to assist with this. Annie Llewellyn also went on to set up her own private school, The Heath House Boarding and Day School for Young Ladies, in Cowbridge in 1870, with the help of £50 provided by the Governors, and this lasted until the early twentieth century.

Miss Baldwin appears not to have been influenced by feminist education ideas and the work of Miss Buss and Miss Beale in England. She had aimed to educate the girls to become cultivated middle class wives, mothers and governesses rather than prepare them for entry into the professions and thereby challenge the position of men. Nevertheless, her achievement at Llandaff was remarkable. Her industry, dedication, successful working relationship with Bishop Ollivant and George Woods, together with her constant badgering of the Governors for improvements, meant that by the time she retired, the school had developed from a charity foundation into a highly successful and sought-after establishment. Even by the mid-1860s, there were forty applicants for the six orphan vacancies each year. The term "Charity" had disappeared by 1872, reflecting in part the changed background of the pupils. In 1860, only four were the daughters of professional men, whereas by 1872 there were thirty six, as well as several clergymen's and army officers' daughters. The entry in the Dictionary of National Biography in 1995 referred to Miss Baldwin's personal qualities: "She ran the school efficiently and with authority. Her régime, however, unlike that of many of her contemporaries, was characterised by kindness and common sense . . . She taught the girls herself, gave rewards for achievement and encouraged pupils with problems to come to her personally." Of course, she was fortunate to have the outstanding George Woods and a strong team of educated and interested Governors to support her. Between them they had laid the foundations on which a very successful school was to continue to develop.

5

MISS EWING (1872-80): SUCCESSES AND PROBLEMS

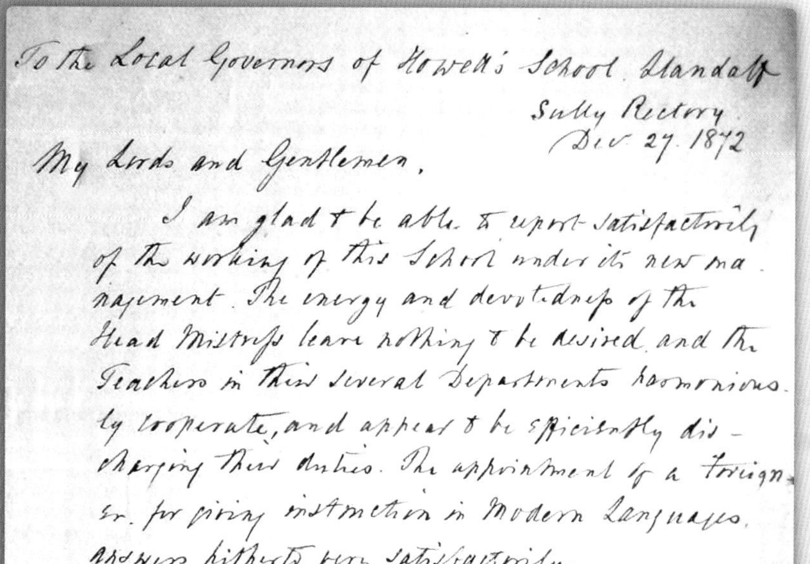

To the Local Governors of Howell's School, Llandaff

Sully Rectory.
Dec 27. 1872

My Lords and Gentlemen,

I am glad to be able to report satisfactorily of the working of this School under its new management. The energy and devotedness of the Head Mistress leave nothing to be desired, and the Teachers in their several Departments harmoniously cooperate, and appear to be efficiently discharging their duties. The appointment of a Foreigner for giving instruction in Modern Languages answers hitherto very satisfactorily.

Facing page
Miss Letitia Ewing, 1872-80.

Left: The beginning of George Woods' report to the Governors, December 1872.

Letitia Amelia Ewing became Howell's second Headmistress at the age of thirty-eight. Although probably the obvious successor to Miss Baldwin, her appointment was not automatic: it involved applying and being interviewed, along with two other applicants, by the Drapers' Court of Assistants, who then held a ballot. Born in Hythe, Kent, she had spent most of her early life abroad as her father was a surgeon in the Army Medical Service. At the age of ten, she had moved with her widowed mother and younger sister to Ruthin, to be joined soon after by her widowed aunt, Mrs Booth, who later became the first Chief Matron of Howell's School, Denbigh. She went to a small private school and then stayed on as a pupil governess before becoming one of the first members of the Howell's staff. A delicate woman and gentle in manner, she was extremely conscientious and intellectual.

By the time of Miss Ewing's appointment as Headmistress, a landmark in the history of education had been reached with the passing of Forster's Education Act in 1870, which provided for a full education for all children up to the age of 13. It is estimated that by 1872 about one third of the children in Cardiff were receiving a primary education, although in the county of Glamorgan as a whole the proportion was little more than one fifth. During the 1870s, several other girls' private schools existed in the Cardiff area but the nearest rival to Howell's in terms of prestige was the one in Cowbridge run by Annie Llewellyn, one of the first orphans, who modelled its curriculum on that of her former school. In 1872, coinciding with Miss Ewing's appointment, the Girls' Public Day School Company Ltd. was set up, with its primary object that member schools should be "places not only of instruction, but of education in the true sense of the word, and a training of the individual girl by the development of her mental and moral faculties". This organisation (reconstituted as The Girls' Public Day School Trust Ltd. in 1905), of which Howell's became a member in 1980, had no representation in Wales until one of its schools was opened in Swansea in 1888. By that time there was just one more endowed girls' school in Wales, Dr Williams' at Dolgellau, founded in 1878.

In Wales, the number of women in professional occupations such as teaching, nursing and local government had increased from 3,144 in 1861 to 9,568 by 1871 but there was still a long way to go. The Taunton Commission of the 1860s had stressed the need for changed parental attitudes towards female education and the desirability of external examinations, inspections and teacher training. In 1868, the Cambridge Higher Local Examination had been established, this being the only educational qualification available for women at the time. Between 1869 and 1879 the Oxbridge Colleges of Girton, Newnham, Lady Margaret Hall and Somerville were opened for them although they were not admitted to degrees, London being the first university to make women eligible in 1878.

In general, the Taunton Commission made a less significant impact in Wales than in England but Miss Ewing was well aware that Howell's could not ignore the developments occurring in England. She almost immediately asked the Governors for permission for the older pupils to attend the new University Extension lectures in Chemistry, held in the Prebendal House in Llandaff, and since these were sponsored by Bishop Ollivant and by some of the wives and daughters of other Governors, unsurprisingly this request was granted. She also recommended that the girls be allowed to sit the Cambridge Local Examinations but the Governors would not agree; they were unwilling to abandon the traditional public examination at the midsummer prize-giving.

Under Miss Ewing's leadership, all went well at first. George Woods reported positively to the Governors on the new régime. Miss Ewing was a kind and inspiring teacher to the pupils in the First Class. She had a particular interest in Science and Natural History and read to the girls from *The Times*. Successive prize-giving speakers praised her highly, and there is no doubt that she was very diligent in all her administrative work, keeping very detailed records. She introduced a few minor changes, including a new serge dress for the orphans, and the quaint poke bonnets were replaced by brown headgear. The growing reputation of the school – or The College, as it was known at that time – resulted in an increasing number of applications, which enabled the Governors to be more selective.

Many of the traditions established by Miss Baldwin were continued. As the girls filed in twos out of the Schoolroom each evening, they curtsyed to Miss Ewing, who sometimes called them aside to encourage or reprimand them. Every day they went *en masse* in crocodile, after lunch, to the turnpike, with two mistresses half-way down the line and two at the rear. The same happened on Sundays when, on arrival at the Cathedral, the pairs parted, forming two rows with an aisle in between, along which Miss Ewing and her companion walked in order to lead the school in.

Not surprisingly, the day the boarders went home for the holidays was eagerly anticipated. George White, the House Steward, and his wife supervised their departure, standing on the stone steps and trying to make themselves heard above the girls' excited voices. Cabs and omnibuses arrived at the school door and the latter, a novelty at the time, were more popular. Kitty Morgan was overheard to announce to a friend, "I'm not going in the cab. I'm going in the omnibus", and when the friend responded, "But supposing Miss Ewing says you must?" she proudly countered, "I shall say, 'Miss Ewing, what does omnibus mean?'"

Unfortunately, the changes made by Miss Ewing were only of a minor nature. It may have been her delicate health and deferential attitude towards the Governors which prevented her from forging ahead with more radical measures that were needed to keep the school abreast of developments in the best English schools, with

Below: An orphan's outer clothing, c.1870.
Below right: First page of a boarder's letter home, 1876.
Below, centre: An advertisement for a mistress, 1876.

HOWELL'S SCHOOL for GIRLS, Llandaff, South Wales. — REQUIRED, in the above school, at or shortly after Midsummer next, a LADY, not under 26 years of age, a member of the Church of England, experienced in tuition, and competent to teach the Englih language and literature and arithmetic to advanced pupils, and to give instruction in musis. Salary £55 per annum with a share, which averages aubot £15 per annum, of the payments made by the day scholars who attend the school, maintenance, and laundry expenses. Address the Clerk of the Drapers' Company, Drapers'-hall, Throgmorton-street, London, E.C.

their pupils sitting the Cambridge Higher Local Examinations and their better qualified, university-educated staff. From 1875, the Public Examiner, J H Thompson, expressed concern about declining standards. By 1879 his report was very unfavourable, commenting that work was "less and less thoroughly done in every department of the school." George Woods too was critical of the younger girls from 1875. Both men disapproved of Miss Ewing's decision to amalgamate the two lower forms to produce a class of twenty-six girls, which they considered too large. In 1880, George Woods' criticisms reached a peak, with comments that ". . . the classes are too large, the teachers too busy to help the backward, the Third class are worse than ever and the First mediocre."

The academic problems could in part be attributed to health problems among the pupils. Although, remarkably, no-one succumbed to smallpox, diphtheria, whooping cough or scurvy, skin complaints were common and in the early spring of 1875 a great epidemic of scarlet fever broke out, which lasted until June. There were also two measles epidemics, in each case involving one in six boarders, and Miss Ewing herself supervised their nursing. A number were affected by St Vitus' Dance and lung diseases, which sadly led to the deaths of four pupils, three orphans and one pay boarder, in 1878 and 1879. Two of these deaths, those of the orphan Caroline Farr and the pay boarder Anne Lucy White, occurred within a week of each other in April 1879, and Caroline, who had tubercular peritonitis, died in school.

Miss Ewing became increasingly irritated with her pupils, as her reports in the book on the *Character and Conduct of the Orphans*, which she completed so diligently to 1878, testify. All her comments about their work and conduct in the later entries are unfavourable. Annie Page was described as "troublesome, being very much spoiled at home", while Henrietta Jones was "very disobedient indeed". Several of them were described as "backward". Since even Lilian Laybourne, the first girl from Howell's to go to Newnham College, Cambridge, was criticised for her academic work, it appears that these comments reflected her increasing frustration caused by other difficulties more than the true ability and behaviour of the orphans.

Various additional matters bothered Miss Ewing. There were delays in the arrival of cheques from the Drapers' Company for running expenses and improvements to the building. It took two years of correspondence between architects, the Drapers, the builder and the Archdeacon for six new lavatories to be built in the yard. Another sanitary issue in October 1879 related to the "effluence of offensive vapour" from the Ely Paper Works. George White, who had kept very good control over the household staff, was unwell and he and his wife eventually retired in 1878. His successors were much less competent, resulting in unsupervised servants who did not work diligently at repairs.

Overshadowing all these problems was the deteriorating health of Miss Ewing from 1877. Her friend and assistant Miss Haynes did her best to hold the fort. Miss Ewing experienced alternating periods of weakness and recovery. While expressing sympathy for her, the Governors lamented on 4th December 1879 that "the school is still practically without a Headmistress" and suggested that she should be asked to retire if she could not resume her duties. Sadly she died at the home of her aunt, Mrs. Booth, in Dulwich on 29th January 1880, ten months before her predecessor Miss Baldwin. On 5th February 1880, the Governors duly placed on record their appreciation for her years of devoted service to the school.

Miss Ewing had been beset by problems which were largely not of her own making. Maud Patterson recalled "the dark stern face . . . a sternness, however, so often dispelled by a charming smile" and "how bravely and how nobly she struggled on to the end." Mary Litchfield recorded, "Her classes were a delight. She was an absolute encyclopaedia of knowledge, and dullness and boredom (when she was teaching us) were unknown." According to Mary

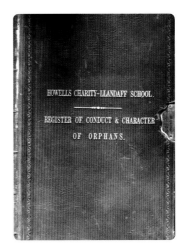

Left: Cover of Register of Conduct and Character of Orphans.
Below: The disgruntled House Steward complains to Clement Waldron, 1876.
Bottom: Governors' concerns, 16th January 1879.

Facing page
Laura Kernick in Paris in the late 1870s.

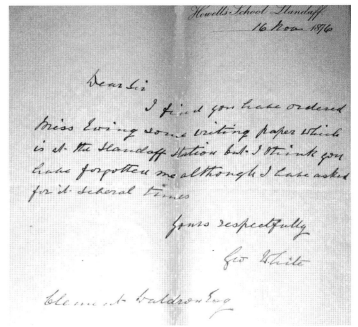

Clarke, "The tone of the school was good. To be clean, straight and play the game was the kernel of all our teaching. To try our best to win prizes, but not to be disheartened if we failed, and to aim at what was better worth having – the approval of our own conscience and the approval of God."

'The great feature of the teaching of those days was learning by heart, and woe betide the unfortunate girl who had to be corrected twice in one lesson! Not only did she lose her place in the class every time she missed (the girl who knew the answer taking the place of the one who did not), but she also had to endure a punishment far greater – the side table! It meant that as the girls filed into the dining room, the unfortunate one slipped out of rank and took her seat at the side table, i.e. the middle table of the three lower ones in the dining room, and in due course a plate of dry bread was put before her! Had she a fellow delinquent, it was endurable, but had she to sit there in solitary state, she was convinced in her miserable self-consciousness that every soul in that room possessed at least six pairs of eyes, every one of which was fixed upon her unhappy self!

Old Mrs Riches came from Cardiff twice a week to drill us and teach the elder girls how to dance the Minuet! I see the little lady now, standing on a form, shouting at the top of her voice, making scathing remarks, calling out to some inattentive girl. If we wanted gymnastics of another sort, we invented our own, and well do I remember a girl, trying to see how far she could get through the bars of the Sixth Form windows, and getting so tightly wedged, she could neither move backwards nor forwards! Amid screams and shouts from the others, two girls seized each a leg to help her out of her difficulty, and, as ill-luck would have it, when the uproar was at its height, the door opened and our Headmistress appeared! Instantly, dead silence. "Come down from there at once!" she ordered, but the girl's almost hysterical "I can't" was mercifully too much for her; with a set face she turned and left the girl to herself and us!

We had to find some outlet for our exuberant spirits, and seized the opportunity of the temporary absence of our Headmistress and the Second Mistress at some local dinner party to have a high old time, as we expressed it. When all lights were out, a certain lot of girls in the West Dormitory dressed up in each other's dressing gowns, got on to the top of the lockers, and to the execrable sounds produced by the beating of tins and mouthing of tissue-paper-covered combs, they danced the wildest quadrilles one ever saw! Don't imagine we were never caught – we were – and innocent and guilty alike brought before Miss Ewing, who insisted on "the truth, the whole truth and nothing but the truth." '

Maud Patterson (1875-1880). Written 1912.

Miss Ewing's background in overseas travel and cosmopolitan outlook inspired many of her former pupils to find employment in other parts of the world. These included the orphan Eva Constance Fosbery, who sailed for New Zealand in April 1877 but was shipwrecked and lost everything. She received a grant of £50 from the Endowment Fund and, undeterred, sailed again, this time with much better fortune. Another pupil who went abroad after her Howell's schooldays ended was Laura Stevens Kernick, who had been admitted in February 1870, aged twelve. She was given permission to remain at school for another six months after her seventeenth birthday, whereupon she went to a school in Brittany to improve her French. The link with Howell's continued through her great-nieces, Patricia and Elizabeth Kernick, who attended in the 1930s.

Regrettably, Miss Ewing did not enjoy the robust health or the qualifications needed to take the school forward to the standard which the best English girls' schools were achieving in the 1870s. It is unfortunate that she did not try harder to persuade the Governors of the benefits of the pupils being allowed to sit the Cambridge

Higher Local Examinations, especially as the Headmistress of the Denbigh school succeeded in this matter. In addition to Dr Williams' School at Dolgellau, changes to a few other schools, such as Tasker's in Haverfordwest, enabled them to admit girls, and in January 1880 Carmarthen High School for Girls was opened, aiming to educate "girls of the middle class and lower high class, something on a similar footing to what existed at Llandaff and Denbigh", according to the Aberdare Report of 1881. Howell's was doubtless still the foremost girls' school in South Wales in 1880, but it would not be able to rest on its laurels if it were to maintain its reputation in the years ahead.

6

MISS KENDALL AND THE RAISING OF ACADEMIC STANDARDS, 1880-1914

Left: Extract from Miss Baldwin's report on the unsatisfactory state of the school, 1880.

I think it will be useless to enlarge on the unsatisfactory state of the Education, as that you have doubtless heard from the Examiner. Unhappily I have to inform you of what the Examiner could not, viz. that I found the discipline and morale of the School in still worse condition than the education - the low state of morale being a natural consequence of the laxity of discipline. Instead of going into details, it will I believe be more profitable to submit to you my plans for bringing about a better state of things.

The appointment of Miss Maria Kendall, at the age of thirty-six, to the headship on 14th April 1880, marked the beginning of a new era. Miss Kendall did not hail from a scholarly background (her father was a currier in Yeovil, Somerset) but she was well educated, widely-read and an accomplished French and German scholar, having spent time employed as a governess in France and Germany. Whereas her predecessors had no formal qualifications, Miss Kendall held an Honours Certificate in French, German, Latin, English and Scripture of the Cambridge Higher Local Examinations Board, gained at the age of thirty-three when she was working as a governess in St Ives. She taught in various English schools before being appointed as Second Mistress at the reputable School for the Daughters of Naval Officers at Twickenham.

Miss Kendall's wide experience prior to her arrival in Llandaff had made her aware of the changes needed in order for Howell's to retain its reputation in Wales and to compete with the most forward-thinking girls' schools in England. By the 1880s these were aiming to provide a sound academic education to prepare girls for Higher Education and a growing range of employment opportunities. Following the establishment of the London School of Medicine for Women in 1874, a handful of women had become doctors, fulfilling the objectives of English educational pioneers that middle class women should be able to earn a living in the same professions as men. Both the Howell's Schools, while praised in some ways, came in for criticism in the early 1880s, from the Aberdare Committee (1880-1) for not encouraging girls to aspire to the higher qualifications of the university local examinations boards and, in 1882, from Dr Frances Hoggan, the first female doctor from Wales, who lamented the absence of women and nonconformists from the governing bodies.

Miss Kendall's immediate impression was that the school was very backward and she did not mince words in setting out to the Governors her criticisms, which began in a letter of 29th June 1880, with an extremely lengthy and forthright attack on the teachers' ability, the timetable and almost all aspects of school life. She particularly condemned Miss Haynes, who had hoped to be appointed as Miss Ewing's successor, having effectively run the school during her illness and been a member of the teaching staff since 1861. Miss Kendall subsequently turned to the domestic side of affairs and criticised the Steward and his wife for mismanagement, he allegedly being deceitful to the point of taking up torn carpets in the dormitories when the Governors were visiting. Another attack was launched against the teaching of the "accomplishments", and especially the Music mistress, Miss Ewing's sister Mary, who had been at the school since 1863.

Miss Kendall in her Sitting Room.

Facing page
Dr Frederick Evans, the House Surgeon, with Miss Baldwin at the front of the school, c.1884.

HOWELL'S CHARITY.

LLANDAFF SCHOOL.

Under the Scheme for the Management of this School, settled by the Court of Chancery, it is directed that there shall be ADMITTED into the SCHOOL 30 FEMALE ORPHANS as "INMATES ON THE FOUNDATION," and 30 GIRLS as "PAY BOARDERS."

No Girl can be admitted before the age of 7, nor upon the Foundation after the age of 12.

The Inmates on the Foundation are instructed, clothed, and maintained at the expense of the Charity; and the Charge for board, washing and maintenance of the Pay Boarders is at present £20 per annum.

The Course of Instruction includes the principles of the Christian religion, reading, writing, arithmetic, English grammar, geography, biography, history, music, drawing, and languages. The Girls are also taught needlework, and to cut out and make their own clothes, and are instructed in such other subjects of the like nature as the Head Mistress with the assent of the Local Governors, may from time to time direct.

Forty Day Scholars are also received into the School, on payment of an entrance fee of 10s., and £2 a term for Girls under 12 years of age, and £2 13s. 4d. for Girls above that age, and arrangements may be made with the Head Mistress to receive Day Scholars as Day Boarders on payment of such a sum for their Board as the Governors shall direct.

The School Terms commence 15th January, 15th May, and the 15th September.

Candidates who are selected are required to pass a Test Examination, particulars of which may be obtained on application to the Clerk.

When Vacancies occur, they are advertised in the *Western Mail*, at Cardiff; *The Cambrian*, at Swansea; *The Monmouthshire Beacon*, at Monmouth; and *The Monmouthshire Merlin*, at Newport; and printed forms of application (which alone will receive attention), and all necessary information may *then* be obtained from "C. R. WALDRON, Solicitor, Cardiff," the Clerk to the Local Governors.

Llandaff, 1884.

The ensuing shake-up brought about major changes in procedures. Wednesday and Friday visits to the Cathedral soon came to an end, and no longer was the catechism recited every Sunday. The practice of curtsying to the Headmistress was abolished, as was the reading of the orphans' letters to parents by a governess. The First Class became known as the Sixth Form. New regulations relating to boarders' exeats were issued and a change from two semesters to three terms a year began in 1884. For the first time, girls were allowed to speak at meal-times. Miss Kendall later recalled her early days at Howell's: "There was no talking at meals. I found that very trying, and used to wish that we had a reader as they have in Convent refectories. But that was soon altered, and it was not long before I had to call sometimes for less talking." Another innovation was the introduction of school reports for parents.

After a few months, Miss Haynes and Miss Ewing left, having been virtually forced out. By the end of 1882, not a single governess

from Miss Ewing's day was left, and most of the replacements did not last long either. Two other influential figures, who had been associated with the school from the start, also soon disappeared from the scene. Bishop Ollivant, who had been instrumental in securing the site for the school and guiding it successfully for many years, died in December 1882, and a few months later so did the old school surgeon, Dr Thomas Evans. The link with that family was retained with the appointment of his son, Dr Frederick William Evans, to succeed him in September 1883.

The House Steward inherited by Miss Ewing was given a month's notice in December 1880. His successors were equally unsatisfactory, leading to the decision in 1897 to replace them and their wives with a resident Housekeeper, aged at least thirty-five years, "to keep the books, pay the household bills and assist in the management of the servants and institution". Soon Miss Kendall herself took over responsibility for approving all expenditure. Another change came that year when the Governors agreed "that no Servant be engaged for the future who is not prepared to do without beer". Soon it was decided that no more beer was to be ordered unless it was needed for the Dining Room.

The House Steward was severely admonished for having disobeyed express orders as to giving away beer to persons not belonging to the Establishment.

Reprimand for the House Steward, 17th August 1882.

Miss Kendall sought to be more selective in the girls admitted to the school. She recorded details about the standard of new entrants in the Admissions Register, noting for example that eleven-year-old Mary Elizabeth Price from Llandovery, who joined in April 1881, was "fairly advanced but has a shocking accent". A new entrance examination was introduced; and seven-year-old Annie Gertrude Gaskell, who started on 1st February 1883, was the first pupil to be examined under the new system.

The tradition of the Christmas prize-giving soon came to an end and the Midsummer Public Examination gave way to the written examinations of the Oxford and Cambridge Examining Board, Howell's being only the third girls' school (after Edgbaston and Clifton High) to be admitted. Miss Kendall thus succeeded in gaining the Governors' consent on an issue where Miss Ewing had failed. As the Reverend W Bruce succinctly stated at the June 1883 prize-giving, "Hitherto the examination had been a public one by a private individual, and it was now a private one by the representative of a public body", which he considered would carry more weight outside the school.

Miss Kendall later recalled this reform, showing clearly her views about the old system: "The only examination they [the girls] had was at the Summer Prize-giving, when the girls were examined publicly

'My first recollection of HSL is coming away from an interview and a kind of viva voce examination. On my first day in September 1885, my mother and I were interviewed by Miss Kendall, who was a bit awe-inspiring to a small girl, and I was then handed over to an older girl to look after me. Miss Kendall always read prayers at 8am and 8pm and the whole school assembled in the large Schoolroom for a psalm, also presided over by Miss Kendall. She always was perfectly dressed in a quiet fashion and looked thoroughly well-groomed, and this perfection of neatness was enforced in the school. I think we all took great pride in our neatness in appearance and the way we kept our clothes and books.

Shakespeare plays were a yearly feature in the last three years of my schooldays. I took part in *Twelfth Night*, *As You Like It* and *The Merchant of Venice*. Miss Cook, who was Music mistress (piano and class singing) seemed to be the one who grounded us and gave us what is now known as elocution but which we called reading and reciting. On All Hallow's Eve, Miss Cook did a sort of fortune-telling. She organised all sorts of fun for us. Miss Maudson, who taught Needlework, looked after our general health and there was a kind of children's matron who nursed us in the sick room when we were ill and bathed the youngest children.

In 1887, Queen Victoria's Jubilee was honoured by the school by making the summer uniforms especially colourful – cream or beige with red velvet facings on the collars and cuffs. The hats were trimmed with orange pompoms. The day was celebrated with a picnic. We went by wagonette to St Fagans. The boarders sat in a hayfield and watched Miss Kendall cut up a large veal and ham pie. There was a special cantata for prize-giving and an extra week's holiday.

We were allowed visitors twice a term and we could go out with them for a couple of hours or so. Sometimes Mabel Harré went for tea with her aunt [Miss Kendall] and on occasions I was invited too, which was a great honour. The school in every respect was thoroughly well-organised and the food was excellent, all due, I am quite sure, to Miss Kendall's skill and forethought.'

Gertrude Kathleen Robertson (1885-1894, Head Girl 1893-4). Written 1960.

viva voce in the school-room, form by form, in the presence of the governesses, the parents, and any other friends of the school who were invited to attend. I suffered this ordeal only once for though there was an examination the following year by a private examiner it was not viva voce. Then the school was put under the Oxford and Cambridge Board. Thus we got on modern lines." In his report to the Board in 1885, the Examiner said that he was "struck by the rapid intellectual advance of the school, and that it would compare favourably with the best High Schools". The Drapers' Company sent a special letter of congratulation. Miss Kendall was, of course, very proud. This was the year in which Howell's won its first Open Scholarship, to Bedford College, London.

In Wales in general during the 1880s and 1890s, the cause of women's education was advanced considerably, notably by the Association for Promoting the Education of Girls in Wales, set up at the instigation of Dilys Davies in 1886 "to raise the standard or ideal of girls' education and arouse public opinion to a fuller appreciation of its value". The Association advocated "the claims of girls to be educated as men are educated" and stressed their economic importance to society. At Howell's, the Governors heard on 1st February that two girls, Lilian Laybourne and Ethel Griffiths, had gained places at Newnham College, Cambridge. In addition, Mabel Geach, a day scholar, achieved the highest score in Mathematics in the Higher Certificate examinations of the Oxford and Cambridge Board at the age of sixteen and won a scholarship to Girton College. Two girls gained exhibitions at

Cardiff and Aberystwyth and therefore were among the earliest female students at those institutions. The Master of the Drapers' Company could report proudly at the prize-giving in the summer of 1890 that "Girls from Howell's were not unknown at the great university centres of Girton and Newnham". These were remarkable achievements considering that the school had only had a few years' experience of preparing pupils for public examinations.

Among the boarders of the 1890s were Miss Kendall's two nieces. Mabel Mary Kendall Harré, who started in September 1891, spent a year as Junior Assistant after completing her schooling and in 1906 became one of the founder members of the Hywelian Guild for former pupils. Her sister Gertrude Eleanor Harré, a pupil from January 1893 to July 1898, was one of the first two Howell's girls to be awarded a County Exhibition on the basis of good conduct and academic progress. She studied Science at Cambridge and later qualified as a doctor, subsequently becoming the first female Medical Registrar at St Mary's Hospital, Paddington, and then a consultant pathologist.

The rise in standards came about largely because of the improved calibre of the staff. One of Miss Kendall's first appointments was Mr James Bush, a teacher at the Cardiff School of Art (and founder of the Cardiff Rugby Club) who, at the rate of five shillings an hour, in October 1880 began to teach senior pupils perspective and geometrical drawing in the Dining Room, in preparation for the Oxford and Cambridge Board and other examinations. Girls had to have a chaperone in his lessons, as they did for all male members of staff. In 1892 he was succeeded by his wife Fanny, who taught several very large classes until she retired in 1920. In that period it was, of course, relatively uncommon for married women to teach, but Mrs Bush also worked for the School of Art and was involved with the Cambridge Local Examinations Board. Their daughter Ethel, who was a pupil at the school from 1886 to 1892, gained a first class honours degree in English from London in 1896 and returned as a mistress in September 1908 to teach English and Scripture.

Miss Alice Georgiana Winny, who came to be highly respected for her scholarship and teaching ability, joined the school in January 1889 to teach Botany and spent her entire teaching career at Howell's. One of the earliest students of Newnham College,

Cambridge, in Natural Science, she also taught Geography and Scripture. Her value to the school was quickly recognised by Miss Kendall and she was appointed Second Mistress after only one year. She soon initiated Shakespeare recitations, which later developed into the annual production of a full play. At first acted in the Schoolroom, where a heavy red curtain was used to separate the performers from the audience, these plays were each performed three times: for the day scholars, the parents and finally for invited guests on "Miss Kendall's night". The guests wore evening dress and had supper in the Board Room with the cast afterwards.

Another prominent staff member was Hester Bellamy from Bristol, a former Orphan of the Foundation, who had been admitted, aged ten, in July 1882. She became Head Girl and as soon as her days as a pupil were over in August 1887 she was appointed as a Junior Assistant. In 1890 she gained the Oxford and Cambridge Higher Certificate and she remained a member of the Howell's staff, with Geography as her main subject, until her death in 1933. She was to become one of the founding members of the Hywelian Guild and its Vice-President from 1909 to 1933.

Miss Fanny Louisa Cook, the Music and Elocution mistress, was famed for her methods of endeavouring to make the girls sing and speak correctly. They had to put corks, for which they paid 1d a term, between their teeth, lie on the floor and say clearly, "Spanish ships at sea". Miss Cook also helped Miss Winny prepare the girls for the Shakespeare plays and worked hard to train the girls for prize-giving; in appreciation, Lord Tredegar presented her with a silver-mounted ivory baton for conducting. Mr George Galloway Beale, the organist at Llandaff Cathedral, joined the staff in September 1894 as a visiting teacher of piano, singing and harmony. After the Hall was built in 1900, Miss Kendall was known to stand outside as girls went in for singing or piano lessons there, to make sure that they were suitably clad.

In 1889 two substantial changes affected the school. George Woods tendered his resignation as Examiner on 24th June, at the age of eighty-one. The changes to the curriculum had been largely of his making and he had successfully taught thousands of pupils. Following his retirement there was a dispute between the Governors and the Drapers, the latter wanting Miss Kendall to take over most of his responsibilities, including conducting the

examinations for admission to the school, "as is the almost universal practice of the other schools of this standing". The Drapers stood firm although the Governors voiced their objections strongly, and one, Mr Jonas Watson, resigned in protest. They then asked the vicar of Llandaff, the Reverend James Rice Buckley, to conduct the test examination.

The other great development of 1889, which had far-reaching consequences, was the passing of the Welsh Intermediate Education Act, in the wake of the setting up of county councils. It established county joint education committees, which were to draw up plans for county schools (later grammar schools): these were to be financed from a combination of the rates, a treasury grant, fees from pupils and the reorganization of old endowments. This was the first time that public money was spent on specifically Welsh intermediate education. The Glamorgan authorities submitted proposals to the Charity Commissioners to give them control of Howell's School and to take any surplus income beyond an amount to be set aside for its needs. Of the Charity income, 60% would go to South

Wales (36% to Glamorgan and 8% to each of Cardiff, Newport and Monmouth) and 40% to Denbighshire, after setting aside a sum for the maintenance of each school. The administration of the school would be transferred to a Governing Body on which a large representation would be given to Glamorgan County Council. There were plans to have at least one hundred day scholars as well as the sixty boarders.

The Governors objected to the inclusion of Howell's in the new Scheme. Most of their protests were in vain, though they did succeed in resisting the abolition of the name Howell's School "considering that the whole foundation is due to that Benefactor". From 1895 the orphans were replaced by thirty Howell's scholars and a sum of money was provided for their maintenance. There were twenty-three Governors; apart from three co-opted, fifteen places went to members of the Glamorgan Education Authority (of which at least two had to be women), three to the Drapers' Company and two to the University College of South Wales and Monmouthshire. The Education Authority was given the surplus income from the

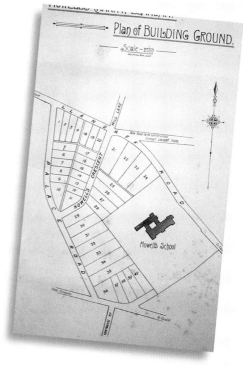

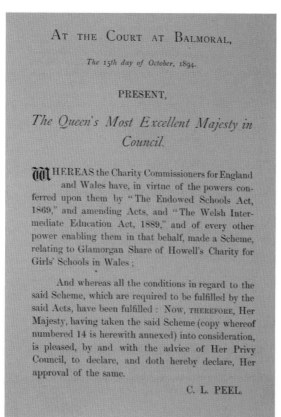

AT THE COURT AT BALMORAL,

The 15th day of October, 1894.

PRESENT,

The Queen's Most Excellent Majesty in Council.

WHEREAS the Charity Commissioners for England and Wales have, in virtue of the powers conferred upon them by "The Endowed Schools Act, 1869," and amending Acts, and "The Welsh Intermediate Education Act, 1889," and of every other power enabling them in that behalf, made a Scheme, relating to Glamorgan Share of Howell's Charity for Girls' Schools in Wales;

And whereas all the conditions in regard to the said Scheme, which are required to be fulfilled by the said Acts, have been fulfilled: Now, THEREFORE, Her Majesty, having taken the said Scheme (copy whereof numbered 14 is herewith annexed) into consideration, is pleased, by and with the advice of Her Privy Council, to declare, and doth hereby declare, Her approval of the same.

C. L. PEEL.

Thomas Howell Trust but was to pay any deficit the school might incur. By contrast, the Bishop of St Asaph encouraged the House of Lords to petition against the new Scheme for Howell's School, Denbigh, so it continued to be managed by the Drapers' Company, while retaining the 40% of the income of the Trust allotted to it.

The 1894 Scheme also allowed women and those who were not members of the Church of England to be Governors. Orphans already at the school, of whom there were twenty-five in January 1895, were to remain there on the existing terms. The school became known as Howell's County Glamorgan School for Girls and from that time the Drapers' Company had much less control over its administration. It was to cater for pupils between the ages of ten and seventeen years, but it was possible to seek permission to stay until eighteen. No particular religious doctrine was to be taught and children could be exempted from prayer or worship if their parents or guardians so requested. For the first time there were scholarships available for day scholars. Girls who had spent at least three years in a public elementary school in the County of Glamorgan or in the County Borough of Cardiff or Swansea were eligible.

On 10th January 1895, twenty-two Governors assembled in the Board Room under the new Scheme, including the first female Governors, Miss Hughes and the Hon. Miss Pamela Bruce. Lord Tredegar, great benefactor and veteran of Balaclava in the Crimean War, was chosen as the new Chairman. The Governors delegated to a Finance and House Committee the responsibility of dealing with school business, including the signing of cheques. At the prize-giving later that year, Lord Tredegar distributed the prizes and in his speech stated that "Howell's had always had a great reputation and under Miss Kendall . . . had attained a noted excellence." As the era of the orphans came to an end and the new order began, this reputation was to continue into the twentieth century. The last orphan to leave was Edith Hooper, whose matriculation fees the Governors agreed to pay on 25th June 1905.

The Governors also passed a motion in April 1895 "that steps be taken to develop the land belonging to the Foundation", by which they meant leasing out part of the field around the perimeter in suitable lots for building. The Charity Commissioners agreed, instructing them to organise the building of roads and sewers, and then divide up the land and work out suitable rents. This resulted in the creation of Howell's Crescent and new houses on part of Palace Road and Pencisely Road. It was decided that no building over six feet high should be erected within thirty feet of the back wall adjoining the school and that a gate should be built at the school end of the lane running from the tennis courts to Howell's Crescent.

The obvious effect of this building was that the amount of open land for the use of the school decreased. Fortunately, as Miss Kendall was keen to encourage girls to play organised games, a sizeable amount of land was preserved for playing fields. Over the year, leases were renewed and permission had to be sought for any changes to the properties. It was not until the 1970s that many of the freeholds began to be sold, following the Leasehold Reform Act of 1967, which gave the leaseholders the right to purchase the freeholds.

Another significant change came in 1896 with the establishment of the Central Welsh Board (CWB) for Intermediate Education. This Board was responsible for overseeing the Welsh Intermediate Schools through an annual examination and triennial inspection, and so Howell's severed its connection with the Oxford and Cambridge Board. As the CWB had both the examination and inspection of schools under its jurisdiction, many inspectors came to know the school and its pupils well and took a strong personal interest in its development.

The Association for Promoting the Education of Girls in Wales came to an end in 1901, having achieved its objectives. The Cambrian News of 7th February 1902 praised its achievement: "The girls in Wales now possess a system of education extending from the Elementary School to the University." It was, of course, mainly the daughters of middle class parents who were benefiting from access to secondary girls' schools and to universities. By this time, the two Howell's Schools and Dr Williams' School were acknowledged to be the premier girls' schools in Wales, and on a par with the best English girls' schools.

Although in 1901 and 1903 Miss Kendall lamented the low standards of those admitted with day scholarships and thought that pay boarders should also be able to qualify for awards, the school continued to receive good reports from the CWB. The inspectors in 1905 stated that "order and discipline were excellent" and praised the standard of teaching and achievement. As far as English was concerned, this would have been due in large measure to Miss Faraday, a relation of the famous scientist, who joined the school in 1903. Her academic credentials were quite remarkable. She had a BA degree with first class honours, an MA with distinction in English Language and Literature and had studied Sanscrit at Oxford as well as doing research into Old Irish, Icelandic and diplomatic charters, about which she had produced several publications. She was also a Fellow of the Victoria University of Manchester.

Leaving Exhibitions were introduced in 1906 for those who had passed matriculation examinations for university and for those who had studied "a fitting combination of subjects in order to study for a degree". The school expanded numerically in 1906 when Miss Kendall secured the Governors' agreement for the opening of a preparatory department for girls of eight to ten years old, with an entrance fee of ten shillings and fees of £2 a term.

The first decade of the twentieth century was not completely devoid of problems, nonetheless. Early in 1907 the Clerk to the Governors was instructed to write to parents about pupils "being sent to an establishment of this character in a state of personal uncleanliness". In 1908 a rat infestation required the services of a professional rat-catcher and the Dental Surgeon reported to the Governors that "the condition of the teeth of new pupils coming to the school was invariably poor", with an average of eight and a half teeth defective in each mouth. One unfortunate girl aged fourteen had twenty-six defective teeth, of which nineteen were "past remedy". In December 1909, a major outbreak of measles in school forced Miss Kendall to postpone the Christmas theatricals and to change the date of the holidays.

Nevertheless, in the spring of 1908 the CWB concluded that "The general impression left by the school is most favourable. The organisation of the school is very satisfactory, the higher work in all departments being entrusted to a specialist." After a similar report in June 1910, the Board of Education gave recognition to Howell's as an "Efficient Secondary School", and from 1st August 1910 it was added to the list of such schools.

7

BUILDING IMPROVEMENTS AND A DISCIPLINED RÉGIME, 1880-1914

Facing page
The first Chemistry Laboratory, in a loft above the stables, 1890s.

Above: Tiles from the ground floor of the Sanatorium.

Miss Kendall was concerned with physical as well as academic improvements, but in the early years she faced a number of battles with the Drapers' Company. Her first major request was for a separate Sanatorium but the Drapers resisted for several years, largely on grounds of cost. It was not until 1887 that it was built, together with a Covered Way linking it to the main school. The siting of new music rooms was also a bone of contention. Miss Kendall strongly objected to the Drapers' suggestion that they should be built in the quadrangle. An alternative location, proposed by the Governors in September 1883, between the shed in the playground and the Dining Room and thus sufficiently far away from the Schoolroom for the sound not to travel, also came to nothing. The lack of response to letters by the Drapers' Company was most frustrating and it is small wonder that Miss Kendall twice informed the Governors that she was applying for another post.

Science teaching in girls' schools in the nineteenth century was quite unusual and a Laboratory was a rarity. However, by 1890 Howell's had both. In October 1884, the Governors agreed to the establishment of a botanical garden at a cost of £25 after an examiner from the Oxford and Cambridge Board sent Miss Kendall a hamper of labelled plants, which the gardener planted under her watchful eye. The first Presbyterian mistress, a Miss Lloyd, was appointed to teach Natural Science in September 1885. Early in 1885, Miss Kendall asked for gas to be laid on in the Experimental Room for Chemistry. As there was no money for the building of

a Laboratory, the former bacon loft above the stables or coach-house was fitted with gas and water and adapted for that purpose. The first person to teach there was Miss Rich, who was on the staff from September 1887 to December 1888. In this dark room the grooms had previously waited during Governors' meetings, and the only means of entry was by a ladder. Gertrude Robertson (Head Girl 1893-4) recalled how, on a winter's evening when there was moonlight, the boarders would pelt across to it, averting their eyes when they passed dead pigs hanging up.

Since under the new Scheme there were plans to have more pupils, an extension was required, to provide more facilities. The Governors resolved to have a Cookery School and Laundry for the subject entitled Domestic Economy, the latter to be used for the instruction of the girls in laundry work. These were built opposite each other off the Covered Way in 1896. However, the Laundry was never used for its intended purpose and was used instead initially as an additional classroom. The following year, the school applied to be connected to the Llandaff Telephone Exchange; the number allocated was Llandaff 10.

It was during Miss Kendall's time that, for a few years, some of the pupils first boarded in a hostel away from the main school building. The increasing demand for places led, in November 1885, to the Governors considering the idea of providing accommodation for day scholars, whose numbers they were keen to increase. Unsuccessful applicants for places as pay boarders were invited to apply for places as day scholars and stay in the hostel. This opened on 15th May 1886, probably in a vacant inn on Llandaff Green, with a widowed mother of eight, Mrs Fanny Tennant, as the manager, bringing her three youngest daughters with her. The fee charged, £30-£34 a year, was considerably higher than the amount paid by the boarders in school. After about fifteen months, Mrs Tennant was replaced by Miss Jane Staines from Cheltenham. There was an outbreak of scarlet fever in October 1887 but by the end of that year there were eleven girls and an assistant governess, who helped with preparation and accompanied the girls to school. When Oaklands, which was larger and more convenient (being opposite the school), became available for rent, Miss Staines moved there with her boarders, who numbered nineteen by the beginning of 1889. She announced her decision to resign in 1892 and was not replaced, so the girls who had lived there had to find lodgings with other people considered by the Governors to be respectable. The idea of a hostel was briefly revived in 1897 and plans were made for one to be built on land adjoining the school grounds, but it never materialised because of conditions imposed by the Charity Commissioners which the Governors felt unable to meet. Oaklands was purchased by Mr John Duncan, whose four daughters, Agnes, Ethel, Violet and Mabel, all attended Howell's. Ethel later returned for a time as Gymnastics mistress and Agnes was one of the founder members of the Hywelian Guild; much later, in 1950, as Mrs Challenor, she had the distinction of becoming the first female mayor of Abingdon. Mr Duncan always showed a

great interest in the school, offered lavish hospitality and became a Governor. Oaklands was bought by the school for use as a hostel again in 1925, after his death.

The year 1900 was marked by the completion of a new south wing, for which the diocesan architect George Halliday was responsible. Two hard courts and a wych elm with a circular seat had to be sacrificed to make way for the new building. It included a Hall (now called the Great Hall), a Lower Hall, mistresses' rooms and the music rooms which Miss Kendall had been asking for since 1883. This enabled all the pianos, which had previously been scattered throughout the school, to be located in one area. To cater for the growing number of pupils there was also increased cloakroom and bedroom accommodation and improved heating and hot water systems. In addition, there was a new bicycle shed outside.

The main development was the construction of the Hall, complete with a platform, and designed to seat about four hundred and fifty people. It was opened on 26th June 1900 by the educationalist Margaret, Lady Verney, a member of the Council of the University of Wales, in a ceremony presided over by Lord Tredegar. As befitted such a grand occasion, the Master and Clerk of the Drapers' Company and other dignitaries as well as parents, the girls and various friends were also present. The day girls wore white frocks for the ceremony and the boarders were allowed to wear white silk and lace fichus (triangular shawls) with their new

Facing page
Left: *The first Laboratory.*
Above right: *Microscopic preparations box, early 20th century.*
Below right: *Early 20th century slides from microscopic preparations box.*

Right: *The Hall, c.1920.*

"AS YOU LIKE IT."

PERFORMED BY THE

GIRLS OF HOWELL'S SCHOOL, LLANDAFF,

December 19th and 20th, 1900.

green Sunday frocks. Lady Verney was presented by Lord Tredegar with a splendid engraved silver key, which was used to open the Hall door.

Miss Kendall was clearly very pleased with the new Hall. From this time, the Shakespeare play was performed there annually at Christmas instead of the Schoolroom, where there was no scenery. The showing of lantern slides in the Hall, initially to provide illustrations for Geography and Botany lessons, became a frequent occurrence for many years. Drill was also conducted there by Miss Ada Steiner, wearing a gymslip, rather than in the Day Room as before. Miss Kendall succeeded in persuading the Governors that a grand piano was needed there, and Mr Beale taught the senior girls to play it; previously his lessons had taken place in Miss Kendall's waiting room.

However, in 1902 she lamented the "bare appearance of our beautiful Great Hall", which led to the submission of a scheme for its decoration in the form of cartoons by Mr J M Staniforth (1863-1921), printer, art reviewer and Western Mail cartoonist, at a cost of about £350. The task of creating the murals, which depicted Shakespearian scenes, was finally completed by September 1905. Exactly two years later the Governors granted permission for a stage, at a cost not exceeding £20.

Improvements took place in other areas of the school. The years of climbing the ladder to the loft above the stables for Science lessons came to an end in 1904 when a new Chemistry Laboratory was built off the Covered Way. An Art Room, complete with a dark cupboard for photography and a modelling room, was also constructed nearby. Following the CWB Triennial Inspection of the school in 1905, Owen Owen, the Chief Inspector, commented, "The buildings are excellent in every respect. A very fine wing has been built, containing laboratories, art and modelling rooms."

Mr Halliday was appointed in 1906 to construct a Gymnasium and a Study for the mistresses, as their former Sitting Room had been partly absorbed into the approaches to the new Hall. The new Gymnasium was used for the first time as the new school year started in September 1907, after weighing and measuring machines and other apparatus had been purchased and the merits of the English and Swedish Physical Education systems considered. Girls wore plimsolls, navy bloomers and a navy skirt and blouse.

Miss Kendall was committed to making games and physical education an important part of school life. In her first year, two lawn tennis courts had been laid out on a part of the field to the north-west of the school. By the early 1890s there were hard courts, at one side of which there was a large shed with two swings and at the other a small plot of garden. Matches were played occasionally with Cardiff University College students; the team wore long pale blue skirts and white blouses. A pavilion was built at the side of the grass courts in 1901. Meanwhile, a field for hockey was planned in 1897 and the new game proved very popular. By 1903 Miss Kendall

was able to report to the Governors that the team had won every match of the season, and this success continued in future years. The girls wore the navy gymnastics outfit with a red belt and red tie. In October 1904 Miss Field was appointed to teach physical exercises and drill, and basketball was introduced. Miss Kendall was also eager for girls to learn to swim and in 1908 secured the use of the public swimming baths in Cathedral Road for the sole use of thirty boarders on a Wednesday afternoon.

Despite the improvements in teaching facilities, boarding conditions continued much as before, Miss Kendall's Victorian ideas of comfort not changing even by the late 1910s. The girls slept in large dormitories in the school building, with little privacy. When it was cold, maids entered before the girls were due to get up in order to light the fires. One former pupil later recalled seeing Miss Cook appear in the West Dormitory at 6.30am and, using a piece of chalk, draw a semicircle near the grate, forbidding the girls to step inside it. Each night boarders who had "sinned" in any way had to tell Miss Kendall in French what they had done wrong or failed to do.

Above left: The new gymnasium.
Above: The hockey team which won the South Wales shield, 1907. Back row, left to right: Phyllis Cox, Olive James, Mabel Duncan, Euronwy Hill. Middle: Kelly Hammond, Violet Duncan (Mabel's twin), Ethel Duncan, Ernestine Phillips, Christine Forbes. Front: Bronwen Jones, Bronwen Thomas. Far left: Miss Kendall (at centre of picture, in black) watching tennis and croquet, early 1880s. Left: Two of the earliest hockey players, c.1898.

'Cleanliness and Godliness went hand in hand. On rising we stripped to the waist for morning ablutions and duly brushed our hair, then bedside prayers before going down to do our homework. The same process being repeated on retiring, only this time under the supervision of a mistress. Saturday afternoons from 4 to 5 o'clock were devoted to Toilet of the Hair – hair-brushing for an hour! We only washed our hair twice during the term.'

Lily Abbott, née Bell (1899-1905). Written 1972.

All the boarders' leisure time indoors at the weekends was spent in the Schoolroom, with the wooden partition pulled back. The girls sat on hard benches, with no backs, and were supervised by the one housemistress. They were allowed to speak in the dormitories once a year, on the last night of the Autumn Term, when they were unsupervised as all the staff were involved with the school play on "Miss Kendall's night".

Discipline was very strict. The girls were not allowed to speak to the maids. Miscreants faced the humiliation of being sent to sit "under the clock" – the central timepiece in the large Schoolroom – for a period of ten to twenty minutes. Printed rules, dubbed the Ten Commandments, were read every Saturday. There was one set for boarders, read in the evening before family prayers, and one for the day scholars, read in the morning before lessons started, the last of these being: "No day scholar may take any letter, book, flower or any communication whatsoever to or from a boarder. Anyone breaking this rule is liable to have her attendance at the school suspended and to be eventually expelled." Dora and

Winifred Kyte were day scholars in the 1890s and Dora's daughter, Nesta Morgan, recalled her mother telling her that on Saturday mornings, after the rules had been read, "Several girls would be sure to be reprimanded because they had been seen going down the drive the previous evening without wearing gloves, or because they were late. Miss Kendall often got hold of the wrong name.

Miss Kendall's bark was worse than her bite. Dora Kyte's duty as cloakroom monitress involved having to lock the cloakroom door after morning Prayers, causing her often to be slightly late for the first lesson. One day she had hardly sat down at her desk when there was a crash and in came Miss Kendall, crying, "Who was that late girl? I distinctly heard her footsteps. My dear Miss –, why do you let that wicked girl into your class at this late hour? Who is she? Stand up, my dear, and explain why you are so late. I cannot allow such conduct to continue in the school. . . . Miss –, you must not allow her in. But first, explain yourself. Why are you late?" "I'm cloakroom monitress, Miss Kendall." "Oh!" was Miss Kendall's only comment and then there was a further crash as the door banged behind her. The girls used to say, "Hark to the sound of her feet before her" as Miss Kendall crossed the Stone Hall to the Dining Room, where some of the girls would be doing prep. She would fling open the door, the train of her dress thrown over her arm, and immediately begin to shout, "You wicked girls! You wicked girls! My dear Miss Maudson [the Needlework mistress], why do you let these wicked girls do such things?" They never knew what they were supposed to have done wrong. Agnes Wood, née Crouch, recalled that naughty girls were sent to sit on the coal box and that once when she was there, Miss Cook came past, checked that no-one was looking and popped a large sweet into her mouth!

Every ailment, ranging from a sore throat to a chilblain, was treated with Gregory Powder by Miss Maudson and the sewing maid, who looked after the girls' general health. This maid, who lived in the Sanatorium, was the only one not to wear a cap, and was regarded as superior to the others. Anyone who complained of a medical condition also had her ration of sweets on Sundays withheld. The timetable for this "Day of Rest and Gladness" was recalled in 1949 by Lily Abbott (née Bell), a boarder from 1899 to 1905:

Facing page
The Schoolroom in about 1910.

Below right: Beatrice Violet Thomas in 1891, wearing the Orphans' uniform of the time.
Right: Beatrice Violet Thomas's Confirmation certificate and St John's Ambulance Certificate.

8am	Family prayers, breakfast and bed-making
9 - 9.30am	Scripture learning – Collect, Epistle or Gospel for the day
9.30 - 10am	Get ready for service at the cathedral at 11 a.m., proceeding thereto in three or four "crocodiles"
12 noon - 1 pm	Back home at 12.30p.m. or thereabouts, change from best dress to everyday one and get ready for dinner
2 - 2.45 pm	Read library books accompanied by the weekly ration of sweets (one's own)
3.30 pm	Service at the Cathedral, preceded by preparation as before
5 pm	Tea (with rock cakes)
7 pm	Preparation of more Scripture, the lower forms learning the catechism, the middle forms the communion service with explanations by the mistress who presided, and the upper forms learned the why and wherefore of the creeds or studied a book called "Evan Daniel", this class being taken by the Head Mistress
7.30 pm	Singing practice of psalms and hymns for the following Sunday
8 pm	Evening prayers

The outdoor clothing worn by the orphans on Sundays was described by Olwen Davies (née Jones), a pupil from 1894 to 1902, as consisting of a heavy black cloth jacket coming well below the waist, a pair of black heavy boots, dark gloves, grey worsted wool stockings kept up with garters, a white silk neck-tie tied in a bow, and a black straw hat trimmed with black velvet and with two orange pompoms. The pompoms had to be removed because young boys from Llandaff used to run alongside the crocodile of girls heading to the Cathedral, accompanied by their bonnet-wearing mistresses, mocking them and shouting, "Oranges, two a penny!" The girls disliked having to change into different clothes at least four times a day, but Miss Kendall used to say, "Think how many times a day the Queen has to change!"

In school on weekdays the orphans wore black alpaca pinafores and sleeves, but on Sundays and Committee days (when Governors' meetings took place) the black pinafores were replaced by white linen ones. Indoors they wore heavy black Oxford lace-up shoes; for the playground they changed

'It was a dreadful offence to possess anything at school not marked with the owner's name. This was firmly – if painfully – impressed upon me, my first night at school, Friday, Sept. 21st, 1894, to be exact. A certain mistress much-loved or much-feared for her eccentricities was on dormitory duty, and asked us if all our toilet requisites were marked. We said yes. Later, an inspection took place and my sponge was discovered unmarked, and vials of wrath descended on my head! I was amazed to find what an evil thing I was! To make matters worse, I was impudent enough to say in self-defence, that I did not know that a sponge *could* be marked. For this I spent many unhappy hours "under the clock" – *accompanied by the sponge* (to the entertainment of the other girls) until an angel from heaven in the form of one Gertrude David, my "mother", rescued me by sewing on to the offending sponge, a tape bearing my name.'

Olwen Davies, née Jones (1894-1902). Written 1920.

into special old boots and coats. In summer they had frocks of a light material in shades of blue and green. These had a staff neckband with a lace or embroidery "tucker" tucked in, and the "mothers" of the little ones had to sew in clean tuckers weekly. All the dresses were made by the sewing maid and her assistants. The summer hats were cream or white, and umbrellas and mackintoshes were issued. This uniform did not change until Miss Trotter became Headmistress in 1920. Day girls wore no uniform.

The end of each term was heralded by the "Train Letter". Miss Winny appeared with a timetable and established the time of each girl's train home. She then returned a couple of days later to dictate the letter which, apart from variations in the date, always read: "The holidays begin on Friday, July 21st, and Miss Kendall has arranged for me to travel on that day by the train leaving Cardiff at – *fill-in-the-time-for-yourself*. Kindly send me the money for my travelling expenses as soon as possible. My cab fare will be one shilling – *full-stop-new-paragraph*. School reopens on Tuesday, September 16th, and I must be back on that day before 6pm unless prevented by illness, in which case a medical certificate must be sent beforehand to Miss Kendall."

For old girls of the school, the year 1906 is synonymous with the establishment of the Hywelian Guild. A letter from Miss Kendall dated 3rd July 1905 was found in an unaddressed envelope by Miss Trotter late in 1933. It included these words: "I should very much like to see the formation of an Old Girls' Guild and the institution of a biennial gathering of its members at the old school. I believe it would not only be a pleasure to you to meet and renew acquaintanceships amid the old familiar scenes, but the Guild would also be a medium for mutual help, which might be valuable." An informal meeting was held in December 1905, at which it was proposed that Miss Kendall should be Guild President and Laura Roberts, née Hurman, Vice President. Eleven ex-pupils would form the committee with one, Lilian Laybourne, as Secretary. These included Mabel Harré, Miss Kendall's niece; Gladys Jones, who was briefly appointed as Miss Kendall's successor in 1919; and Agnes Duncan, the eldest of the four sisters who lived in Oaklands, who became the Guild's first Treasurer. The name Hywelian was chosen from the Welsh word for Howell. There was an annual subscription of one shilling or a life membership fee of one guinea. The badge, which was to be worn at meetings, depicted the arms and motto of the Drapers' Company, for which permission was granted in 1908.

The early committee meetings took place in Miss Kendall's drawing room. The members were attired in long narrow hobble skirts, black woollen stockings, button boots and enormous cartwheel

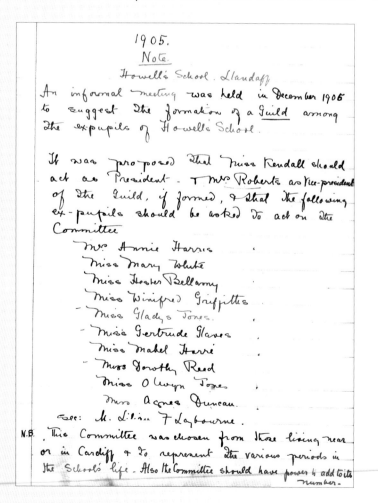

HYWELIAN GUILD.

FOUNDED 1906.

REPORT

FOR THE YEAR 1910–1911.

INCLUDING

Treasurer's Report, Rules, and List of Members.

BARGOED:
PETER WILLIAMS, THE BARGOED PRINTING WORKS.
1911.

Howell's School, Llandaff.

The Governors and Head Mistress request the pleasure of the Company of

Mr & Mrs Frewer

at a Garden Party, to be held in the School Grounds, on July 29th, from 3.30 to 6.30 p.m., to commemorate the Jubilee of the School.

HOWELL'S SCHOOL, LLANDAFF.

Garden Party,
IN THE
School Grounds, to commemorate the Jubilee of the School,
JULY 29TH, 1911.

PROGRAMME OF MUSIC
By ROBERTS' CITY ORCHESTRA, 3.30 to 6.30.

1.	...	...	"Grand Coronation March."	
2.	VALSE	...	"The Count of Luxemburg"	...
3.	OVERTURE	...	"Light Cavalry"	... Lehar.
4.	SOLO (Cornet)	...	"Softly Awakes my heart"	... Suppe.
			(From Samson and Delilah.)	Saint Saens.
			Mr T. BAMBOOM.	
5.	SELECTION	...	"Reminiscences of the Savoy"	... Sullivan.
6.	VALSE-LENTE	...	"The Quaker Girl"	... Monkton.
7.	(a) Entr'acte	...	"In the Shadows"	
	(b) Piccolo Solo	...	"Echo du Bois"	... Fucik.
8.	THREE DANCES	...	"Nell Gwyn"	... Damaire.
9.	VALSE	...	"The Chocolate Soldier"	... E. German.
10.	FANTASIA	...	"Faust"	... Strauss.
11.	MARCH	...	"The Children of the Regiment"	... Gounod.
				Fucik.

Conductor - - Mr. FRED. G. ROBERTS.

Marching, English and Swedish Country Dancers, and Part Songs, by the Scholars of the School.

Facing page
Left: The first page of the Hywelian Guild Minutes Book.
Right: An early Hywelian Guild Report, showing the Drapers' Coat of Arms used as the Guild's badge.

Top left: Senior boarders on Botany trip with Miss Winny to Peterston bog, 1910, wearing black ribbons on their hats in mourning for King Edward VII.
Above: Expedition to Penarth, 1914.
Top right: Admission letter, 1911.

Above: Garden Party invitation,1911.
Right: Garden party programme, 1911.

hats secured with long decorated hatpins. Miss Kendall's personal maid, Mabel, served the tea, wearing a stiffly starched and frilled cap and apron, as befitted the formality of the occasion. The Guild flourished, with summer meetings which included tea on the tennis lawns followed by a display of morris dancing and a match between pupils and Hywelians. It also developed a hockey team, which played several matches a year against local teams, and a Dramatic Society which gave an annual performance. At a committee meeting in May 1909, it was decided to provide two General Knowledge prizes from Guild funds to two pupils, one senior and one junior, the papers to be set and marked by Hywelians. This tradition lasted until 1983, when prizes were given for Current Affairs instead. In 1910 the first Annual Report was printed, from 1912 there was a New Year's Letter and the first winter meeting took place in January 1913.

The year 1910 marked the fiftieth anniversary of the school's opening but this landmark appears to have gone unmarked, although Miss Kendall had hoped that it might be possible to build a swimming pool. The Governors did not take up the suggestion put to them in writing by the Secretary of the Hywelian Guild that an extra week's holiday be granted to celebrate but they agreed to commemorate the jubilee the following summer. On Saturday 29th July, 1911, there was a Garden Party, which included a gymnastics display, morris dancing and a band. The Hywelians arranged their summer reunion to coincide with the event. Fortunately it was almost over before a massive dust storm blew up, bringing proceedings to a premature halt.

That year, the school celebrated George V's coronation with a day's holiday. For the boarders there was a special tea and entertainment in school. In June 1911, the new King and Queen passed the school on their way to Llandaff Cathedral, their car slowing down as they were driven past the entrance to enable the pupils to see them.

In the years leading up to the First World War, Miss Kendall's enthusiasm for improvements continued unabated. She obtained what she called "modern single desks" to replace the old long ones, a bookcase for the library to hold the scholars' books, a stereoscope and the necessary slides for the teaching of Geometry and an umbrella stand for the pupils. Mr Halliday prepared plans for new store rooms, larders, a bakehouse, the housekeeper's room and bathroom, and there were new electric bells at the tradesmen's entrance. In March 1914, the Board of Education sanctioned the building of two new bedrooms and fifteen cubicles to accommodate twenty extra boarders, together with substantial improvements to the servants' quarters, which raised the north wing to three floors. Miss Kendall's desire for a Culture House for Botany, situated near the Laboratories, was also satisfied; she had written to the Governors during the summer holiday of 1913, "We have before been the only school which has had distinction in Central Welsh Board Botany."

Three familiar faces disappeared during this period. In August 1911, Dr Frederick Evans resigned after twenty-eight years' service. He was replaced by a female Medical Officer, Dr Erie Evans, who had the distinction of being Cardiff's first female doctor. As well as her medical duties, she took an active part in the women's suffrage movement. Miss Alice Maudson, Needlework mistress since September 1885, was forced to retire through ill-health in December 1912. She was delighted to buy a fur-lined coat with money raised for her by the Hywelians. The third loss was the popular Chairman of the Governors, Lord Tredegar, who died aged eighty-two on 11th March 1913. Chairman since the new Scheme came into operation in 1895, his annual distribution of the prizes had always been eagerly anticipated by the pupils. In his honour, the poem *The Charge of the Light Brigade* had been recited with precise diction at every prize-giving. The occasion reflected his fondness for military tradition, with the girls entering the Hall by marching in pairs down the centre, in height order, and then dividing to take their places. It was through his influence that Lilian Mary Rogers Thomas of Ystradgynlais was a pupil at Howell's from 1906-9; her father, like her grandfather before him, was his agent for the Palleg estate in Ystradgynlais. Lilian's granddaughters, Catherine and Ruth Price, followed in her footsteps and were pupils at Howell's consecutively between 1975 and 1987.

By the beginning of 1914, Miss Kendall was seventy years old and retirement beckoned. However, with the outbreak of World War I in August, she nobly agreed to continue in her post until it was over. Little would she have thought that it would be six more years before her time as Headmistress came to an end.

some of us went to a Missionary Exhibition at Cardiff last Saturday & some of us are going this afternoon, I went last Saturday. We are going to the Theatre on Saturday to see "as you like it". Sybil has gone up to the Upper III. Miss Clark has made me monitress this term. until you come back. Mother wrote to Miss Kendall last week & asked if I should leave off drawing, & Miss Kendall said I could. The Upper III have got a new mistress, Miss Raigner, instead of Miss Milne. Miss Field is giving marks for the gardens

Left: Part of a letter to Lilian Mary Thomas from her friend Phyllis Jenkins, written soon after Lilian's mother had died, May 1908.

Facing page
Above left: Father's letter to Lilian Thomas, January 1908.
Above right: Staff group, c.1914.
Left: Miss Winny in the Staff Study, c.1910.
Right: Lilian Thomas's school report, 1909.

Tyr Roger
Cphadgynlas
31. I. 08

My Dear Lillie

Glad to hear from you I am writing instead of Mama who is not very well

I Mama wants to know the reason why you have not replied to her question as to you seeing Miss Cook.?

II I am enclosing the tape with your name on it but we have no black tape here Mama will send you some watch key herewith

III Mama wishes me to impress you as the absolute necessity of looking after your head well

IV We were delighted to hear that you had a hat

HOWELL'S SCHOOL, LLANDAFF.

REPORT

O. L. Mary Roger Thomas   for the Summer   term 1909.

Form Up. III   Number in Form 23

SUBJECT.	POSITION IN FORM.	PLACE IN EXAMINATION.		REMARKS.
Holy Scripture	1st	1st	I	She has worked satisfactorily throughout the term.
Arithmetic	7th	15th	Fail	
Algebra	6th (br)	7th	Pass	
Euclid	7th	8th	Fail	
English Language	} 7th	13 (br)	Pass	
English Literature				
History				
Latin	2nd (br)	8th	III	
French	6th (br.)	2nd	Pass	
German	2nd	9th	Fail	
Geography				
Botany	1st (br)	1st	I	
Chemistry	7th (br.)	6th	II	
Elem. Physics	3rd	5th	Fail	
Music Theory	6th	7th	Fail	
" Piano	}	She has done her best.		
Drawing		Fair		
Needlework		Very fair.		
Cookery				

Weekly Form Places 4th, 5th, 2nd, 7th, 2nd, 4th, 2nd, 1st, 3rd, 2nd, 3rd
Number of Times Late

" Absent

Conduct Good. She has been a very reliable Monitress.

School will re-open at 9 a.m. on Wednesday Sep. 15th when every girl must attend. Boarders must return before 6 p.m. on Tuesday Sep. 14th

Every girl must bring her Health Certificate properly filled in and signed

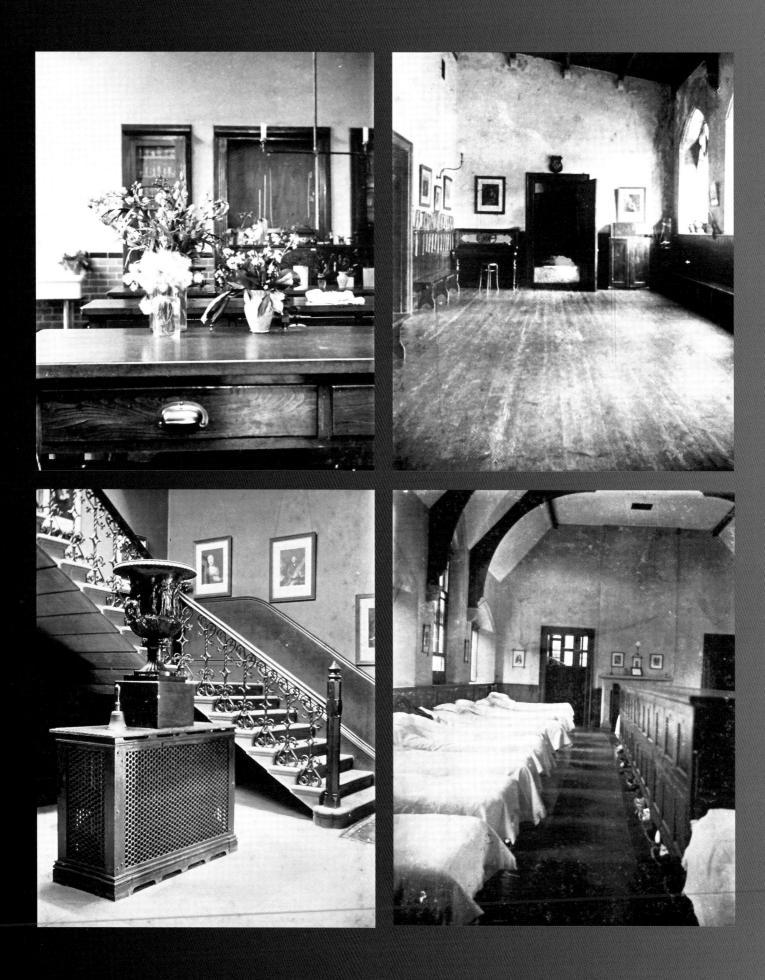

8

THE FIRST WORLD WAR AND MISS KENDALL'S LAST YEARS, 1914-20

Facing page
The school in about 1914
Clockwise from top left: The Botany Laboratory; The Day Room; The East Dormitory; The stove in the Stone Hall.

Above: Form V, 1914-15.
Above left: Boarders who left in 1915.

The first signs of Welsh patriotic feeling at Howell's seem to have been shown in the months before the First World War broke out. One of the Governors, the Reverend D H Williams, suggested that the school should celebrate St David's Day in some way, and it was agreed that a flag depicting the Red Dragon should be bought and unfurled. On the day, fifth and sixth formers performed *tableaux vivants*, illustrating scenes from traditional Welsh history, for the younger pupils in the evening, following a half-day holiday with a walk in the afternoon. The question of introducing Welsh was also raised for the first time but was shelved because the curriculum was already crowded.

As usual, Empire Day (24th May) was celebrated by the singing of patriotic songs to begin morning school but in 1914 the pupils sang Kipling's *Children's Song*, which was adapted as the school song, and remained so until the 1990s. The idea for this had come in 1909 from the Hywelians, who had wanted "a poem worthy of the traditions of the school" in order to "take away the reproach that a School so famous as ours has been all these years destitute of a School Song", and had invited suggestions from current and former pupils. The music was composed by the Music Master, Mr Beale.

During the war, the day-to-day running of the school continued much as before and, for those whose family lives were greatly affected, the element of stability provided must have been extremely welcome. A new range was supplied for the Cookery School, which Miss Kendall was eager to have in place before the visit of the CWB inspectors in 1915. Although she recognised that the war years were not the time to have a new room specifically for Geography, which was taught in the Botanical and Physical Laboratories, she produced a lengthy list of requirements for modern methods of teaching the subject, to much of which the Governors agreed.

Inevitably the war impinged on the school in some ways. Mademoiselle Jeanne Rolin, who had joined the staff in 1913, lost two of her three brothers and her French family home was

Children's Song (The Howell's School Song)
By Rudyard Kipling
arr. Mr George Beale, Music Master

Land of our Birth, we pledge to thee
Our love and toil in the years to be;
When we are grown and take our place,
As men and women with our race.

Father in Heaven who lovest all,
Oh help Thy children when they call;
That they may build from age to age,
An undefiled heritage.

Teach us to bear the yoke in youth,
With steadfastness and careful truth;
That, in our time, Thy Grace may give
The Truth whereby the Nations live.

Teach us to rule ourselves alway,
Controlled and cleanly night and day;
That we may bring, if need arise.
No maimed or worthless sacrifice.

Teach us to look in all our ends,
On Thee for judge, and not our friends;
That we, with Thee, may walk uncowed
By fear or favour of the crowd.

Teach us the Strength that cannot seek,
By deed or thought, to hurt the weak;
That, under Thee, we may possess
Man's strength to comfort man's distress.

Teach us Delight in simple things,
And Mirth that has no bitter springs;
Forgiveness free of evil done,
And Love to all men 'neath the sun!

Land of our Birth, our faith, our pride,
For whose dear sake our fathers died;
O Motherland, we pledge to thee,
Head, heart, and hand through the years to be!

Facing page
The Dining Room, c. 1914.

Left: *First part of the original manuscript of the school song, with the music composed by George Beale, visiting teacher and Llandaff Cathedral organist.*
Below left: *Certificate awarded in place of a prize, 1917.*

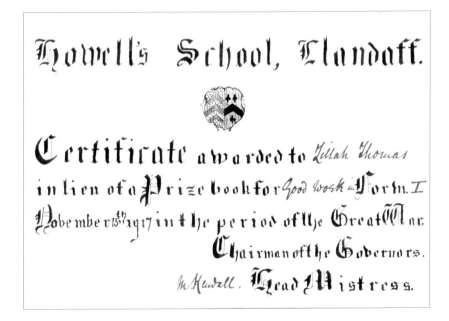

destroyed. The "odd man", Mr R G Martin, who had served the school faithfully for many years, began service with the National Reserve and resigned his position in September 1914. Miss Kendall agreed to accept a ten-year-old Belgian refugee as a day scholar, free of charge. The costs of building work increased because of the rising costs of timber. In November 1915, the girls themselves suggested that, instead of prizes, they should receive certificates at prize-giving. The girls were involved in designing the certificate and the £15 15s 0d saved was sent to the Kitchener Memorial Fund and the Navy League. This practice continued until the war ended. New blinds had to be purchased and all lights had to be subdued on account of the new Lighting Order in 1916.

Right: Miss Winny carrying corn which she grew at school, 1915. Far right: Group of boarders, c.1917. Dorothy Harrison, later Head Girl, member of staff and Senior Mistress, is at the top right.

The school contributed to raising funds for war charities, such as the National Fund for the Welsh Troops, Disabled Welsh Soldiers and the YMCA work at the Front. The girls also gave concerts for wounded soldiers at the Red Cross Hospitals in Llandaff. Hannah Reynolds (Head Girl 1917-8) won the violin solo at the National Eisteddfod at the age of fifteen. During the war, Lloyd George called her to 10 Downing Street to play in concerts and *At Homes* organised in aid of Welsh serving members of the armed forces. The annual Shakespeare play performed at Christmas continued but from 1916 it was decided that proceeds from the sale of tickets should be donated to a war charity. From 1916 to 1918, vegetables grown in school which were ready to eat during the summer holidays were sent to the Convalescent Military Home at The Lodge in Llandaff.

The Hywelian Guild also made financial contributions to worthy causes during the First World War. In particular, on 1st July 1916, it organised a huge Sale of Work. The whole event was quite an occasion, including dancing, competitions, tea and other entertainments. A brass band played in the Stone Hall and its members were invited to sample the refreshments first. They were obviously so delighted to see these, at a time of food shortages, that they consumed them all, leaving none for the Hywelians, to the dismay of Gladys Clark (née Mullin), who had worked in difficult circumstances to prepare them. The sale raised £200 for British Prisoners of War and £26 for both St Dunstan's Hostel for blind ex-servicemen and Russian Prisoners of War. The following year another event was organised for war charities, called an American sale, with old girls asked to donate an item to the value of 6d, to be sold at that price.

Not surprisingly, fewer Hywelians attended the meetings during these years as so many of them were engaged in war work. The activities in which they were involved are testament to their independent spirit, leadership qualities and bravery. Doris Bryson was involved in an unusual occupation for a woman at the time, producing gunwork and engines for tanks with an engineering firm in Lancashire, and recorded her fascination in seeing a tank on trial, going through trees "as if they were not there". Marjorie Williams served as a Voluntary Aid Detachment (VAD) in French Military Hospitals for five years, was mentioned in Lord Haig's dispatches and in 1920 had the distinction of being invested with the Royal Red Cross by George V at Buckingham Palace. Another VAD, Olive Sheppard, had a remarkable escape after the ship on which she was sailing from Southern Italy to Egypt was mined off the coast of Alexandria, and she was in the water for about twenty minutes. She was picked up first by a little Japanese lifeboat and then hauled up on to a destroyer on the end of a rope. Another Hywelian nurse in Egypt, Gertrude Roskell, was less fortunate. She died in October 1915 while working as a VAD under the auspices of the British Red Cross and was accorded a military funeral in Alexandria. The other Hywelian known to have died on war service was Kate Banks, who was working at a Voluntary Aid Hospital in Somerset. Tragically, soon after she had been involved in organising an afternoon entertainment for the patients, she died as a result of poisoning a finger while washing bandages.

During this period, the school had to contend with other issues not directly associated with the war. Miss Kendall found that, by

1914, she could not insist that all mistresses be resident and wrote to the Governors that it would be essential to appoint some as non-residents. She recognised that "It is an outcome of the spirit of the age, and must be met." The only long-serving mistress to leave during this period was Miss Cook, artistic teacher of Music and Diction, who had painted sprays of apple blossom on the panels of Miss Kendall's sitting-room, but she later returned as a guest. Rats continued to be a problem, despite the setting of traps, and the servants were instructed to put all flour into bins rather than leave it in sacks on the floor. A shortage of ordinary flour meant that it had to be mixed with barley flour in the making of bread from March 1917. There were ongoing problems with the school's heating and, probably for this reason, in February 1918 it was decided that every girl should be given a cup of cocoa at night and a bowl of porridge for breakfast. Food rationing was not introduced until the end of the war and the school hardly seems to have been affected.

There seems no doubt that every possible step was taken to care for the girls' welfare during these years but an issue which must have caused Miss Kendall a great deal of anxiety towards the end was a complaint made by a parent, Mr J B Finlay, that his daughter Frieda was suffering from the consequences of malnourishment.

Eventually the case came before the Cardiff Assizes, with the school accused of neglecting the girl. The verdict was given in favour of Howell's but the judge added a rider that details of its menu should be drawn up and approved by the Medical Officer. The Hywelians and current pupils, meanwhile, had passed a resolution expressing their total support for Miss Kendall and the administration of the school. Olwen Jones recorded, "For eight years I was a Foundationer at the old school (1894-1902), and I feel nothing but the profoundest gratitude for all I received during that time, and I should have been only too happy to have had a chance to record, at the recent disgraceful lawsuit brought against the school, my own experience there as a boarder."

After Miss Winny had read the terms of the Armistice in the Gymnasium, girls and staff celebrated in November 1918 with a day's holiday and evening entertainment. It was then decided to make an application for the school to be put on the list of those recognised for grants by the Board of Education, an issue which had first been raised in March 1917. Howell's was duly added to the Grant List from 1st August 1919. There were certain conditions: fifteen free places were to be given; the fees must include stationery; there was to be a maximum of thirty pupils in a class; and provision must be made for the teaching of Welsh.

Left: Tennis players in the pavilion, c.1919.
Above: Prize list, 1919. Of the girls listed, three – Madeline White, Phyllis Hicks and Dorothy Harrison – returned to teach at Howell's.

Far left: Miss Kendall's resignation letter, 1919.
Left: The Kendall Memorial in Llandaff Cathedral.
Above: Letter of recommendation for Madeline White who, as Mrs Davies, returned to teach Geography at Howell's from 1954-68.

Not surprisingly, by that time, at the age of seventy-five, Miss Kendall was more than ready for retirement. It was not until 10th October 1919 that the new Headmistress, Miss Mary Gladys Jones, a former pupil and founder member of the Hywelian Guild, was selected, and Miss Kendall agreed to hold the fort until she could take up her new post. Unfortunately, Miss Jones was soon diagnosed as suffering from "severe nerve strain" and in January decided to resign. She went on to have one of the most distinguished academic careers of all Hywelians, gaining a doctorate, becoming Professor of History and later Director of Studies in History, Law and Economics at Girton College, Cambridge.

On 12th March 1920, five candidates were interviewed by the Governors, of whom Miss Eleanor Trotter was selected to be the new Headmistress. Miss Kendall retired to Arundel, where she died aged 89 on 3rd February 1932. Concurrently with her funeral at Binstead, there was a memorial service in Llandaff Cathedral, attended by over two hundred Hywelians. The Guild soon decided that, as Miss Kendall had hoped to have a swimming pool at Howell's but had not been able to see this dream realised, they would raise funds for one to be built in her memory. They also erected a tablet in Llandaff Cathedral, which was dedicated by the Bishop of Llandaff and unveiled by Miss Kendall's niece, the Hywelian Dr Gertrude Harré, on February 20th 1937. It bore the coat of arms and motto of the Drapers' Company, an inscription and the school crest.

By the time of Miss Kendall's retirement, Howell's was recognised as the most prestigious secondary school for girls in Wales. Under her leadership, the facilities had increased considerably, with a Gymnasium, Art Room, Laboratory, Cookery Room and Hall. By 1920 there were far more girls in the school – 95 boarders and 162 day scholars – as well as ten resident mistresses. Since 1906, it had been possible for girls to stay on until the age of nineteen. The curriculum had changed considerably; by 1920 it included Mathematics and Science, and there were organised games, swimming and gymnastics. Miss Kendall herself was enormously hard-working and, although physically small, had a very strong constitution. She had no secretary and she wrote her letters when everyone else had gone to bed, making an ink copy of every single one.

The staff were much better qualified – indeed, the younger ones had had the chance of a higher education not available to Miss Kendall – and some, such as Miss Wood and Miss Holmes, had gone on to become Headmistresses themselves. No longer were the girls prepared only to be good home-makers and governesses. They were entered for public examinations and gained honours for the school; many had secured places at university and had gone on to the professions. Hywelians were to be found all over the globe. Of course, to a large extent Miss Kendall's changes reflected the shifting attitudes towards women in society at large. Female emancipation, including the right for those over thirty to vote in general elections from December 1918, and greater educational opportunities went hand in hand.

Miss Kendall wrote, some four years after she retired, that she was afraid that "I upset many by my changes" but went on to say that "Changes are necessary and inevitable, though they do give a shock to hallowed associations. And who knows? The next generation may look on what is at present modern as out of date and needing reformation." That was indeed the case and Miss Trotter considered that a great deal of modernisation was needed. The routines had hardly changed since Miss Kendall's measures of the early 1880s, but there is no doubt that she was viewed with great affection by her former pupils. She continued to serve as the President of the Hywelian Guild and wrote an annual letter or article for the magazine until the year of her death.

'I was a day girl and started under Miss Kendall. One day she sent for me and I thought, "What have I done?" I was in the Upper Third and she said that they were starting to have form leaders and asked whether I would be the form leader. I said I thought I'd done something wrong and she commented on my expression of relief! She was a very warm person and very nice.

We went up to the Hall for prayers every morning and for our singing lessons. We had singing lessons with Georgie Beale who was the organist at Llandaff Cathedral. He stopped the singing one day and said, "If Marguerite Milner would be quiet we might be able to hear the others singing!" I loved singing and he was very good. Another teacher I remember was Gwladys Williams. We all had a crush on her! Miss Winny was very austere but nice. She only taught the senior girls. Mademoiselle Rolin ("Maddie" Rolin, as we called her) was also firm but very nice. Miss Bush lived in Romilly Road. She taught Scripture and put me in the corner for having chocolate! We met many years later and remained friends. Hester Bellamy was lovely – warm and clever too.

I remember some girls – Joyce Drewett of 3 Howell's Crescent, Muriel Doxsey of Canton, Jessica Frewer of Palace Road and Constance and Mavis Diamond who also lived in Palace Road. Mary Walker and I were close friends. I lived in Pencisely Road and she lived next door but one to me. We used to walk to school together. One day we decided to climb the rubbish dump at the end of my father's garden, walk along the wall, and then climb over it – that was a short cut to school. We found two mistresses waiting to greet us on the other side! Mary married Bernard Morgan of David Morgan's at The Hayes.

I enjoyed subjects like Cookery and Housewifery. Howell's made a feature of good manners, which were generally expected. Howell's was strict but it wasn't a silent place – it had an atmosphere like a good residential home. It was a very happy period in my life.'

Marguerite Desmond, née Milner (1917-1924). Interviewed October 2009 (aged 99 years, 7 months).

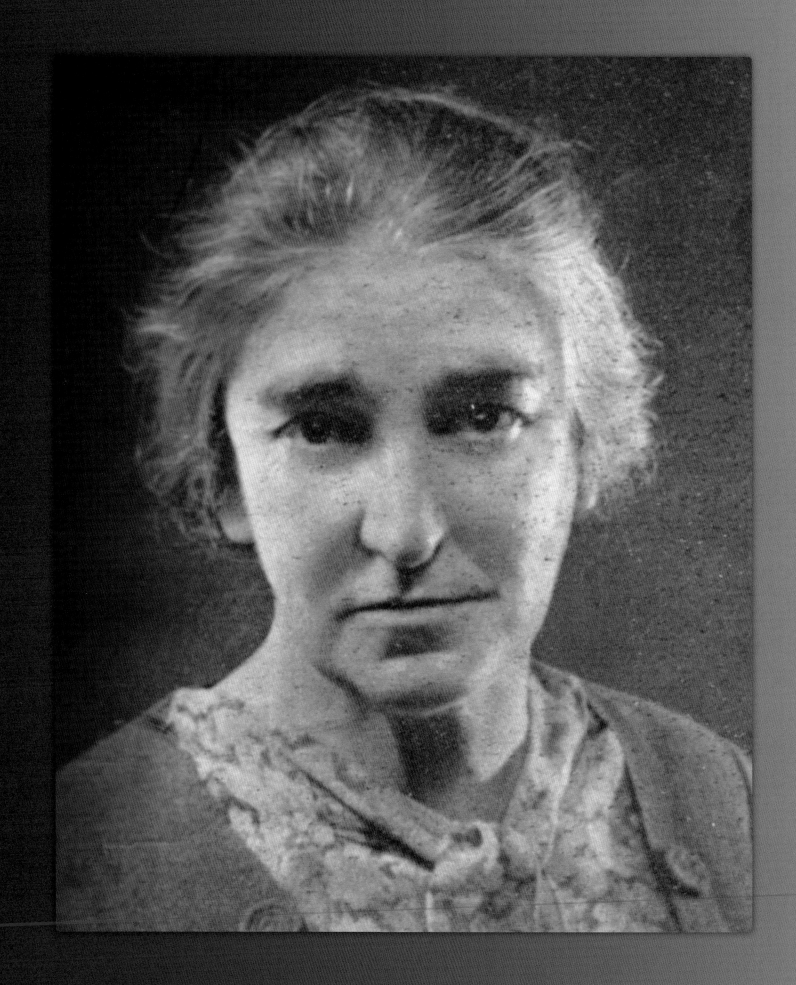

9

MISS TROTTER AND THE UPDATING OF PRACTICES AND FACILITIES, 1920-30

Facing page
Miss Eleanor Trotter, 1920-37.

Left: *Cover of Miss Trotter's book*
Seventeenth Century Life in the
Country Parish, *published in 1919.*

Described by one of her earliest Head Girls, Mary Hewart Jones, as "a breath of fresh air", Eleanor Trotter was the first Howell's Headmistress to have had previous experience of that role and to hold a university degree. Born in Yorkshire, a farmer's daughter, on 16th March 1875, she attended schools in Darlington and Hereford. Her first teaching appointment was at Magdalen College School, Wainfleet, after which she studied Latin, Greek, English and Pure Mathematics to gain her first degree, an external BA from London. She subsequently taught at Hinckley Grammar School and Dalston, London, during which time she gained first a BA Honours degree and then an MA at University College, London. Armed with these qualifications, she served as Headmistress of Darlington High School for seven years. She was forty-five years old when she became Headmistress at Howell's in September 1920. By this time, she had several publications to her credit, of which the best-known was *Seventeenth Century Life in a Country Parish*.

Eleanor Trotter's period as Headmistress of Howell's filled almost the whole inter-war period and saw a huge shake-up in all aspects of school life. Before she took up her appointment, the Governors had agreed that Domestic Science and Physical Science mistresses could be appointed and that Welsh could be taught to those who desired it. This subject, first considered in Miss Kendall's day, soon appeared as an alternative to German, and in the autumn of 1926 Beti Rees became the school's first pupil to read Welsh at university. She went on to open the first university and Welsh language bookshop in Cardiff, in Castle Arcade, in 1950.

Miss Trotter wasted little time in starting to make changes. She

appointed the school's first secretary, Miss June Williams, almost immediately. Mr Arthur Waldron, who had replaced his elder brother Clement Richards Waldron as Clerk during World War I, resigned in October 1920, thereby bringing to an end the long family connection with the school, their father Clement having held the position before them. The next long-serving Clerk was the solicitor Mr T P Pritchard, appointed in April 1922. One of his tasks was to sit in the Hall on the first day of term and receive the fees from the girls before they were allowed to go to their form rooms. The tuition fee had risen from £8 to £13 in 1920 and the boarding fee was set at £40. Most Day Scholar Scholarships and Leaving Exhibitions had ended but the County Committee was still willing to provide these in cases of need. The girls had to deposit the fee cheques in a large aspidistra pot and hand medical certificates to Miss Bellamy, who always dressed on these occasions in a green jersey suit with little bone-stiffeners in her lace collar and a gold watch on a chain tucked into her waist-belt.

Facing page
Top: Miss Trotter's Sitting Room, 1922.
Below: Front page of prospectus, December 1920.

Right: The first prefects, 1921.
Far right: Prefects' invitation to Miss Trotter, 1922.

Lessons on Saturday mornings were soon abolished, though the boarders did three hours' study and Miss Trotter expected the day girls to do likewise. Detention was held at the same time, so any day girls punished in this way had to return to school – a practice which persisted until the 1980s. From the outset, Miss Trotter encouraged day girls to take part in all activities, including organised games, from which they had previously been excluded (they had been permitted to spend an hour on Wednesday afternoons on the field unsupervised), and for the first time they began to wear the uniform, which she soon modernised. In August 2009 Mrs Dorothy Wickett (née Clarke), aged 98, recalled the change: "*My first uniform was a long-sleeved dress with high neck, rather Victorian. Very soon after, Miss Trotter changed the school uniform, introducing a dark navy blue gym slip with a red sash, with white blouse and red tie in the summer and black high neck jumper under the gym slip for the winter. We wore black woollen stockings in the cold weather, which we were allowed to wear with knees darned (accidents always happening), then beige lisle stockings in the summer. The long boots were changed for shoes. My mother was quite put out that she had just bought the new uniform dress only to find she then had to get new uniform again. In the first year, it was permissible to alter the dresses into gym slips. I remember the large navy blue knickers with elastic around the bottom of the legs. As time went on they became a very convenient way to harbour things.*

I remember a gobstopper dropped out and it rolled down the classroom floor. I had to own up as it was obvious where it had come from, but I was not sent out because we were in the middle of an examination." The red girdles were tied in bows at the back, the bows and ends having to be of equal length. On Open Days the girls wore special white dresses, with their house colours pinned to their chests from the late 1920s.

Although Howell's had had a Head Girl since early in Miss Kendall's day, very few other girls had responsibilities. In her first term Miss Trotter introduced a system of prefects, and the sixth form girls appointed came to play a major role in the running of the school. They assisted with house activities and had supervisory functions, with the power to enforce discipline and to issue order marks to younger pupils. Miss Trotter entertained the boarder prefects informally in her room every Sunday evening.

Miss Trotter's Head Girl for her first two years (1920-1922) was Dorothy Harrison, who later joined the staff. Her next appointment broke with tradition: she selected a day girl (or "day bugs", as the boarders disparagingly called them) as Head Girl. Mary Hewart Jones had, amongst her responsibilities, the task of setting out Miss Trotter's gown in the morning and the senior boarders hoped that she would not arrive in time to do this so that they could demonstrate her unsuitability for the post.

'I was born on 26th August 1911. I started at HSL as a day girl in 1920. It was in Miss Trotter's first year. We had to pass an entrance exam to get in. I remember very clearly on my first day being met by Miss Bellamy who said, 'I hope you are not going to be like your Aunt Marjorie Clarke, who was very badly behaved'. Marjorie apparently did her best to be disruptive and she was subsequently sent to boarding school to "try to mend her ways"! She lived too near to Howell's to be a boarder; the school must have been relieved.

I remember at first that the school was not quite sure what to do with the new juniors and we sewed the edges of handkerchiefs, while being read to. I particularly recollect with fondness listening to *The Wind in the Willows*. In those early days we learned to use script writing to develop our 'hand'. We were taught Arithmetic, History with *Piers Plowman* as a text book, and Geography with a large globe on a stand in the classroom.'

Dorothy Wickett, née Clarke (1920-8). Interviewed August 2009.

'We couldn't run or speak in the corridors. We used to get order marks, which were dished out by the prefects. That was why I wanted to become a prefect – and I did, and dished out several! Mistresses would give you lines and detention. If you transgressed three times in a week, Miss Trotter would read out your name in Assembly on a Monday morning and you were sent out, in front of the whole school, to stand in the corridor outside her room. If you were young, you had to walk right down the Hall from the front. It happened to me several times in the first term as I started late, because I was ill, and I didn't know the rules.'

Catherine Powell, née "Minnie" Morgan (1927-34). Interviewed May 2009.

A report made by Miss Trotter to the Governors in 1923 reveals how her educational philosophy was diametrically opposed to that of Miss Kendall. She wrote that her predecessor's system "gave an excellent training to girls in habits of order and neatness. It produced in them a quiet manner and it made them pay attention to their lessons." She continued, "The whole trend of my educational training has been to consider the child as an individual" and "with the giving of as large a liberty as possible to the girls there was frequently noise and untidiness and confusion such as had never happened before because the children had so little self-control . . . the only way to make a child want to practise self-control is to give her liberty of action . . . that is my way of training character." Her methods seem to have paid off.

The school was hit by a tragedy that year: a day girl aged eleven, Rena Hoffman, drowned in the River Taff on 26th February while trying to collect alder specimens for her Botany homework with her friend Mary Rees. South Wales had just experienced its heaviest rain for thirty years and it appears that she fell from the sluice which fed the mill stream running through Llandaff Cathedral churchyard. Despite the efforts of a local police constable, who jumped into the river, she could not be saved. A portrait of Rena, whose sister Joyce was also a pupil, was put up in the Stone Hall but was unfortunately destroyed in the fire which engulfed the school in 1932.

The school experienced significant financial difficulty in the early 1920s. Miss Trotter inherited a heavy debt and in 1922 the Board of Education agreed to an amendment of the Scheme so that the tuition fees could be raised to £16 and the boarding fees to £48. It was also necessary to ask Glamorgan County Council to grant an annual sum for a few years, but the Drapers' Company was unable to provide the £700 requested on account of the state of its own finances. Hoped-for purchases therefore had to be deferred and in March 1922 the Clerk was asked to hold back as many tradesmen's accounts as possible for a fortnight.

Temporary help to alleviate the situation came with the new Burnham salary scale for secondary school teachers. Initially, all the staff salaries at Howell's were reduced by 5% but since they could now rise to a maximum of £400 a year for graduates and £320 for non-graduates – and more for the Senior Assistant teacher – the savings benefit did not last long. Nevertheless, the effect of the increase in fees, a saving on the light, heating and fuel bills and the grant given in recognition of the Advanced Courses the school was offering in Science and Mathematics meant that there was a small surplus in April 1923. Unfortunately for Miss Faraday and Miss Esmé Underhill, who taught Gymnastics, the new pay scale meant that their salaries were too high for the school to be able to afford to retain them.

'No dropping of rubbish was allowed; someone dropped a bus ticket at the school gate and the whole school was punished with no games for a week and 'walks only' during the lunchtimes. Discipline was very strict, there was no running or talking in the corridors and walking was on the left. Prefects were on duty at each end of the corridors and in the main hall and other gathering places. Those breaking the rules were reported and order marks were given, leading to possible detention. I found it hard not to talk and so I remember having to write lines and learn the Kings and Queens of England off by heart, which I knew very well. I eventually became a prefect and I remember that we had our own room in the music cells under the Hall.'

Dorothy Wickett, née Clarke (1920-8). Interviewed August 2009.

The School in 1922
1: *The Dining Room.*
2: *The Botanical Laboratory.*
3: *The Schoolroom.*
4: *The Assembly Hall.*
5: *The Board Room.*
6: *The Day Room.*

1

4

2

5

3

6

'Rena entered the school at seven years old and I went the following year. Miss Bellamy helped me with my maths in the entrance exam and I wanted to do another in the afternoon as I had enjoyed it so much! We were weighed and measured on the first and last day of every term, much to my dislike. I remember marching in for dinners to a Sousa march and the smell of cabbage. One day, staying for lunch, I passed the message along the table to Mademoiselle Rolin for a very small portion of rice pudding – back came my dish with one grain of rice in it! In the gymnasium I was good at balancing and ribstall climbing but poor at squeezing between the ribstalls! In craft lessons, we went outside in turn to wet the canes for the baskets we were making.

My mother went to Miss Trotter to say that my parents would give up the grant given to Rena as the most outstanding junior pupil so it could be given to someone more needy, but the grant stayed with Rena. Her death was a terrible tragedy for Howell's School. Afterwards, my parents sent me away to boarding school.'

Joyce Davey, née Hoffman (1920-1925). Interviewed February 2005.

Nevertheless, the 1920s saw the appointment of several young and well-qualified staff whose length of service is remarkable. They included Miss Myfanwy Williams (History) in 1921; Miss Elsie Fowler (Geography and Botany) and Miss Edith Tickner (Classics) in 1923; Miss Hilda Taylor (English and Latin) in 1924; Miss Daisy

Walters (Welsh) in 1927; Miss Barbara Ruby Phillips (English) and Miss Dorothy Harrison (Botany), Miss Trotter's first Head Girl and later the holder of a research scholarship in Botany at Swansea, in 1928; and Miss Elizabeth Taylor (Mathematics

and Biology) in 1929. All these stayed for at least thirty years and some considerably longer, notably Miss Tickner, who retired in 1970 after forty-seven years. Miss Madeleine Holland, who became housekeeper in 1927, also remained for forty years. A new Medical Officer, Dr Constance Griffiths, who on her marriage later that year became Dr Parry, also arrived in January of that year. She succeeded the suffrage campaigner Dr Erie Evans, who after the war also played a part in the furtherance of the ideals of the League of Nations and the spread of Esperanto. For the next quarter-century Dr Parry showed a particular interest in the boarders' welfare. In 1931 there were no fewer than six Hywelians on the teaching staff, comprising almost one quarter of the total; Dorothy Harrison, Rose Davenport (later Vice-President of the Guild), Verna Reynolds, Daphne Gardiner, Ruth Longdon and Ethel Bush.

One of Miss Trotter's major concerns was to improve the residential conditions, which were uncomfortable for both girls and staff. Many rooms were lit by candles and it was often impossible for the staff to have a hot bath. Great fires burned at each end of the Schoolroom and uniformed maids scurried around carrying buckets of coal. The girls below the sixth form spent all their spare time indoors in the Schoolroom, and there were no comfortable chairs. In the summer months, from the beginning of Miss Trotter's headship, the older girls were allowed to sleep out on the flat roof outside the East Dormitory. However, after one unfortunate girl, Hilda Roberts, was found on the ground with a broken leg by the Art and Craft mistress, Miss Winifred Gill, early on the morning of 2nd July 1921, the Governors declared that this practice was to be discontinued until the parapet was more efficiently protected.

Electric lighting and new heating apparatus were urgently needed, as the gas was in a poor state of repair. It was decided to have both major installations done simultaneously to avoid two

Facing page

Top: *Staff, early 1930s.*
Left to right: *Miss Verna Reynolds (History), Miss Winifred Elliott (Chemistry), Miss Hilda Taylor (English and Latin), Miss Ruth Longdon (History) and Miss Mary Bromley (English). Verna Reynolds (Head Girl 1925-6) and Ruth Longdon were Hywelians.*
Bottom: *Tea party with Miss Bellamy, Miss Faraday, Miss Walters, Miss Page and Miss June Williams (Secretary), March 1922.*

Left: *Side wing, showing the parapet with the flat roof behind, where boarders sometimes slept during the summer.*
Below left: *The Stone Hall in 1922, showing the stove.*
Below right: *The Rise, 1926.*

periods of disruption. The work began in March 1923, with one central boiler in place of the four sets which had always seemed to break down when there was a frost. Floorboards were pulled up, as were the flagstones of the Stone Hall; noise, dirt, dust and pipes abounded. The old stove – on which boarders' post had been placed daily – disappeared from the Stone Hall. An anonymous pupil recorded both the advantages and drawbacks of the new electric lighting in 1924: *"There is no more anxious groping in dark lockers for lost books, when one has fears of not being seated in time for the last tinkle of the preparation bell; all is light as day. On the other hand, there is this disadvantage; it is more difficult to camouflage untidiness."*

Concurrently with these improvements, discussions about acquiring a hostel for boarders were taking place. As Miss Trotter wished the school to expand, more accommodation was essential so that classrooms could replace the dormitories in the building.

Options considered were buying a property – either Tynewydd, on Fairwater Road, or Oaklands – and building a hostel in the school grounds. In 1923 a new opportunity presented itself: The Rise, on the corner of Penhill and Cardiff Road, became available for renting. Painted chests and furniture were bought from the Lord Roberts' Memorial Workshops. Miss Bellamy, Miss Margaret Hole and the nurse lived there with the first group, mainly from the West Dormitory, and the girls were delighted to be in what was described as a "home from home" atmosphere. Miss Bellamy, who loved gardening, supervised the girls and a tradition of girls caring for the schools' gardens began. One of the first residents, Jane Evans, recorded: *"Twenty-three girls, including three prefects, were chosen to live there, all of whom were thrilled at the idea of living in a real, ordinary house from which they walked to school in the morning like day girls. The house and the garden, the bedrooms, which were newly-furnished, and above all the sitting-room, appealed to everyone."* The Rise was also used by the youngest pupils of the preparatory department who, under Miss Hole's supervision, spent their mornings in the schoolroom at the hostel. This room, furnished with small chairs and stools, had two French windows leading into the garden. However, the numbers in the kindergarten were small and in May 1925 the decision was made to close it.

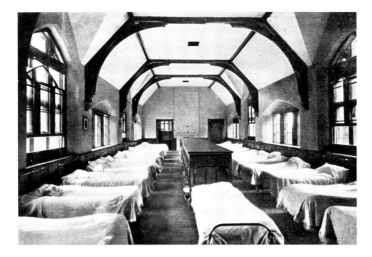

Far left: The East Dormitory, 1922.
Left: Dormitory sketch by the Art mistress, Miss Emily Mason, late 1920s.
Below: The edge of the playing field, 1922.

Once some boarders were members of The Rise, it was decided that those who were accommodated in school should also belong to a named house. Thus, in the summer of 1923, the girls in the East Dormitory became members of Kendall House and those in the North wing constituted Tredegar House. The houses composed their own house songs, held house concerts and competed for the Challenge House Picture to hang on their wall; it was awarded for "general behaviour and tidiness".

The new heating system, electric lighting and hostel were not the only changes greeting the girls and staff when they returned from their summer holidays in 1923. The old West Dormitory had been partitioned by a sliding door to create two large classrooms. The East Dormitory had also been divided, the western half now providing a form room, while the eastern section still had its rows of white beds. As there were by then only nine resident mistresses, some of their former bedrooms had been converted to girls' bedrooms. A new Arts and Crafts Room had been created, Miss Maudson's former bedroom became a sixth form classroom and other forms found themselves in new locations. In the kitchen there was new steam cookery apparatus and there was an extra bath for the staff. Most of the large windows had also been repaired. At weekends, the boarders enjoyed more comfort: rooms were adapted as sitting-rooms for them, with deck-chairs, table-cloths and rugs. For the first time, they could also choose to go home at weekends. In the

later 1920s, all the boarders still resident in school had cubicles for greater privacy. The vacation of former dormitories in the main school paved the way for two extra classrooms, and there was also a small Physics Laboratory and Craft Room combined, a Laundry for the Domestic Science department, a Welsh and History Room and a Science Study by 1926. There were also constant additions to the furnishings and equipment, such as new desks, pianos and boot lockers.

During the early 1920s, great improvements were also made to the playing field. Miss Trotter liked the girls to spend as much time as possible out of doors. Previously, the hockey pitch resembled

'A few months before my seventh birthday, I became a pupil [in January 1921], without examination or even interview. I had a sister in the school; my mother said I could read. That was enough. The First, Lower Second and Second Forms were housed in one room at three long tables of graduated heights. On the mantelpiece were two clay heads on which we grew green hair of mustard and cress. We had no swimming baths, no library, no French windows, no cinder track round the hockey field until we made it ourselves, and the hockey field was our only field, for it was many years before any but the most senior girls were allowed near the tennis courts, and the Head's garden was holy ground.'

Bronwen Jones (1921-31). Written 1959.

a hayfield when the grass grew long, but the purchase of a motor mower and the creation of a running track made tennis, cricket and athletics in the summer possible. The girls helped with the building of the track, standing in long lines to pass on buckets of earth, and those who were fitness-conscious ran around it before breakfast. Netball began early in Miss Trotter's day and 1926 saw the first series of cricket fixtures, the batting side sewing or knitting while waiting to play. Junior girls enjoyed rounders.

In May 1923, the Cardiff Corporation agreed that Howell's pupils could use the open-air baths in Llandaff Fields two afternoons a week. During the year 1925-6 a few hardy boarders were prepared to brave the cold to swim there before breakfast. Lacrosse was first introduced in the spring of 1929 and was taught by Miss North, who played for Glamorgan. The very first fixture, against Glamorgan and Monmouth Ladies' Lacrosse Club's First XII, resulted in a loss but the sport grew and became very popular. For gymnastics and games, the girls did not change out of their school uniform but, to prevent their tunics flopping down over their faces when they were upside down on the ribstalls in the Gymnasium, they wore a piece of elastic under their girdles which they pulled down.

Around the edge of the playing field, the wilderness of weeds was replaced by a herbaceous border and a rockery sheltering rare plants. All the work was undertaken by girls and staff, under the enthusiastic direction of Miss Trotter, Miss Bellamy and Miss Winny. The latter also supervised senior girls in creating a peat bog

as part of the botanical garden at the far end of the grass courts, where the swimming pool was built in the late 1930s. Miss Trotter could often be seen walking around the school field with a stick, which she used to point to flowers or weeds, asking for them to be named or cleared respectively. Flowers adorned the Dining Room and the Hall and, on

'One of the first changes Miss Trotter made was to open up windows in all the rooms in the whole school, including staff rooms; until then none of them opened. I remember this clearly as my father's firm had the contract to make the changes. Miss Trotter would come into class and say "Good morning girls – open up all the windows"; this was in all seasons. I remember one very hot summer when the boarders slept out on the Day Room roof. Miss Trotter was a fresh air fiend and started up many of the sports, which she was very keen on, and brought them up to date. We played netball, hockey, cricket, rounders and tennis and as time went on, tournaments were organised with other schools. We had gymnastics lessons as well.'

Dorothy Wickett, née Clarke (1920-8). Interviewed August 2009.

special occasions, the Stone Hall and the main staircase as well. Between the hockey field and the main school, along one side of the Gymnasium, there was a large kitchen garden, where all sorts of vegetables were grown.

Two years after The Rise was rented, Oaklands was bought for £4,000 and opened in September 1925 for thirty-five boarders, including three prefects. Girls were involved in painting furniture and putting patterns on the partition curtains, and those who had worked most diligently on the needlework for the new hostel were chosen as the first residents. Miss Bellamy moved to Oaklands and was replaced by Miss Hilda Susannah Millburn at The Rise. The large gardens with their tennis court and dingle "where rare botanical specimens may be found" particularly delighted the girls.

Catherine Powell, née "Minnie" Morgan, a boarder in Oaklands from 1927-34, recalled in 2009: *"The worst thing you could do if you were in Oaklands, which I was, was to cross the road unaccompanied if you weren't a prefect or sub-prefect. We had to change out of school uniform into what we called our light clothes for tea. If you were left in school after playing games, you were caught between the devil and the deep. You were in trouble if you were caught in your uniform*

yet you couldn't cross the road on your own to change out of it. I did once and sailed straight into the arms of my housemistress, Miss Bellamy. She was lovely but she only had to look at you and you felt like crawling under a stone. When I was a junior, every Saturday night we used to get our laundry back and we had to check whether there were any holes in our stockings, and we used to sit round a huge fire and darn them. Miss Bellamy would read to us – Lorna Doone and The Secret Garden, that sort of thing. She was always a form mistress of Form II and she was very knowledgeable."

In 1930, the school acquired another hostel. In January a purchase price of £3,500 was agreed for Hazelwood and, as usual, the girls were involved in the decorating. Twenty-six girls from Tredegar House moved their belongings into the rooms, which were sectioned off into cubicles, and they delighted in the sitting room and the gardens with the lawn tennis court. There was no heating in the bedrooms and on cold mornings there was sometimes a thin layer of ice on the water. Miss Hilda Taylor was the housemistress and Miss Trotter moved there herself, thereby making available two extra rooms in the main school for classrooms. In 1933, she obtained a dog, Ung, who enjoyed going for walks with the girls.

Right: Miss Mason's sketch of Miss Bellamy with her young pupils.
Far right: Oaklands.

Facing page
Top: Hazelwood.
Centre left: Staff bedroom, probably Miss Trotter's, in Hazelwood, early 1930s.
Centre right: Cubicles in Hazelwood, early 1930s.
Bottom left: Miss Trotter's Sitting Room in Hazelwood, early 1930s.

Her Sitting Room was used by the boarders of Kendall House, still resident in school, where there were carpets and easy chairs. The older girls could also use a library and small study so conditions for them, too, were more comfortable. The vacated East Dormitory was transformed into two classrooms.

As well as the physical improvements, there were some curricular developments. For a short while in 1924 the school experimented with the Dalton Plan, the revolutionary first attempt to encourage independent learning, in which girls were given a programme of work to follow at their own pace, assisted by staff as necessary, but it was abandoned as being incompatible with examination requirements. For a few years, there was a third class for each of the sixth form years in addition to the arts and science forms. A Domestic Science course included Household Management, Craft

Right: Concert programme for 1923-4, almost certainly designed by Esther Grainger, whose name appears at the top. She later enjoyed a distinguished career in Art. As Principal Lecturer at Cardiff's College of Education, she taught drawing, painting and embroidery.

Facing page
The kitchen garden with the Sanatorium (later School House) behind, 1930s.

and Needlework, Horticulture and Social and Economic History. Those hoping for careers in Art or Music also followed a general course.

There were also elocution and voice production lessons. By the end of the 1920s, Biology was replacing Botany in the Senior School, with girls in the Junior School doing Nature Study, although in the sixth form Botany and Zoology were taught separately. A few girls in the sixth form studied Italian, and History of Art became an increasingly popular option for the School Certificate examination. Lantern lectures were given by Miss Trotter on a wide variety of topics: she was determined to educate girls in the broadest possible sense and make them more aware of the world outside Wales.

In the later 1920s, financial difficulties re-emerged but fortunately Cardiff and Glamorgan agreed to pay the deficit for the foreseeable future. In addition, Miss Trotter herself needed an operation in London in October 1928. She did not return until the Summer Term of 1929 and during her absence Miss Winny, the Second Mistress, was in charge. The following year, Miss Winny herself was ill and decided to retire after forty-one and a half years. She was replaced as Botany mistress by Miss Emily Willey, and the Senior Mistress, Miss Bellamy, succeeded her as Second Mistress. In addition to her teaching, Miss Winny had coached tennis and hockey and had been the driving force behind no fewer than thirty-five Shakespeare plays at Christmas. She had also been responsible for setting up a school branch of the League of Nations Union, another enthusiastic supporter of which was Miss Bush.

Miss Winny was praised for introducing modern methods of Geography teaching, which involved field survey work, and a Governor, Mr Charles Morris, wrote that she was "one of the great teachers of Wales . . . her teaching of Botany is known throughout Wales". The Hywelians honoured her by making her an Honorary Vice-President of the Guild. She retired to her new cottage on Anglesey where she died in May 1944. The Hywelian Guild donated a leaving scholarship (the Winny Memorial Scholarship) to the best scholar of the year. The first recipient, announced on 14th November 1946, was Joan Ede.

10

THE GROWTH OF EXTRACURRICULAR ACTIVITIES, 1920-31

Facing page
Miss Mason's sketch of a League of Nations party in the Hall, late 1920s.

Above: Form IV League of Nations party, 24th May 1921.

Not only did the conditions become much more comfortable during the 1920s; there was also a wider range of activities and events outside the classroom. Armistice Day (11th November) was celebrated in 1921 with Kipling's *Song of the English* and the girls dressed to represent different countries of the League of Nations. This developed into an eagerly anticipated annual party, The format varied slightly from year to year, reflecting the work and problems of the League, but the girls always dressed to represent different member countries and there were prizes, a sumptuous tea and dancing. At the end of events like this, Miss Trotter would dance with the Head Girl or one of the prefects or staff, and would play games with the younger children. On Friday afternoons there were form concerts, made up of samples from work done during the week: poems, playlets in foreign languages, songs and piano pieces. Miss Trotter revelled in all these occasions.

The idea of having houses for the day girls was first mooted in 1923 but they did not come into existence until the end of the Summer Term of 1926. All girls from the Upper Third upwards became members of a house. To mark the new units, members of each house, rather than each form, filed past Miss Trotter for the customary farewell handshake at the end of term. The names of the six houses all had a Welsh or Howell's connection. St David's and St Dyfrig's were named after the Welsh patron saint and, according to legend, Wales' first archbishop respectively; Founders represented Thomas Howell; Drapers provided a link to the original management of the school; Buckley took its name from the Archdeacon of Llandaff who for many years prepared pupils for Confirmation; and the surname of John Lowdon, a Governor from 1904 to 1925, provided the sixth. Each house had a Head Girl and a housemistress, and met briefly once a week. The girls wrote their own house songs and a strong spirit of loyalty soon developed, with house concerts and inter-house matches. The annual Sports Day, with rivalry between houses, included light-hearted as well as serious races.

Another innovation was the annual publication of a school magazine. There had earlier been an unofficial magazine, *The College Mirror*, intended for private circulation only, but in July 1924 the first detailed official record of school events was produced, combined with the school roll, Miss Kendall's reminiscences and pupils' original contributions. That year, the girls held their first Flower Show and from 1925 this formed part of an Open Day, at which visitors could inspect the girls' work.

'On Friday afternoons we had Form Concerts, which were made up of samples from our form work. When these were replaced by House Concerts after the day girl houses were founded, they became much more entertaining and reached a high standard. . . . Prompting was absolutely forbidden and if memory failed one left the platform with ignominy.

No make-up was allowed in any play, not even to Shylock or Caliban; we were to be neither horrific nor glamorous. A helpful mistress was once shaping Viola's bodice with darts, but Miss Trotter, as she unpinned them and restored shapelessness, tapped the actress's bosom and said severely, "We must get rid of *all this*."'

Bronwen Jones (1921-31). Written 1959.

PROGRAMME
FORM U.P. III

PROGRAMME
FORM IV.A
CONCERT

~TREDEGAR~

PROGRAMME
BUCKLEY HOUSE CONCERT

"Forward the Light Brigade"

PROGRAMME

K IS FOR KENDALL AND KENDALL ALONE
AND STILL WE "DARE NOBLY" TO KEEP
UP ITS TONE

1. **E** IS FOR EXTRACTS FROM BOOKS YOU ALL KNOW
AND IF YOU CAN GUESS THEM WILL YOU
PLEASE LET US KNOW?

2. **N** IS FOR NONSENSE, THE CENTRE OF FAIRS
WHERE THERE'S DANCING AND SINGING AND
SELLING OF WARES

3. **D** IS FOR DANCING, UNIVERSAL DELIGHT
WHICH WE HOPE OUR PERFORMANCE WILL
MERIT TONIGHT

4. **A** IS FOR ARTS, ONE IS MUSIC YOU KNOW
OUR NEXT ITEM WILL BE A VIOLIN SOLO

5. **L** IS FOR LUPO, BROTHER WOLF HE IS CALLED
WHOM THE GENTLE ST FRANCIS FROM HIS
VENGEANCE RECALLED.

6. **L** IS FOR LAST, OUR WELL KNOWN HOUSE SONG
WE TRUST WE HAVE PLEASED YOU NOR KEPT
YOU TOO LONG.

Left: Miss Mason's sketch of Miss Trotter directing a rehearsal of Hamlet, *1926.*
Right: Julius Caesar, *1927.*
Left to right: Enid Owen, Marjorie Gurney, Nest Phillips, unknown, Peggy Luke, Peggy Charters.
Lower right: Portrait of John Lowdon, Governor 1904-25, painted by Miss Mason.

Miss Trotter enthusiastically assisted with the preparations for Miss Winny's annual Shakespeare Christmas productions, which served to further the girls' cultural education. The play was chosen and cast each year before the summer holiday and the girls were expected to be familiar with the text by the start of the Autumn Term. The costumes were recycled each year and the footlights were nailed to a plank placed on the front of the stage. The Art mistress, Miss Emily Mason, spent time at the weekends perched on a ladder, painting the backdrop. There were just a few breaks in this tradition; for instance, in 1931, there was a concert involving the whole school instead of a Shakespeare play. A prominent part was played by Miss Gwladys Williams, a member of staff with a fine singing voice.

Prize-givings were always very grand occasions, the military precision matching that of Lord Tredegar's day. They were always followed by tea, a display by the Star Gymnastics class and dancing by the boarders after the parents had gone home. In 1924, Miss Mason presented the eighty-year old John Lowdon, a Governor since 1904 and Chairman from 1920-5, with his portrait, which she had painted in oils; he then handed it back to the school to be hung in the Board Room. In 1927 the Governors were the only guests and the Chairman distributed the prizes, reviving briefly the tradition of Lord Tredegar. The prize-giving of October 1930 was a particularly memorable occasion as the guest of honour was a former pupil of the school, Edith Sankey, who was a Justice of the Peace in London and sister of the Lord Chancellor.

For the first time, St David's Day was celebrated in 1927 with an impromptu concert from each house. Empire Day festivities also took place in May each year. Maretta Madge described what happened in 1928 after a performance of *The Song of the English*: "After the play, Miss Trotter told us a little about the Empire, and the responsibility which rests upon its citizens. The representation was heartily applauded, and *God Save the King*, sung by the school, gave the audience also an opportunity to express their patriotic love of the Empire."

'The entrance exam was very simple in those days. There were only about six of us and we had English and Arithmetic papers which we did sitting around the Board Room table. We were supervised by Miss Bush.

I loved being a boarder at the weekends, when we had the school to ourselves. We did prep on Saturday morning in school and in the afternoon there were games or we went for long walks with the Bug [Miss Hilda Taylor] – all the way to St Fagans and back by a circuitous route, a long way for little legs. We used to be terrified of her when we were young – she was quite a forbidding character – but you got to know and like her when you were older. In the Autumn Term, if you were old enough, you helped to make props for the school play. I remember making flowers in the Board Room for *A Midsummer Night's Dream*. I was Celia in *As You Like It*. We just had a row of footlights and there was no make-up at all. We dressed in the music cells. I was sickening for something and looked dreadful. I can remember an older girl, Verna Reynolds, who was later on the staff, saying, "You can't go on like that. I'll put some of my own make-up on you." Trott came down to inspect us and she said, "Take that off at once!"

On Sundays we got up later and had sausages, which we loved, then we went to the Cathedral. Nonconformists went to a Presbyterian chapel in Cathedral Road. In the afternoon we played games. On other days we got up at seven, walked around the field unless we had to do piano practice, had breakfast at eight, then went back to Oaklands to make our beds and then came back to school.

Miss Trotter designed for herself a sort of ceremonial robe, like a medieval robe, for special and social occasions. We used to be proud of our blazers but Miss Trotter introduced ghastly Grecian tunics. They were all right if you looked like a reed but if you were rotund, as I was, they made you look like a balloon! For prize-giving we all wore white dresses, which we also wore to church in the summer, with a white coat and hat. We used to rehearse and rehearse. The school song music was composed by Georgie Beale, the Cathedral organist. It was nice at first – sung staccato and very quickly – but much later on it became more like a dirge.'

Catherine Powell, née Morgan (1927-34). Interviewed May 2009.

'The richness of my school life during eleven years under Miss Trotter's rule was astonishing. Her energy, vitality and readiness to experiment were phenomenal; and everything was on a grand scale. My earliest memory was a Christmas party for children from the poorer districts of Cardiff. Every girl in the school invited a child individually. . . . There was a concert in the Hall and a giant Christmas tree in the Gym, on which were hung the gifts each one of us had brought.

Then I remember the full-scale dancing display. Mme Gaultier and Miss Yapsley taught us – but Miss Trotter produced powder-puff dance, Dutch dance, Old English minuet framed in the open hall doors, and the tiger-lily ballet with butterfly and bee soloists, costumes all created in the Art Room.

About this time the gym competition was inaugurated, together with the Star Gym and Star Folk-Dancing, under the auspices of Miss Hutchinson. The gym competition was held every year and every form competed for the shield with a ten-minute programme, comprising marching, exercising and apparatus work in sections. The Czechoslovakian dances were a feature on Sports Days. Miss Trotter and Miss Winny brought back from Czechoslovakia authentic costumes and these were copied at school and the dances taught.

HOWELL'S SCHOOL, LLANDAFF.
HYWELIAN GUILD FETE
Czechoslovakian Songs & Dances
BY
THE BOARDERS' TROUPE.
WELSH, IRISH, SCOTCH & SWEDISH DANCES in the FIELD on FRIDAY, July 20th at 6.15-6.45 p.m.
Entrance - SIXPENCE.

We had experiments in the classroom, too. In 1924 it was the Dalton Plan, when we were not to have formal lessons but received typed slips with the week's schedule of work. . . . When I was in the fifth form the idea that mistresses should help us during examinations was tried. I remember being paralysed for the first hour of the English exam, with the fear of my effort being read over my shoulder.

I have not mentioned the annual form picnics to the seaside in char-a-bancs, expeditions after the summer examinations to Caerleon, the Castle, Castell Coch etc. In my final year in the sixth, the great pageant was held in Cardiff Castle, and I well remember in the summer evenings swotting Cicero on the turret steps between rehearsing. There were evenings, too, when we went back to Hazelwood for an English lesson in Miss Trotter's Drawing Room.'

Mavis Adler, née Diamond (1920-31). Written 1960.

Left: Outing to Marcross in 1929 with Miss Elsie Fowler, who taught Geography and Botany from 1923 to 1965.
Above: Outing to the coast, c.1931. Megan Anthony is on the left in the second row, kneeling. She became Head Girl 1933-4, Chemistry Mistress at Howell's from 1943 to 1953 and then Headmistress of Queen Elizabeth School, Carmarthen.
Left: The great gale, 16th November 1928 – an illustration from the school magazine.
Right: Miss Trotter dressed to take part in the pageant at Cardiff Castle, 1931.

Facing page
Hywelian Guild fête ticket, 1930s, showing dances learnt by the girls.

A party of nineteen girls, with just one member of staff, enjoyed Howell's first overseas trip during the Easter holiday of 1922. Miss Rose Davenport, a Hywelian whose four sisters were also at school, organised a three-week visit to Paris and Rouen. Considering the less sophisticated means of communication that existed then, this must have been a massive feat of organisation. It was very successful and was repeated for many years. Closer to home, there were many other excursions. Senior girls were taken on a four-day walking tour of the River Wye by Miss Fowler and Miss Bellamy in 1925 and a walking tour at Easter became an annual event, with a different destination chosen each year. By the early 1930s, girls were increasingly involved with events outside school. In the autumn of 1931 they took part in a grand pageant of the History of Cardiff at Cardiff Castle, organised by the university.

These years saw extremely difficult times in Britain for many people, with the effects of the Great Depression. Families in the South Wales valleys were hit very hard, with mass unemployment and sickness. Howell's adopted the Girls' Council School of Trehafod, and sent clothes, boots and cakes for the pupils and their families. The girls worked hard for Dorcas, which involved knitting and sewing garments, and sent parcels to Dr Barnardo's, the Waifs and Strays, Treloar's Crippled Children and other worthy causes. An awareness of the needs of others and practical citizenship was also inculcated through the making of Dorcas garments and "surprises" such as toy shops, farms, a Noah's Ark and dolls' hospitals for local homes and hospitals as well as collections for disadvantaged groups.

Despite all these activities, academic work was not neglected; the CWB produced consistently good reports following inspections and a steady stream of girls went on to university. In January 1931 the school heard from the Director of Education that Howell's girls would be eligible for Cardiff scholarships in Art and Science and that studentships could be awarded for courses at the University of Wales.

'We had to walk round the hockey field before breakfast at eight – nice in the summer, not so good in the winter. The girls who were in The Rise were exempt from that as the trail up to school from their house at 7.30am was considered a good substitute. There were games or walks (in crocodiles) in the lunch hour, and games after afternoon school. Everyone had to change from school uniform into her own clothes for tea; The Rise brought their things up in the morning, but Hazelwood and Oaklands had to go back to their houses to change. Prep was in our own houses – done in silence; baths were taken out of our prep. Time – maximum of fifteen minutes from the time one left prep. to the time one resumed one's seat. The food was plain to say the least and our supper consisted of bread and butter/beef dripping, and cocoa in the winter or milk in summer. "Lights out" was at nine and no talking afterwards.

One curious omission from our diet was fresh fruit. We had it stewed but never fresh and parents of most of the boarders used to place a weekly order for fruit at the beginning of term from Bale's, the fruiterers in the village. We all queued in the Covered Way after lunch on Wednesdays, received our bags of fruit, were allowed one piece each, and there and then the bags of fruit were stowed in lockers in the Covered Way and we went every day to take one piece. We were strictly rationed as to sweets. We were allowed ten every Sunday from our tuck-boxes, but lost one sweet for every misdemeanour discovered during the previous week. These sins ranged from untidily-made beds to talking after "Lights" and I often went sweetless.

It wasn't all work and no play. Every Christmas term we (and I mean day girls as well) put on a Shakespeare play. The whole school was involved in some way and I vividly remember sewing on the feathers of the "Shapes" costumes in the Board Room on Saturday nights when we did *The Tempest*.

In the Spring Term the big thing was the House Concerts. There was great competition about these; all plans were kept very secret and everyone in the house from the lowliest to the highest took part. Miss Trotter used to sit in her chair half-way down the centre of the Hall, which was a bit intimidating, but one tried to rise above that and ignore the piercing look.'

Catherine Powell, née Morgan (1927-1934). Written 1990.

Above: Hywelian summer meeting, 1929.
Above centre right: Hywelian blazer, early 1930s.

Above far right: Gong presented to school by the Hywelian Guild in 1931, to celebrate the Guild's twenty-fifth anniversary.
Right: Rosalind White wearing her school hat, late 1920s. Her sister Madeline was also a pupil at school and, as Mrs Davies, taught Geography from 1954 to 1968.

On St David's Day 1931, the school held its first Eisteddfod. Before the day itself, there were various subject competitions and on 1st March the girls enjoyed music, recitations in several languages, competitions in creative work, handwriting, puzzles and a science lecture. During the 1930s, the Urdd Gobaith Cymru movement began to flourish in school.

The year 1931 also marked the twenty-fifth anniversary of the Hywelian Guild. During the 1920s, it had continued to expand in size and in the range of its activities. With Miss Trotter as Deputy President, it initiated a Loan Fund, which lent money to both pupils and Hywelians to assist them with the costs of higher education, while the Helping Fund gave charitable assistance to old girls. On 25th July 1922, the Guild organised a massive bazaar in aid of the Loan and Helping Fund, using all parts of the building and grounds. In 1923, a Hywelian Dramatic Committee and a Games Committee were formed and the Guild members had their own blazer. In the same year, an annual magazine replaced the report.

By 1931, the Hywelian Dramatic Society, with its annual performances, had raised almost £450 for the Loan Fund. As members of the Guild were increasingly living further afield, the idea of having branches in the provinces developed and the first branch outside Cardiff began in London in January 1927. Four years later, there were also branches in Swansea, Manchester (the Northern branch) and Southampton (the Southern branch). In 1931 it was decided to begin a Needlework Guild and in its first year two hundred articles of clothing were made and sent to the Queen's Nurses in Cardiff as well as a donation to Barnardo's.

To celebrate the quarter-century of the Guild, it was decided to hold a weekend of events at school in July. These included the presentation of a series of tableaux representing the founding of the school, "At Homes" at school and in all the hostels for Hywelians and their families, and a service in the Cathedral. There was also a dinner, during which girls entertained the former pupils with Czechoslovakian dances, and the newly-formed Hywelian orchestra made its début performance under the direction of Mrs Edith Richards (née Novello-Davies). It was decided to make a gift to the Children's Corner of the Cathedral, and a copy of the Sistine Madonna was dedicated at the Sunday service. The Hywelians also presented the school with a very fine inscribed gong.

At the end of 1931, everything seemed to be going well for the school. Plenty of planning for the future was taking place, with Governors' sub-committees discussing such matters as reorganisation and furnishing. Little did anyone know that, after the celebrations of the twenty-fifth anniversary of the Hywelian Guild, Howell's was to face a calamity in 1932.

THE GREAT FIRE AND ITS AFTERMATH, 1932-7

Photographs taken on the night of the Great Fire.

The year 1932 was the most momentous in the school's history. At the beginning of February came the news of Miss Kendall's death. Just two weeks later, on the night of Friday, 19th February, a major fire broke out. Miss Trotter was in London attending a Headmistresses' Conference, leaving Miss Bellamy in charge. At about 9.45pm, with the boarders of Kendall House sleeping in the school, the matron, Miss Yardley, smelled smoke and raised the alarm. Six fire engines were on the scene within minutes, pumping thousands of gallons of water into the building, but the fire spread quickly through the Stone Hall, Dining Room, Sanatorium and several classrooms, studies and cloakrooms. The main turret and the former East Dormitory were also destroyed; thankfully, there were no longer any girls sleeping there.

The fire is believed to have started in a flue above the boiler house and to have smouldering for an hour before the alarm was raised. An official of Cardiff Corporation, who happened to be passing, dashed into the boiler house and turned off the gas. All the meters near the school were also quickly turned off. Very soon after the official's brave action, the boiler house went up in flames. The chief constable directed the fire-fighting operations from the highest rung of the water tower and managed to prevent the fire from spreading to the kitchens, the main entrance and office, which contained all the school records. Fortunately, the Hall also escaped destruction as it happened to be on the leeward side. The greatest destruction occurred on the first floor, as the fire travelled quickly along the roof.

At the time of the fire, five mistresses, the housekeeper, eleven other members of the domestic staff and twenty-four boarders were in the building. The boarders were quickly roused and, dressed in what clothes they could find in the darkness (as the electric lights had fused), were led to the Board Room. After a roll-call they were evacuated immediately to the nearby hostels, private homes and the nearby Llandaff School of Dancing in Cardiff Road, carrying their bedding. Their sleeping quarters in school were not destroyed in the fire. School staff, the older girls, servants and other willing helpers salvaged what they could, and items such as clothes, sports

Recollections of the fire

'I noticed outside the school several boarders wearing coats over their night attire, walking along in an unperturbed manner, carrying their bed-clothing. . . . Standing in the kitchen gardens we watched the Lower V Science form room being entirely destroyed; we heard the dry crisp crackle of the flames as they licked higher and higher over the walls; the roof fell in with resounding crashes, and the flames . . . leapt up to the sky, devouring the walls at a tremendous pace, a blaze of gorgeous colour. All around us were curious sightseers; they trampled across the gardens regardless of plants, they climbed up the fruit trees, and on the wall of the hockey field stood a dozen press photographers. . . . Firemen and police seemed to be everywhere, and on the ground lay a network of huge hosepipes. In the centre of the lawn lay a heap of clothing, books and pictures. Some mistresses were salvaging articles from the bedrooms, some of the maids and the policemen rescued hockey sticks, crosses, hats, coats and shoes from the cloakrooms, which were quickly being flooded with water.'

Sybil Clark, a day girl, lived near Penhill and ran to see the fire with some neighbours.

'The occupants of our bedroom were sleeping peacefully when we were rudely awakened. . . . We were told to get up and dress quickly, but were not informed that there was a fire. I thought that I was late for music practice, and started to perform little morning tasks, such as stripping my bed. . . . We hurried down the winding belfry stairs, in the charge of a mistress, Miss Baker, and Dora, a maid. . . . Miss Bellamy took me over to Oaklands. . . . I got into bed, fully clothed, but not to sleep. . . . After a while I got out of bed, and walked round the room, from where I had a good view of the fire. . . . The Tower was lit up by the lurid glare of the flames. . . . The belfry was silhouetted against the blood-red sky. . . . Flames were reaching to an alarming height, and on the top of a tall ladder a fireman could dimly be seen directing a hose into the middle of the furnace. . . . At last, at about half-past two, I dropped off to sleep from sheer weariness. In the morning, I woke to find the top of the Stone Hall and some form rooms, charred ruins, but the main part saved and everybody unharmed.'

Myra James was a boarder in Kendall House (in school).

equipment and pictures were piled up on the tennis lawns. A few of the Governors arrived to give assistance and the resident staff stayed at school most of the night. Parents arrived from far and wide to check on their daughters' safety. It was about 11.45pm before the fire appeared to be under control but it lasted for about six hours and the firemen remained in school throughout the night. The cost of the damage, according to newspaper reports immediately after the blaze, was estimated at about £25,000 but the claim against the insurance company was finally settled at £9,638 6s.3d, excluding the personal property of the staff and pupils.

Miss Trotter returned the next day. The Junior girls spent a week at home but the Seniors missed no lessons at all. On Monday morning, Prayers were held in the Gymnasium and each form was then allotted a room in one of the hostels, which were turned into makeshift classrooms. Some textbooks, which had been soaked, were salvaged, dried and used again; others had been burnt but

Recollections of the fire

'On the morning of 20th February, I awoke to the fact that the empty bed in my room was occupied. . . . I was told of the exciting escape of the staff and girls from the building, and how the drive was crowded with a mixture of firemen, anxious parents, equally anxious staff, and excited girls. I was also told that we were going to have breakfast in Oaklands. . . . I arrived down to breakfast to find Oaklands reinforced by some of the refugees from School House. They were a motley crew, most of them being in borrowed garments that did not fit them particularly well. . . . We had several duties assigned to us, as the maids were busy. . . . We procured a newspaper, and read with mirth one slightly exaggerated account of the fire. "Thrilling Escape" and such-like headlines adorned the paper.'

Minnie Morgan, a pupil from 1927 to 1934, and later a member of staff, was a boarder in Oaklands.

'Early the next morning, some of the non-resident mistresses arrived and helped to serve breakfast to the increased number of inmates in the hostels. . . . Reporters arrived on the scene at an early hour, and desired interviews with both girls and mistresses. All the morning girls were going back and fore to school sorting out the clothes, etc., which had been deposited on the tennis courts. . . . Before the afternoon most of the Juniors had gone home – to remain there for a week. The Seniors who were left spent a busy and interesting weekend. We looked after ourselves in the hostels. . . . When the boarders went to church on Sunday they seemed to be regarded as heroines of the hour.'

Megan Anthony, also a boarder in Oaklands (later Head Girl and Chemistry mistress) recalled what happened that weekend.

Patricia: 'I can remember coming down in a train from Pontypridd and we saw flames in the distance and I thought, "I bet that's my school burning down." '
Elizabeth: 'I was playing with a group of children and someone said, "Your school was on fire last night", and I thought they were pulling my leg.'
Patricia: 'We rolled up to school on the Monday and we were sent down to the Institute. I think we were there for a year, probably longer than that.'
Elizabeth: 'I was sent to Oaklands. There was even a class in Old House, by the Cathedral.'
Patricia: 'The teachers had to walk up and down so we missed bits of lessons all the time, which we thought was lovely! I got up and went to the sweet shop round the corner once but I was caught by one of the teachers.'

Patricia Kernick and Elizabeth Jones, née Kernick (cousins). Interviewed April 2009.

Members of the school staff salving valuable paintings and personal effects from the burning building.

ON SALVAGE WORK.—These girls of Llandaff school make light of their task of sorting out their belongings after the fire of Friday last.

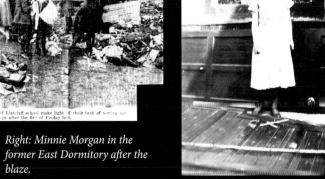

Top: A fire-damaged classroom.
Above: Newspaper reports
following the fire.

Right: Minnie Morgan in the
former East Dormitory after the
blaze.

replacements arrived by the end of the week. When the Juniors returned, they found themselves having lessons in the Llandaff Institute and two rooms in the nearby Llandaff School of Dancing, which the school had hastily rented. The dispersal of forms to different locations necessitated some alterations to the timetable to minimise the distance the mistresses needed to cycle. Miss Trotter made a plan, using flags to show where each form was located. All meals during the first few days after the fire were eaten in the hostels, there being no gas or electricity in school, but by the end of the week the Gymnasium had been converted into a Dining Room. Gymnastics lessons, without equipment, took place in the Hall.

At an emergency Governors' meeting the following Monday, Miss Trotter was authorised to engage temporary extra domestic servants. Workmen began repair work immediately and the girls and staff became used to the noise and to wading through puddles, wearing galoshes and mackintoshes and carrying umbrellas to reach their form rooms. Girls were supposed to wear their hats when walking through the roofless Dining Room, a rule that was impossible to enforce. Occasionally both staff and girls disappeared down holes in the floor but there were no serious accidents. As a reward for their helpfulness, each man-servant was given a gratuity of £1 and each maid 10 shillings. Amidst the noise of rebuilding, school life continued as normally as possible, with all the traditional activities that year taking place.

Above far left: Miss Mason's sketch of staff and pupils walking through the school after the fire.
Top: Form IV Science and Lower V Science on Graig-yr-Allt, June 1932.
Above: Large-scale drill, 1932.
Left: Twins Alice and Grace Cheetham in 1932. Pupils at Howell's from 1926-35, they both went on to gain first class honours degrees in Botany in 1938 and Zoology in 1939 at University College, Cardiff, becoming the first twins to achieve double firsts in the same subjects at the same university. As Mrs James, Alice edited the Hywelian magazine from 1942 to 1963.

Left: Three staff enjoying an outing, 1932. Left to right: Miss Daisy Walters (Welsh), Dr Phyllis Hicks (Botany), a former Howell's pupil who gained a first class honours degree at the age of twenty, and Miss Barbara Ruby Phillips (English).

On the Wednesday after the fire, a house at 122 Cardiff Road was rented to provide accommodation for boarders. After a rapid period of painting and furnishing, some girls moved from Hazelwood, Oaklands and Kendall to what became known as "122", under the charge of Miss Hilda Taylor, and soon became involved in gardening. In June, another new hostel was rented by the Governors. This was the Old House on The Green, reputedly the oldest dwelling in Llandaff. "122" had to be given up the next year but in 1935 the school took possession of yet another hostel, with the purchase of what became known as Kendall House at 128 Cardiff Road. This enabled the remaining boarders' cubicles in school to be converted into a spacious new Craft Room, with the luxury of fourteen basins.

The County Architect produced plans for the re-building, and within a year of the fire much reconstruction work had taken place. The exterior remained much as before but the interior was transformed. There was a new Dining Room and the Stone Hall was beautifully restored, becoming much lighter. The new classrooms on the ground floor had French windows for the first time, so that the girls could see out into the grounds from their new desks. The rooms on the first floor had fanlight windows and skylights in the roof. All the floors had green cork linoleum in place of bare boards, and new corridors outside the upstairs classrooms meant that lessons were no longer disturbed by people passing through. Substantial sound-proof walls replaced the old brown partitions which had previously separated classrooms. The over-riding impression was of light, airy rooms. The west wing also housed a small Physics Laboratory. The paintings, all of which had miraculously been saved, were placed in their previous locations but in the next few years a wonderful new collection appeared in corridors and on classroom walls.

The most prized addition to the school was the Library with its oak doors on the first floor, which replaced two bathrooms, the Craft Room and the staff cloakroom. Some of the girls perched on ladders to oil the woodwork in the new Library and helped to move furniture, pictures and books. The woodwork was all made in the school workshop by the carpenter and joiner, Mr Raymond Window, and his assistants.

Left: The new Library, created after the fire.
Top: The Stone Hall after the fire, with new light paintwork.
Above: The Big Dining Room after the fire, with its new French windows.

Far left top: Miss Hilda Taylor, 1933.
Far left bottom: Miss Mason's sketch of herself on her travels in Morocco.
Left: Miss Sheila Disney, the formidable Physical Education mistress, 1933-54.
Above: Joan Jackson and Olwen Rowlands wearing the unpopular Grecian tunics, in a rough saxe-blue cotton.
Right: Elizabeth Kernick wearing her new school blazer.

Meanwhile, in 1932, the school faced more bad news with the serious illnesses of Miss Bellamy and Miss Harrison, both of whom underwent operations. Miss Harrison returned before the end of the Summer Term and Miss Bellamy at the start of the Autumn Term. Unfortunately, the latter's stay did not last long. She went to her brother's near Tintern Abbey where she died on 16th March 1933. Miss Bellamy had been at Howell's since entering as a ten-year-old orphan in 1882. Apart from her teaching, she was renowned for her gardening, walking holidays with the girls and work for Dorcas. In recognition of her helpful nature, the Hywelian Guild, of which she had been Vice-President, decided to present a named prize each year to a girl who had given good service to the school, and in 1936 a bird-bath was placed in the garden of Oaklands. Miss Bellamy's successor as Second Mistress was Miss Hilda Taylor.

Miss Trotter was also absent with diphtheria for almost two terms from January 1933, and Miss Taylor ran the school during this period, just as forms were moving back into the building following the fire. In 1934 there was another staff death: that of Miss Mason, who had been an artist in her own right, with pictures displayed annually in the South Wales Art exhibition. She had designed covers for various periodicals and had made pottery, bas-reliefs and statuary. In the shrubbery near Miss Winny's peat bog she had created a model village, peopled by nursery-rhyme characters. Among other activities, she had told the girls enthralling stories of her pioneering travels in Africa.

Mr Beale left after forty years in 1934, and was succeeded by Mr Albert Price, the organist of St Germain's church in Roath. Composer of numerous hymn tunes and anthems for the school, including the music for the school song, Mr Beale had also helped with the Christmas play, concerts and Open Days. Sadly, his retirement was short as he died in October 1936.

The Physical Education department received a new impetus with the arrival of Miss Sheila Disney, known as Diz, in 1933. That summer, the Gymnasium was equipped with new climbing ropes, a new balancing bench, repairs to the old ones and a new cover for the vaulting horse. By July 1934 the Governors had hired a new field, Bishop's Field, from the Llandaff Institute, for hockey, lacrosse, cricket and rounders. Part of Llandaff Fields was also used regularly as an "overflow". The extended facilities enabled games to be organised in houses and Miss Disney worked hard to make it possible for all pupils to play at lunchtime. She also organised folk

'The summers in Hazelwood were lovely. We had a large garden with a tennis court and fruit bushes laden with raspberries and loganberries. Some of us got up early to swim before breakfast in the pool in Llandaff Fields. This was of course before we had a school pool. When gardening became an alternative to games on Saturday afternoons a number of us developed a sudden interest in plants. Weeding was a very pleasant occupation on a sunny day and could be carried out while sitting down and chatting. It was due to Miss Trotter that we had a lot of pictures in the house.'

Professor Pat Clarke, née Green (1930-37, Head Girl 1936-7). Written 2002.

dance classes, especially a Czechoslovakian troupe, and ran the Star Gymnastics group which stayed after school on Fridays for special training. By July 1936 the Governors had provided two sheds, in Oaklands dingle and on Bishop's Field, for storing games kit.

The 1930s marked the beginning of organised clubs in school. An extracurricular activity, started in 1933, was the Current News Club, which discussed the League of Nations and other topical subjects. Welsh flourished under Miss Walters, girls in 1933 taking part in an Urdd Eisteddfod at Hengoed in the Rhymney Valley. By the mid-1930s the Urdd Gobaith Cymru was active at school, with games, Welsh folk songs, readings from literature, drama and poetry, and participation in an Urdd camp and cruise.

Minor changes to the uniform occurred in the 1930s. Elizabeth Jones (née Kernick) recalled that during her time in school, starting in January 1932, the white collared blouses became square-necked. She felt very self-conscious having to continue to wear the original design until it wore out but she was very proud of her navy summer blazer. She remembered "those ghastly bluish Grecian tunics with short sleeves which we had to wear in the summer, which was completely shapeless and had a piece of elastic round the waist. And woe betide us if we didn't change into our indoor shoes."

Nationally, there were lengthy discussions about the value of homework between 1933 and 1935, with the issue even being raised in Parliament. The school tried abandoning it in the Summer Term of 1935, on the grounds that there would be more time for other activities, but lower academic standards by the autumn led to its reintroduction. On George V's Silver Jubilee, 6th May 1935, there were no lessons either; the girls went out picking bluebells in the afternoon, and many joined in the evening celebrations in town and watched the fireworks display on Llandaff Fields. Less than a month later, on 1st June, the school was honoured by the presence of the Lord Chancellor, Lord Sankey, at prize-giving, and rejoiced that the Head Girl, Doreen King, had won an Open Science scholarship to Girton College, Cambridge, and that Aline Kyle had been awarded a League of Nations travel scholarship to Geneva. After the ceremony and the ensuing dancing and gymnastics display, Lord Sankey planted a tree in the grounds of Hazelwood. In July his sister Edith Sankey became one of the Governors, the first former pupil to do so.

That summer saw a great deal of time spent out of doors, as Miss Trotter always liked, with games on the fields, picnics, lessons under the trees and evenings – and even nights – spent by the boarders in the gardens. As Miss Trotter edged towards retirement, there was no let-up in the amount of activity. The girls enjoyed their regular lectures on Wednesday afternoons, illustrated with lantern slides, the League of Nations Party, Empire Day celebrations, confirmation classes, the Dorcas distribution at Christmas, Open Days (which were organised on a massive scale, that of 1935 being attended by no fewer than a thousand visitors), carol singing and concerts.

Right: Lord Sankey, the Lord Chancellor, visiting Hazelwood to plant a tree after Prize-giving, 1935.
Far right: League of Nations party, mid-1930s.

Far left, top: The Swimming Pool, opened in 1937.
Far left, below: Swimming pool memorial tablet.
Above: The stone seat donated by the Hywelians in memory of Miss Trotter, 1946.
Left: The Trotter Cup.

Miss Trotter announced her resignation in September 1936. The first advertisement for her replacement produced no suitable applicants and it was decided to re-advertise, omitting the words "Experience in a residential school essential". Miss Trotter agreed to stay until the end of the summer term and in March 1937, Miss Edith Knight was appointed on a starting salary of £600.

From 1934, the Hywelians had been preoccupied with raising funds for the indoor swimming pool in memory of Miss Kendall. That year they had held their first, very successful dance, followed by supper in the Dining Room. They also put on a concert and held another huge bazaar. At the end of Miss Trotter's final term, on 17th July, the pool was formally opened, five months after the memorial tablet to Miss Kendall in the Cathedral was unveiled. Built on the area formerly known as *The Bog*, beyond the grass tennis courts, it had taken longer to build than expected. However, finally everyone was well satisfied as the Governors donated £2,100 to the project on top of the £1,700 raised by the Hywelians, meaning that the pool had a roof and could therefore be used all year round. The opening ceremony concluded with a display of swimming and life-saving by a small group of Hywelians. An anonymous donor gave a solid silver cup, known as the Eleanor Trotter cup, for achievement in swimming, and a competition was duly organised a few days later; Drapers House emerging victorious.

Miss Trotter lived at Rhosneigr on Anglesey until her death from a heart attack in 1946. Her health was not particularly good but, against medical advice, she devoted herself to growing all kinds of fruit and vegetables during the Second World War and donating the proceeds to the Red Cross, as well as making children's clothes. A stone seat for the School Field was provided as a memorial to

her, paid for in part by the funds remaining from the Rabbit Club run by Miss Disney during the war. She herself left money in her will for a Shakespeare prize.

Under Miss Trotter, the school had almost doubled in size to 479, the greatest increase being in the number of day girls, of whom there were 358 in 1937. In terms of material improvements, the contrast with the situation when she arrived was remarkable. An article in the school magazine for 1946 stated: *A girl entering the school twenty-six years ago would have found no swimming baths, no hostels, a much smaller library, no French windows, few pictures, and those without colour, no path round the hockey field, high windows with iron bars, no craft room, no class rooms upstairs but instead long dormitories and bedrooms with rows of beds almost touching, no electric light or modern heating system; the form room floors were bare board and benches were used in the Dining Room.*

The prospectus of 1935 described the enhanced facilities, which must have seemed impressive at the time by any standards: *The original building accommodation within the school has been converted into additional class rooms, which have been constructed on modern hygienic principles to admit the maximum of light and air. Three Laboratories for Physical and Life Sciences, a Domestic Science Kitchen, an Art Studio and Modelling Room, a Craft Room, Music Rooms, a Gymnasium, a Library and a large Assembly Hall have been added to the original buildings. Electric light and a new heating apparatus were installed in 1923, and extended in 1933.*

The Boarders are accommodated in five Houses with pleasant gardens, large sitting rooms and airy bedrooms; the latter are divided and furnished so that each girl has a separate bedroom. Care has been taken in the furnishing of the School Houses and in the arrangement

Above left: The Cookery School, 1930s.
Above right: The Art Room, 1930s.
Right: The school in the 1930s.

'On the first day of term we had to kneel on the ground and check that our tunics just touched the floor. If they were a bit long or too short we were sent home forthwith to have them altered to the right length.

We used to go straight to The Rise on a Monday for House-keeping lessons. You had to make your own polish by stirring something in a saucepan and then you more or less cleaned the house. We had to learn how to wash clothes and we washed and ironed all the pillow-cases. Our teacher was Miss Thomas, whom we called "Gawd Thomas" because she always said "Gawd our father" when she took Prayers. Originally we did Cookery at The Rise and then we went up to the Cookery School in the main building. I remember being in the Cookery School one day when I cracked an egg and dropped it on the floor. "Gawd Thomas" made me scoop it up and put it in the pudding.

Miss Trotter was strict but you knew exactly where you were with her. She used to come down the corridor in her gown and when you heard the rustle of her gown you jolly well sat up and paid attention. But she wouldn't do anything that was unjust. She used to come round on Friday afternoons and you'd have to line up in the form in order of merit, as she read out your name, according to the marks the mistresses had given her that week. I was usually about third and if I was lower than that I made sure I worked really hard the next week to climb back up.

If you were at school at lunchtime and you didn't play games, you had to go on a walk and you had to speak French or German.'

Patricia Kernick (1930-7). April 2009.

Above left: The Games Field.
Left: Girls of The Rise, 1937.
Above: Miss Trotter.

of the Class Rooms to train the taste and to foster an appreciation of order and beauty. In addition, by the time of Miss Trotter's departure, there was also, of course, the new large swimming pool.

Unlike both her predecessor and successor, Miss Trotter did not have to lead the school in wartime, but on the other hand she had to face the challenge of the 1932 fire – which she turned to the school's advantage through the improved facilities afterwards. By 1937, life for the boarders was infinitely more comfortable and the day girls were regarded on equal terms. Miss Trotter's hospitality was legendary and her enthusiasm for fresh air knew no bounds. One warm summer, she, Miss Bellamy and Miss Winny slept outdoors for six weeks near the Covered Way. She herself was enormously energetic, imposing seemingly impossible demands at times on both staff and girls. Highly respected, she also struck awe into the hearts of those who had done wrong but she was always prepared to give praise for effort as well as achievement. At house concerts, she sat half-way down the Hall. No-one was ever allowed to take a book, paper or music on to the stage. The girls were well

used to memory work; they all had to learn a few lines of poetry or prose each night and were tested at the end of term.

During Miss Trotter's period, a huge variety of career possibilities had opened up for educated women, and the Howell's staff, amongst the first to have gained university degrees themselves, strove above all for academic achievement for their pupils. Whereas in 1924 seventeen girls had taken the School Certificate, by 1936 this figure had risen to sixty-two, and there was a regular succession of girls to university. With features such as prefects, a house system and an emphasis on games, Howell's, like other prestigious girls' schools, was by 1937 echoing the traditions of boys' public schools. The curriculum had been expanded and the school was recognised beyond Wales for its cultural as well as academic achievements. Miss Trotter had provided infinite opportunities for participation in musical and dramatic events, for exercise, for developing a love of art and an international outlook. Howell's girls must have been as well prepared as young people anywhere else to take on the responsibilities and challenges which would be required in the impending war.

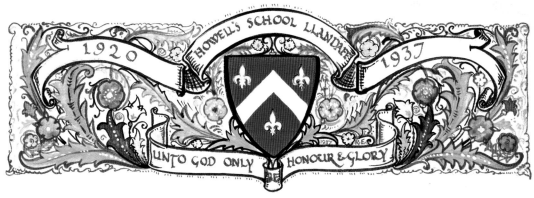

PRESENTATION TO

MISS · ELEANOR · TROTTER

ON THE OCCASION OF HER RETIREMENT.

WE, the past and present members of the Staff of Howell's School, Llandaff, ask you to accept this gift as an expression of our affection and esteem. We should like at the same time to place on record our appreciation of your friendship and generous sympathies, your ideals of conduct and education and the single-hearted devotion with which for seventeen years you have guided the destinies of the School.

12

MISS KNIGHT (1937-41) AND THE PROBLEMS OF WAR

Facing page
Miss Edith Knight, 1937-41.

Above: The Old House boarders,
Summer Term 1938

Howell's fifth Headmistress, Edith May Knight, took the helm at the age of forty-one, having been born on 3rd May 1896 at Malvern, Worcestershire. She had been educated at Worcester Secondary School for Girls and Royal Holloway College, London University, where she gained a first class BA Honours degree. She had taught at Barnsley High School and had become Headmistress of Portsmouth Southern Secondary School in 1931. With excellent academic credentials and previous experience of running a school, the Governors must have hoped that the school would be in good hands for a long time. Unfortunately, her time as Headmistress included the beginning of the Second World War and her tenure came to be the shortest in the school's history. A very different type of character from Miss Trotter, she was quiet and had a much less dominant personality. Miss Taylor referred to her "gentle and kindly rule" and appeared grateful that the pace slowed down after Miss Trotter's "whirlwind activities".

At their first meeting under Miss Knight, on 6th September 1937, the Governors decided that in future they would appoint male members of staff, including gardeners, and that no more pupils would be admitted without their consent. A fee increase was soon sanctioned by the Board of Education: for the Senior School it was to be £22 a year and for the preparatory department £25.

Initial signs of the new régime were promising, with the Governors supporting Miss Knight's plans for change. One immediate proposal was to convert a Cookery Room to a Biology Laboratory. A drinking fountain in the girls' cloakroom and repairs to the playground were sanctioned. There were improvements to the stage lighting and new electric irons in the Domestic Science kitchen. Plans were made for renovations to Hazelwood, including the installation of a telephone; electric power points and meters were fitted in the bedrooms of all resident staff; and day girls were to receive milk under the Milk Marketing Board Scheme. By the end of January 1938, repairs and renovations to the scullery, pantry and laundry had been carried out.

Miss Knight continued the cultural traditions established by Miss Trotter. Parties were taken to Stratford and to the theatre in Cardiff. Apart from the Urdd and the Current Events Club, there was a new Literary Society. In the holidays there were Geography trips to Plynlimmon and expeditions to Holland and Belgium. Basque refugee children from the Spanish Civil War were entertained in school.

Before life became greatly affected by the outbreak of the Second World War, Miss Knight made a few changes to existing practices. From her second week in the school, the prefects were asked to take turns in reading the Lesson at morning and evening Prayers. At her first prize-giving in May 1938, the orchestra played in the Stone Hall as the girls marched into the Hall and afterwards the members of the Star Gymnastics team put on a display. The house concerts became limited to performances by boarders. During the year 1938-9, instead of the traditional Open Day, three Open Evenings were held. The Armistice celebrations took the form of a service in the Hall, followed by a Peace Party in the Dining Room. At Christmas 1938, the usual Shakespeare play was replaced by John Masefield's Mystery Play, *The Coming of Christ*, which was performed very successfully, with music specially composed by the Music Master, Mr Price. Thursday afternoons were given over to Greek and ballroom dancing and to swimming in the new pool. Surprisingly, Miss Knight met opposition when she proposed a new summer uniform of cotton dresses in place of the Grecian tunic with its sides slit to the waist, revealing the matching bloomers

'I had a scholarship to Howell's School like my elder sister Irene. I remember having an exam and interview. My father had to pay fifteen shillings a term for my books. I was a day girl and I started at the same time as Miss Knight, who was very quiet. I used to cycle to school from the far side of Cowbridge Road until I had my bike stolen, and then I had to walk.

The school outfitter was Evan Roberts. My mother made a gymslip for my sister as there wasn't much spare money – there were five children – and Miss Disney said, "Couldn't your mother have bought one?" She was able to tell because one of the seams was on the diagonal. I was once told off by Miss Disney for wearing cream socks instead of white. At lunchtimes we had to play games – netball, hockey, lacrosse – and then I had to cycle home, have my lunch and then cycle back. When I got home, I used to take off my gymslip so that I wouldn't risk dropping any food on it and one day, when I got back to school, I took off my raincoat and discovered that I hadn't put my gymslip back on! Miss Disney found me and I had to cycle home again to put it on.

Once the war had started, we had to carry our gas masks to school and keep them with us.'

Beryl Lowman, née Box (1937-43). July 2009.

'We wore a vest, a liberty bodice, combinations, knicker linings, thick knickers, a square necked blouse and square-necked tunics. We each had about nine pairs of shoes for different occasions – Sunday best, shoes with a bar, hockey shoes, gym shoes and so on. Every morning before school we had to walk around the field. We played cricket near the Cathedral School grounds, where there was a green and white hut for changing. We walked up in crocodile. Once, my parents were passing in their car and they drew up and spoke to me. I was told off as we were not allowed to speak to our parents except at exeats, once every half term. On those days, my parents took me to R E Jones' restaurant in Queen Street for lunch and afternoon tea.

There was silence in the corridors. Red posture bars were given for good deportment after a term or so and once awarded it was a disgrace to lose them. At meal-times it was forbidden to ask a neighbour to pass any food – it was up to the girls to make sure that they had served others. The Art teacher inspired an interest in the subject. I also had elocution lessons and piano lessons with Mr Price. I remember being a water nymph in *The Tempest*. Every year, there was an International Day at City Hall and I represented New Zealand in the guard of honour. Most girls went to the Cathedral on Sundays but, as my father was a Baptist, I went to the Presbyterian chapel in Cathedral Road.

I was the youngest in Kendall House and so I had to go to bed earlier than the rest, at about six o'clock. The resident cook used to bring me my supper, which included some leftovers from the housemistress's meal. There was no reading after lights-out.

There was a box under each bed which contained a potty. At end of each term, we had a midnight feast. We took the potties out, put them in a cupboard and stored goodies in them. Once, there was an ant invasion and all our goodies stored in the cupboard were destroyed. We were allowed ten sweets each a week if we were good. Parcels sent from home were stored under the Hall and were opened in presence of the house prefect. Everyone in the house had to share the contents and if there was not enough to go round, the girl who received the parcel had to go without.

I was very happy at Howell's but my father was concerned for my safety once war seemed likely, so I moved to a school near my home.'

Yvonne Watkin-Rees (1936-8). Interviewed February 2008.

worn beneath. Rosemary Tunnell (née Ferrier Williams) recalled in 1996, "I don't know that we had cared for it before, but to replace it with skimpy cotton dresses . . . "

Life for the boarders continued much as before. All parcels received were opened, including birthday presents, and the contents given out in the evenings. Any food received was shared evenly between everyone in the house. Letters, written on Sundays before church or during Sunday afternoon, had to be passed to the housemistress to check that the addresses matched an approved list of correspondents. Friday evenings were spent darning and patching clothes. On Saturdays the junior boarders had their hair checked by Matron, before preparation and folk-dancing. On Saturday afternoons they might be taken for walks by staff such as Miss Disney or Miss Eyre, or do gardening with Miss Taylor. Other activities such as Dorcas work, inter-house music competitions, concerts and the Flower Show continued.

The new pool was well utilised from the start. Miss Knight introduced swimming lessons as part of the curriculum and many girls were entered for the Royal Life Saving Society's examinations. When the pool was first opened, most girls were able to swim only

Left: Boarders in Hazelwood on a Saturday afternoon in the summer of 1939.
Below left: 1st XII lacrosse team 1937-8: Valerie Whiteside, Joyce Thomas, Nancy Tucker, Margaret Tamplin, Elsa Thomas, Mary Gwynne Jones, Ray Johns (captain), Peggy Griffiths, Valerie Jones, Myra James, Dorothy Evans, Myrle Jones.
Bottom left: Cricket team 1938-9: Joyce Thomas, Mary Gwynne Jones, Bronwen Evans, Elizabeth Walsh, Betty Thomas, Anne Evans, Diana Green, Ruth Reed, Sheila Bilbrough, Marcia James, Margaret Sims.
Right: Miss Ethel Bush in 1932.
Below: Mrs Mabel Shaxby.

a little, if at all, so it was a remarkable achievement that in 1938, 138 medals were awarded, and almost one hundred in the first six months of 1939. Miss Knight also made the pool available for the use of Hywelians for three hours every Wednesday evening. Before the pupils went into the water, they were taught the strokes in the gymnasium, lying on the benches. The girls were given one and a half minutes to undress and three minutes to dress, while being questioned about life-saving. Until sweet rationing began, they were allowed to buy a halfpenny bar of Cadbury's chocolate before going to the drying yard, where they would put their red woollen swimming costumes through the big wooden rollers and then hang them on the lines.

Yvonne Watkin-Rees, a boarder in Kendall, greatly enjoyed outdoor games but was very nervous about swimming. When all the other girls had begun to swim at the deep end, Miss Disney ordered her to throw a brick into that end and then pushed her in to retrieve it. She sank to the bottom and Miss Disney had to jump in, fully clothed, to rescue her. This was not the only occasion on which Miss Disney unexpectedly found herself in the pool. Barbara Forte, née Mealing, remembered a girl very nervously obeying the command of "Jump, woman!" but grabbing Miss Disney as she did so. The two sank and then rose again together.

Barbara Forte also recalled that for gym lessons the girls wore blouses, navy blue knickers, brown lisle stockings and plimsolls. If anyone revealed any flesh between knickers and stockings Diz would bellow "Gaps, gaps"! They had to do exercises on the beam, leap the horse and try to shin up the ropes to the top rafter, always to the accompaniment of "Come on, woman!" and "You don't say you can't, you try!"

Unfortunately, the shadow of war was soon cast over the school. The Hywelian and long-serving member of staff, Miss Ethel Bush, was a committed pacifist who had constantly extolled the virtues of the League of Nations in her lessons. She had a stand in Cardiff market and took a portable pulpit into Llandaff Fields, from which she delivered impassioned speeches. Another campaigner for peace and international understanding was Mrs Mabel Shaxby (1880-1939), who had visited school and whose husband Dr John Shaxby, a scientist at University College, Cardiff, donated a prize to school in her memory in 1941.

As early as September 1938, a full year before Britain declared war on Germany, the boarders' parents were sent a letter instructing them to fetch the girls immediately if war broke out. Six months later, Miss Knight was involved in discussions with the Air Raid Precautions (ARP) Officer for Cardiff about procedures to be followed in the event of war, and an ARP sub-committee was set up in school. This met in June 1939 and made various recommendations. The whole school would be evacuated in an emergency, though resident members of the teaching staff and housemistresses could remain if they wished. Maids would be free to go home but male staff would be required to stay. The Clerk to the Governors was to arrange for all school documents to be lodged with the bank for safe keeping.

With war declared on 3rd September 1939, the beginning of the Autumn Term was postponed to 2nd October. In January 1940 the Cardiff and Glamorgan Councils decided to pay the full cost of the ARP work. There were three air raid shelters built in the school grounds: two between the Gymnasium and the Covered Way and a third between the Art Room and the stables.

When the sirens sounded, other locations also served as refuges. The youngest form went to the stationery cupboard and sat under shelves holding hundreds of books, while another gathered under shelves full of china in the pantry. Other classes crowded into the music cells under the Hall, each overflowing outside into the communal area so that it was cheek by jowl with another, the mistresses attempting in these testing circumstances to teach lessons to their particular group.

Boarders in Oaklands disturbed by night-time raids had to grab a blanket and walk down the long flights of stairs in complete darkness to the kitchen, which had a steel-girdered ceiling. The cold tiled floor, the shortage of space and the noise from the anti-aircraft guns on Western Avenue meant that sleep was almost impossible, but the rising-bell always sounded at 7am. In the summer of 1940, all the beds were taken downstairs to the two common rooms but the girls still went into the kitchen during air raids.

Above left: Hazelwood, summer 1939. Mrs Gwladys Morgan Jones, assistant housemistress, is holding the cat and is next to her sister Gwen and pupil Phyllis Evans, with Sheila Hopkins and Valerie Pearce in front.
Left: Hazelwood Seniors with Mrs Morgan Jones, summer 1939. As Miss Gwladys Williams, she taught English from 1918 to 1932.
Right: The air raid shelter between the Art Room and the stables.

'I started at Howell's on 2nd October 1939. The start was delayed because of the outbreak of war. I remember having two written exams and then an interview with Miss Knight, who wore blue-tinted glasses. I was accepted as a scholarship girl. I spent the first fortnight with the other girls putting bandages across all the windows, using horrible glue, to lessen the effects of shattering glass.

You had to have a gas mask. You weren't allowed to enter school without one and you had to carry them everywhere you went. At the sound of a siren we would have to dash, complete with gas mask, to our allotted "safe space". At first we sang "Ten Green Bottles" and the like, and no work was done, but this did not last for long, unlike the air raids. We had to take all the books we would need, together with the gas masks, and lessons would continue.'

Barbara Forte, née Mealing (1939-44). Interviewed August 2009.

Fewer documents were produced in the early years of the war than in any other period in the school's history. Because of the shortage of paper and costs of production, after the Winter Meeting of 1940-1 the Hywelian Guild suspended its business and issued only a brief newsletter. The money saved was used to buy extra War Savings Certificates. The school magazine was not produced at all between 1940 and 1942 and there was no General Knowledge competition until 1942. According to Yvonne Phillips, née Jones, a boarder in Hazelwood, the senior girls were particularly aggrieved that the disruption caused by war meant that there was no Shakespeare play, as they lost their chance to take the leading parts. They formed their own Dramatic Society and put on just one play – *Berkeley Square*.

In June 1940 work to camouflage the swimming pool was authorised and Miss Knight considered the evacuation of the entire school to Canada. In 1939, Cardiff had been declared a neutral area, considered neither so dangerous that people should be evacuated nor so safe that it should receive evacuees, but after bombing raids began, many of the city's children were sent to safer areas. She was also concerned about the risk of falling shrapnel because of the large number of skylights. However, at the end of the Summer Term, all parents were informed that the school would open as usual after the holiday. Apart from the windows with their strips of bandages, there was a supply of sandbags, which were piled up outside the windows of the small music rooms (the "cells") under the Hall, creating a dungeon-like effect. Just beyond these, a blast wall was built in the playground.

At the start of that Autumn Term, about thirty boarders did not return. Day girls were allowed to become boarders for the duration of the war if their parents wished. It was decreed that all pupils must sleep downstairs in the hostels, where more protective work was undertaken. The Hywelian Guild postponed its Winter Meeting until February 1941, to make the most of the longer hours of daylight and to enable everyone to reach home before the black-out. The event proceeded as in peacetime, Hywelian teams playing hockey and lacrosse matches against the girls. Miss Knight provided tea in spite of the rationing and the proceedings culminated in a concert in aid of the Red Cross. The Guild decided to send £3 to help a former maid, Lucy Edwards (known as "Old Lucy"), who had worked for many years under Miss Kendall and Miss Trotter. The unfortunate woman had been injured and had lost all her belongings as a result of enemy action. She died nearly two years later.

Serious danger was very close on 2nd January 1941. A Luftwaffe attack caused the death of some 160 people in the Cardiff area. Llandaff Cathedral was reduced to almost complete ruin by a land mine and Old House on the Cathedral Green was damaged. Fortunately, as this occurred during the Christmas holiday, no girls were in residence at the time and the two maids escaped

Facing page
The last pre-war Hywelian magazine.

Above: Llandaff Cathedral after the bombing, January 1941.
Left: Old House, on The Cathedral Green.

Dorothy Bowen (1941-5). Interviewed 2006.

uninjured. As the land mine fell at the bottom of the bank sloping down to the Cathedral, the blast went straight up, the bank giving considerable protection to the houses on Llandaff Green. The Governors considered the possibility of boarders transferring to schools in their home areas, but this soon proved impracticable. Parents were allowed to remove their daughters from school without financial penalty, and the decline in the number of pupils led to the Governors considering decreasing the number of teaching staff. This was in contrast to the situation one year earlier, when concerns about a possible shortage of teachers had caused them to entertain the idea of employing married teachers if necessary, going against the national practice in the inter-war period of demanding that women teachers resign their posts on marriage. By contrast, there was a shortage of maids, some having left to undertake war work in factories.

After the damage to Old House, Miss Fernie, renowned as a strict housemistress, slept in the school sanatorium and undertook fire-watching duties. The girls were re-housed in Kendall House at 128 Cardiff Road, which from that time was known as Old House and Kendall. The lease on the damaged hostel had been surrendered by April 1943 and the building was subsequently used by the military as a treatment centre for shell-shocked soldiers.

On 22nd January 1941, a full-time fire-watcher was appointed and four men on the staff became part-time fire-watchers. The resident mistresses were also asked to act as fire-watchers in school and Miss Knight herself paced the corridors. Although non-resident, Mademoiselle Rolin went into school during the holidays to assist with fire-watching and on one occasion single-handedly extinguished an incendiary bomb. To add to all the difficulties, in February damage was caused by burglars at The Rise, Hazelwood and Oaklands.

By early March, Miss Knight was so concerned for the safety of the boarders that she wanted the school to remain open to day girls only. At a Governors' sub-committee meeting, she pointed out that since the most recent bombing raid, more boarders had left the school and said that others had intimated that they would do so. She recommended that the scholarships be suspended and that the parents of boarders be asked whether they would like their daughters to travel to school daily or to leave. Eleven days later, the sub-committee was informed that the Board of Education would not permit the closing of the boarding facilities and that a number of parents had indicated that they wished their daughters to remain as boarders. Assistant mistresses and housemistresses were interviewed and were of the opinion that boarding should continue; furthermore, they thought that, given encouragement, many girls would stay. One has the distinct impression that Miss Knight's view on this matter did not coincide with that of the majority of her staff, and the stress was too much for her. The Medical Officer, Dr Parry, reported that she was not fit to carry out her duties and that she had gone home; in the doctor's opinion, she would be unlikely to recover in Llandaff under the circumstances. On 21st March, a specially convened Governors' meeting received the news that Miss Knight had tendered her resignation.

Miss Knight's term of office had been unexpectedly brief and she had been unfortunate to take over at such a difficult time. The Hywelians appreciated the warm welcome and the interest she had shown in all their business. Her disposition, however, made her unsuited to the task of running a boarding school in wartime. Away from the stresses, and living back in Malvern, Miss Knight recovered her health and in 1942 began the study of medical sciences at Aberystwyth. After undertaking a world tour, she settled down in Malvern and remained there for the rest of

Above: Mademoiselle Jeanne Rolin,
French mistress from 1913 to 1948.
Above right: The kitchen garden,
late 1930s.

her life. She maintained her links with the school and re-visited it on special occasions, notably for the Hywelian fiftieth anniversary celebrations in 1956. By the summer of 1965 she was a Governor or Manager of four schools and colleges in Worcester and Malvern. She died on 29th July 1974.

After Miss Knight's sudden departure, Miss Taylor became Acting Headmistress. The fifty or so boarders remaining were all housed in Oaklands, Kendall or Hazelwood. By the end of May 1941, the Cardiff authorities had put stores of food above the garage at Oaklands and proposed to build a cook-house as a "shadow kitchen" near the swimming pool. Miss Taylor's strength of character and courage were immediately apparent. She insisted that lessons and school life should continue with as little interruption as possible, while undertaking fire-watching duties herself at night. She was

subsequently paid a £50 gratuity for her extra responsibilities. She appointed just one new member of staff, the Scripture mistress Miss (later Deaconess) Irene Allen, to succeed Miss Bush, who retired after almost thirty-three years.

The advertisement for the new Headmistress described Howell's as "A Public Endowed School for Girls" with 450 pupils, including 120 boarders, and invited applications from candidates with high academic qualifications, the appointment "terminable by six months' notice and will be annulled by marriage". Four candidates were interviewed on 24th June, following which Margaret Llewellyn Lewis was appointed to the post, which she immediately accepted. The Luftwaffe may have proved too much for Miss Knight but nothing whatsoever appeared to intimidate Miss Lewis. She was to remain at Howell's for thirty-six years.

13

MISS LEWIS AND LIFE DURING THE SECOND WORLD WAR, 1941-45

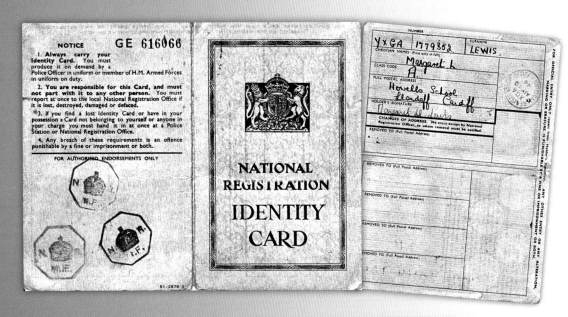

Facing page
Miss Margaret Lewis, 1941-77.

Above: Miss Lewis's identity card, 1944.

Miss Margaret Lewis was, remarkably, only thirty years old when she was offered the post of Headmistress, with the challenge of seeing it through the war years and beyond. Born on 6th July 1910, she was a native of Cardiff and therefore the first Welsh Headmistress in the school's history. Educated at Malvern Girls' School and St Hugh's College, Oxford, where she graduated in English, she subsequently taught at Alice Ottley School in Worcester, Queen Ethelburga's School in York and Pate's Grammar School in Cheltenham. Although she had not had previous experience as a Headmistress, the Governors' confidence in her at such a difficult time was amply justified. A tall and formidable woman, she gave the impression of being indestructible. Indeed, her strong constitution was to enable her to rule the school for more than thirty-six years. She made a great initial impact on the girls on account of her youth and energy, striding around school with bare legs and sandals, her hair straight and parted in the middle. Her first Head Girl, Dorette Gould, recalled that she was "enthusiastic, kindly and above all approachable".

Miss Lewis had a very different temperament from Miss Knight and her policy was not to allow the war to interrupt the girls' education, while at the same time making any adaptations necessitated by the circumstances. This attitude served to engender feelings of security. Except during air raids, the usual timetable was followed; school reports continued to be written; external examinations were taken with great success; and girls proceeded to universities, colleges or found employment. On the other hand, the paper shortage meant that there were no Christmas examinations.

Transport difficulties in 1941 and 1942, caused by air raids and petrol rationing, meant that school started at 9.30am. Day girls went home at the usual time because there was double summer time, so even in winter their journeys were undertaken in daylight. Boarders were required to assist with the cleaning chores because of the shortage of domestic staff. They continued to walk to Llandaff Cathedral every Sunday but after the bombing the Prebendal House and then the Lady Chapel were used for the services. First year boarders attended Sunday School in the village. Despite the rationing, boarders were expected to have every item in triplicate as well as a small attaché case containing a further set of underwear in case their hostel was bombed out. Long cupboards bordering the Covered Way housed a store of uniform, left by leavers and those who had outgrown clothing, and these items Miss Disney passed on coupon-free. When the Government was prepared to give extra clothing coupons to children taller than average, she measured the girls with a "generous" tape measure while they stood as straight as possible. Because of the shortage of fabrics, the navy tunic lost its pleats. Prefects' badges were unavailable but when the new stocks arrived after the war, the former prefects had the opportunity to buy them as souvenirs.

Once a week the girls practised wearing their gas masks. Whenever there was an air raid, the girls were escorted to the shelters. The boarders of Kendall House sometimes spent the night on mattresses in the kitchen if there was an alarm and were given the treat of a cup of cocoa. The girls in Oaklands continued to sleep downstairs until 1943. Day girls were told that, should the siren sound when they

'In 1941 and 1942 the sirens used to go off quite frequently and we used to stop our lessons and go to different places. Otherwise, lessons carried on as normal during the war. My mother kept chickens in our garden and if she was out when I got home from school, I had to make up a mash of potatoes and bran and feed them. My mother gave me some eggs to take to Mademoiselle Rolin's house in Pembroke Road.

I remember Miss Taylor being very kind. When I was about sixteen, my brother and I had chickenpox and I had it quite badly. Miss Taylor had a cottage in East Harptree in Somerset and during the war a teacher and his family from London were evacuated there. She let me go and stay with them while I convalesced and they looked after me for about three weeks.

When I was sixteen, I briefly left school after my exams and went to help out at Severn Road Nursery but my mother sent me back to school. But I only spent two terms in the sixth form as a new lower age was introduced in the war for admission to college, so I went to Furzedown College in Cardiff to train as a teacher. My mother wouldn't let me go away as she thought that I'd only be fed on potatoes. By the time I was nineteen and a half, in 1945, I was a trained teacher. I never regret having gone to Howell's.'

Beryl Lowman, née Box (1937-43). Interviewed July 2009.

were on their way to the buses, they were to go to the nearest hostel and shelter with the boarders there. Girls became used to taking their books to their appointed "safe places" when the sirens sounded and were quite blasé about the potential danger.

In 1942, in response to Lord Woolton's appeal for more home-produced meat, poultry was kept at school. Mr Window, the carpenter, constructed a large hen-house on the side of the tennis courts for five Rhode Island pullets and Kendall house also reared chickens. Miss Disney soon converted the pavilion into a rabbitry and the five original rabbits had become fifty-two by the summer of 1944. All the rabbits were named after characters from Shakespeare and their names were written above their cages. The boarders spent several games periods helping Miss Disney to dig the Headmistress's garden for potatoes and cabbages. Much of Llandaff Fields was given over to allotments and several games pitches formerly used by the school were converted, leaving it with just one. Miss Ruby Phillips, Mademoiselle Rolin, Miss Tickner, Miss Fowler, Miss Mary Bromley and the sixth form rented allotments and girls from Kendall worked on Miss Phillips' each week as well as growing carrots, peas, onions, shallots, radishes and lettuce on their own. In spite of all these efforts, by all accounts the quality of the school food was poor, being badly cooked and served. This was partly because day girls contributed no coupons. Boarders recalled hard prunes on Sundays, accompanied by watery custard.

Barbara Forte, née Mealing, at school from 1939 to 1944, recalled in August 2009: "*The food was diabolical. We had our allotted places in the Dining Room. In the Little Dining Room there was a French, German and Welsh table and there were house tables in the Big Dining Room. The food was served by maids at first and you always tried to get on the good side of your table's maid so that you wouldn't be served burnt rice pudding. A favourite was 'Railway', a hard sponge cut into squares with a rather watery red jam. Later there were no maids – they had gone to better paid jobs or into the Services, and then we had ready plated meals. On one occasion I just couldn't eat it and I had to sit there with it congealing in front of me. Miss Taylor (the one known as the Slug) made me carry it through the kitchens and then to Miss Lewis, who was more sympathetic. She said, 'Can you eat any more, Barbara?' 'No, Miss Lewis, honestly I can't.' 'Do you like sponge pudding? Well, go to the Board Room and I'll send some down.' The usual trick was to cough the tough and gristly meat into your handkerchief and then, when on the compulsory post-prandial walk around the school field, jettison it on the far side.*" Dorothy Bowen, who was at Howell's as a pupil from 1941 to 45, held similar views when interviewed in 2006: "*The food at school during the war was absolutely awful. I can't think how the boarders survived. Rations were very short. The housemistresses used to come and buy what we cooked in Domestic Science lessons. All our cooking was influenced by the war. There was a very big vegetable patch where the Sports Hall is now. Miss Disney ("Diz") kept rabbits in the pavilion, which supplemented the boarders' rations. Boarders had to bring their ration books and the school then took them to the appropriate grocer's, butcher's and so on.*"

Parties of senior girls spent time in the summer of 1943 at various local farms thinning beetroot and picking potatoes, beans and peas. For three weeks during the holidays in 1943 and 1944, Miss Lewis, a few staff and girls went to an agricultural camp at St. Mary's Hill near Cowbridge, to "lend a hand on the land", where they harvested corn, picked potatoes and helped at local farms. Dorothy Bowen recalled the girls' surprise at seeing Miss Lewis standing on a hay wagon wearing trousers! Some girls also took part in the harvest work scheme organised by the Glamorgan War Agricultural Committee. On at least two occasions, girls went to Ball Farm, Rumney, on day trips to pick broad beans and potatoes.

'We were allowed to go for a day to Ball Farm, Rumney, to pick broad beans. We went in full school uniform, with our light blue cotton gym tunics and blouses underneath, complete with blazers and straw hats. We were taken there on the back of lorries, sitting on school benches in two rows facing each other and holding hands behind our backs. If a lorry went over a bump, the bench would roll and you'd lose a whole line of girls! It got hot and eventually the blazers came off and we sat on them for our break. The teachers then said that we could roll up our sleeves and take off our blazers, and it didn't matter that our hats weren't on straight. We went back to school absolutely filthy. The next time we went we did potato picking and were allowed to be in mufti.

Anne Meggitt invited the captain of one of the Baltic ships and some of his crew to her home and a couple of weeks later a letter came to school addressed to her. As she was a day girl, she wouldn't normally receive a letter so the staff thought it was highly suspicious. She had to take the letter to Miss Lewis and read out the contents. It was from the captain thanking her parents for the hospitality.

Mademoiselle Rolin was one on her own. She was a dinky little woman and she wore striped flannel petticoats, which we could see because she used to lift up her skirt to polish her spectacles. She said to me one day, "Barbara, I do not like your face", so I had to sit with my back to her in class and in the Dining Room. Eventually it got beyond a joke and I went to see Miss Lewis, who was very diplomatic and said, "Mademoiselle is French, you know", as if that explained it.

Miss Lewis was absolutely fantastic, the way she held the school together during the war.'

Barbara Forte, née Mealing (1939-44). Interviewed August 2009.

Left: Miss Eileen Allen, Hywelian and Housemistress of Oaklands, in her Fire Service uniform. A popular housemistress, she organised parties and plays for the girls, made costumes and coached netball.

Facing page
Above: Lois Anthony, House Captain, shaking hands with Captain Holmquist, captain of the Danish ship, on one of his visits to school in 1943. The onlookers are the sub-prefects of St David's and St Dyfrig's houses. Back row, left to right: Pat Morris, Joan Lewis, Linda Parker. Middle: Margaret Stocks, Margaret Hunt, Rosalind Chamberlain, Barbara Pritchard. Front: Janet Foster, Lois Anthony, Enfys Jones.
Below: The presentation of the War Savings Cup by Lady Reardon Smith to Marianne Phillips, Head Girl, in 1945. In the background is Miss Elizabeth Taylor, who was in charge of the wartime savings group.

The war served to widen the pupils' international outlook. A number of foreign girls, whose families had fled from occupied Europe, joined the school and subsequently settled in Britain. These included Dorothy Oppenheimer, a Jewish girl from Vienna who came to Britain under the *Kindertransport* scheme in January 1939, Lislott Mendle, Ingeborg Furst and Helenka Toffler. Pupils made garments which were sent to Prisoner of War camps, Russia and places where troops were stationed. The school adopted two French prisoners of war. Miss Willey and Miss Lilian Tonkin took responsibility for selling foreign stamps in aid of the Red Cross. Mademoiselle Rolin stood at the Day Room door one afternoon a week with a collection box for the Free French forces. The staff must have been particularly tired during the war years as they were also involved in fire-watching duties during the night, and some also joined Civil Defence organisations. Miss Disney drove an ambulance.

Five ships – two Danish and one Estonian, Belgian, and British – were adopted by the girls under the Ship Adoption Scheme, different houses adopting different ships. Staff from some of these ships visited the school and the girls were delighted to have the chance to have a chat with dashing naval officers. Two officers from the Belgian ship brought a case full of grapefruit and oranges for the girls of Hazelwood and Buckley in 1943 – a real treat at the time. The captain of the Danish ship adopted by St Dyfrig's, Captain Holmquist, first visited for two days in 1942, and then stayed in Llandaff for a week in 1943, during which he taught navigation to Form VI Science and visited many of the girls' homes. Captain Larsen of the Danish ship adopted by Founders and Lowdon spent a few days at school in the spring of 1945, attending some lessons, and Captain Holmquist even paid a flying visit on VE Day itself.

Pupils knitted comforts for the crew such as scarves, mittens, balaclava helmets, socks and long stockings made from white oiled wool. There was regular correspondence between the girls and staff of the adopted ships as well as the master of a Greek ship.

Left: Banner on Cardiff Castle, 1945.

Facing page
Left: Forces letter sent to Miss Dorothy Harrison, 1943.
Right: Certificate for Life-saving presented instead of the Bronze Medallion in 1942.

A flourishing School War Savings Group saved £25,329 between June 1940 and May 1943. In February 1945 the school had the great honour of being presented with the Lady Reardon Smith Cup for six months, in recognition of its efforts; the girls had raised enough money for five Spitfires. The Lord Mayor, Sir William and Lady Reardon Smith and representatives of the Cardiff Local Savings Committee arrived at school for a small ceremony during which the cup was handed to the Head Girl, Marianne Phillips. Substantial sums were also sent to war charities during the war and towards the end, four hundred garments and sixty pounds of soap were sent to relieve suffering in the Allied countries.

To develop greater international awareness, speakers from overseas were invited to school. In 1944 there were visits from Dr Karel Vogel, the Czech sculptor and art critic, and from his compatriot Dr Kosta from the Czech Ministry of Education. The girls were also fascinated to hear Madame Cathala, the leader of the resistance in a French town, speaking about the French Resistance Movement. Dr Zernov, whose earlier visit had been the inspiration behind setting up a Russian Club, came to give another talk in 1945.

Although games lessons continued every lunch hour, with difficulties caused by the shortage of pitches and lack of tennis balls and lacrosse equipment. The motor mower could not be used regularly because of petrol rationing, so the field became overgrown. The shortage of equipment continued after the end of the war and when replacements finally arrived, they were of very poor quality. One sporting activity which did flourish, however, was swimming. The pool was kept filled throughout the war as it was classed as an Emergency Water Supply. In 1943 the school was proud to be awarded the Mrs Henry Cup for having the best record in Life-saving examinations in secondary schools in South Wales, and this success was repeated in 1945.

In 1942, many pre-war activities resumed, with a Speech Day, an Open Day in the autumn and a Shakespeare play (*King Lear*) and a carol concert at Christmas. The Hywelians' General Knowledge paper was reinstated and Dorcas activities continued, with the

'Once the war had started, we were all asked to write letters to European sailors who had left country and family to fight with the British, and a number of these people with their ships were based in Cardiff docks. Imagine the consternation one day when a very handsome seventeen year-old called Pierre, a Belgian, turned up at school asking for me – because my letter had been passed to him! I was sent for and introduced, but that was that – he was taken away by the staff and I never saw him again!

During the war it was also arranged for anyone who wished to go to Harvest Camp in the holidays. We slept in tents on palliasses, filled with straw. My friends and I went for two weeks and were very lucky as we were allocated a small farm where we helped a lovely old farm-hand called George to hay-make, which meant picking up the hay with a pitch-fork and throwing it on to a cart drawn by a horse. We loved it and were very lucky because lots of the other work was picking beans or pulling up potatoes, which was back-breaking.'

Sylvia Hinton, née Sharman, a boarder in Hazelwood (1937-45). September 2009.

MISS D. M. HARRISON
ARUBA
VAUGHAN AVENUE
LLANDAFF
CARDIFF
WALES

329920

Above space for Post Office use only

Read Instructions overleaf. Write the message in ink very plainly below this line.

Sender's Name and Address :
12th March 1943   Date :

T. King Davies, 27 Air School Bloemspruit, Bloemfontein S.A.

Dear Dorothy,

Very many thanks for your Airgraph which I received today, and also for your good wishes and congratulations. I expect the "news" came as a quite a surprise to you, and as a matter of fact it never even occurred to me when I left home, that I would be getting married out here. But there it is, and believe me I am very happy and consider that I am a lucky man. I hope the day is not too far distant when I shall have the pleasure of introducing her to you all and then I am sure you will agree with me that I am lucky. (By the way, I hope you dont mind my typing this letter to you - but not only is it far quicker, but I hope it is going to be easier for you to read) Many thanks indeed for your offer of a wedding present, but honestly I really dont know what to suggest, as for one thing, I am sure that most things are unobtainable over there now - and you would probably have to surrender some coupons or something any how. So if you would really care to send me a cheque(or a credit note by cable is the best method I think) it would be very welcome indeed.

The weather out here, at this time of the year is almost too perfect - you know - sunny cloudless blue skies day after day, and I cant help contrasting it with the usual March weather we used to have at home. It's a wonderful country really, but give me the Old Country every time. This place is too vast somehow - why - it takes two days to get down to the coast by train, and again, believe it or not, one can have too much sun.

I'm still doing quite a spot of flying - unofficially of course, and I only wish I could get on it permanently, but I'm afraid that's impossible. So I do the next best thing. But this flying business is certainly a thing of the future, for contrast, for instance, the two days mentioned above with three hours which is the normal time taken by air.

Well, I've rattled on long enough now I think, and in any case I'm coming to the bottom of the page. Please give my regards to Miss Walters, and anybody else I used to know, and my very best wishes to yourself. And once again, my very sincere thanks.

Yours,

Love.

Hope you received
the crystalised fruit
I sent again the other day?

This space should not be used.

THE ROYAL LIFE SAVING SOCIETY

INCORPORATED BY ROYAL CHARTER

Patron:
HIS MAJESTY THE KING.

President :
THE RT HON.
LORD DESBOROUGH, K.G., G.C.V.O., D.C.L.

THE BRONZE MEDALLION (token) CERTIFICATE
awarded to

JOAN F.M. JENKINS

Howells School

For Practical Knowledge of Rescue, Releasing oneself from
the Clutch of the Drowning and for Ability to render aid in
Resuscitating the Apparently Drowned.

S. E. Bradford.
Chairman of the Central Executive.

Date June 1943.

Alwyn E. Biscoe.
Chief Secretary.

Please refer to the back of this Certificate

IMPORTANT NOTICE.

Owing to the restriction in the use of Metal during the War, the Royal Life Saving Society is issuing this (token) Certificate instead of the Bronze Medallion to which the holder of this Certificate is entitled. If the holder will forward the Certificate after the cessation of hostilities to the Chief Secretary, it will be replaced by a Bronze Medallion suitably engraved.

NOTE: You should fill in the following details as soon as you receive this Certificate :—

Full name in Block Letters

Name of Class, Club or School
where Examination was taken

Place of Examination   Date

Name and Address to which
Medal is to be sent

The Royal Life Saving Society, 11, Thetford Road, New Malden, Surrey.

Miss D.Harrison,
Aruba,
Vaughan Avenue,
Llandaff, Glam.

Hywelian
Guild
January, 1942

Far left: First wartime school magazine, 1943.
Left: First Hywelian news sheet during the war, January 1942.
Below: Oaklands boarders, 1944.

Facing page
Boarders on the first wartime excursion, Easter 1944
1 At Llandinam. Left to right:
  Dorothea Mitchell, Joan Smith,

Daphne Moore, Audrey Peacock, Audrey Glyn Jones, Phyllis Evans, Sylvia Sharman, Catherine Shaw, Miss Mary Bromley, Miss Margaret Hawkes.
2 On the summit of Plynlimon Fawr. Left to right: Dorothea Mitchell, Sylvia Sharman, Joan Smith, Phyllis Evans, Daphne Moore, Catherine Shaw, Audrey Peacock, Dene Roberts, Linda Steer.

knitting of blanket squares and the making of baby clothes and soft toys for poor and sick children. Enthusiastic groups attended meetings of the Current News Club and Russian Society. The twent-first anniversary of the Urdd was celebrated in the Spring Term of 1943. The boarders' house concerts took place and there was an inter-house music competition. Encouraged by the house prefects, many girls participated in the games, swimming and Flower Show competitions; it was deemed important to uphold the honour of the house. By the summer of 1943, peace-time school hours had been restored and the school magazine was published for the first time since 1939. Miss Lewis was delighted to secure the appointment of Froebel-trained mistresses for both the junior forms, which she considered very important. Although school expeditions had not taken place since the war began, at Easter 1944 it was deemed safe enough for a ten-day trip to Mid-Wales, organised by the Geography department, to take place.

Numerous Hywelians undertook valuable work in many fields during the war. The newsletter of January 1941 referred to Betty Powell and Dorothy Seig at Military House, Llandaff, as well as three members of the Cardiff Air Training Corps and others working further afield. A year later, the list was longer, and included Diana Kerr, a Quartermaster in a St John's Ambulance hospital, Nan Galletly, a sister in an RAF hospital, who later served in West Africa, Leila Howell, a sister in Queen Alexandra's Nursing Reserve with the Middle East forces, and Isobel Bartlett who was in Cape Town with the Women's Auxiliary Transport Section. In 1942 three sisters were actively involved in war work: Mary David was a coder and Lisbeth a wireless telegraphist both in the WRNS, and Anne, Mary's twin, was an Assistant Section Officer in the Women's Auxiliary Air Force (WAAF). Mary was commissioned in 1944 and worked in the Cypher Office in the Cardiff Naval Base before travelling to Colombo, while Lisbeth also became a Cypher Officer and later went to Colombo with her sister. Patricia Green (later Professor Patricia Clarke FRS) was employed in the Armaments Research and Development Establishment, working on the chemistry of various explosives. She later moved to the

1

2

'We adopted Allied ships and two of them, the Danish and Belgian ships, docked in Cardiff. The Danish captain had already visited earlier but then had a heart attack and he stayed in the spare room in school for several weeks. A man staying in school! He was a splendid chap and we got to know him. Miss Drinkwater, our French mistress, brought the French mate from the Belgian ship into our sixth form lessons. He used to sit behind her and wink at us! We were engrossed in catching his eye! Sadly he later went down with his ship. Both ships gave us flags, which the school kept for many years.

I particularly enjoyed my French lessons with Miss Drinkwater and Miss Hawkes, who succeeded her. "Drinks" was superb – the best French mistress I ever met. In the Lower Sixth we didn't read the set texts. She told us who the authors were and told us to go away and read the other books they'd written, as well as other authors. It was an eye-opener. Later she went to work with the relief services which were opening up in Europe after our troops started to go up through Italy. I enjoyed the Current News Club which Miss Myfanwy Williams ran and I eventually became its secretary.

Mademoiselle Rolin was very kind. She sold chocolate icing for the Red Cross and was at the Day Room door every week with her collecting tin. She had lost her brothers in the Great War. Another one who was kind to me was Miss Williams, who taught History. When we had a terrific snowfall early in January 1945 and Cardiff was cut off from the rest of the country, she invited me to her flat in Palace Road and gave me an extra lesson for Oxford entrance. Mostly there was a huge rift between the girls and staff – they were very remote. Many had lost their men-folk in the Great War and they gave absolutely everything to us. It was a quite exceptional time.'

Dorothy Bowen (1941-45). Interviewed 2006.

Wellcome Research Laboratory at Beckenham where she undertook research on immunisation against tetanus and other pathogenic bacteria. Betty Powell and Nesta Gabe were members of Queen Alexandra's Imperial Military Nursing Service and both worked in Iraq. Betty spent time in Persia, India and Indonesia, enduring colonies of flies in the desert, staff and food shortages and nursing war casualties and troops with various fevers and dysentery.

Many Hywelians gained commissions in the forces and the magazine of January 1944 listed about sixty who were serving in the WRNS, Royal Army Medical Corps, WAAF, Auxiliary Territorial Services (ATS), the Land Army and as nurses. Gwyneth Phillips was a Seaman Torpedo Wren, undertaking electrical repairs on mine-sweepers. Noreen Blackford was at GCHQ, Bletchley Park, where her responsibilities included involvement in the plan for the Normandy invasion in 1944 and its misinformation networks. In the New Year's Honours of 1945, Annie Roper, in the Motor Transport Corps, gained the MBE award for looking after the welfare of troops since 1939 along the Kent coast, including thousands of members of the ATS and WAAF.

One Hywelian who had a lucky escape in 1942 was Nesta Morgan, who was torpedoed on her way to the colonies and spent five days in an open boat. She was mentioned in dispatches for the work she did at that difficult time. Sadly, three lost their lives. Barbara Williams and Betty Cooke died of injuries sustained in air raids and Marie Melhuish, a member of the WRNS, was killed when she stepped off the station platform at Barry during the blackout in 1943. Tragic as these deaths were, considering the total number of British people killed in the war and the number of past pupils from many boys' schools who lost their lives, the number is small.

On 6th June 1944, lessons were interrupted as the school was summoned to the Hall to hear Miss Lewis announce the D-Day landings. For the next year the progress of the Allied invasion forces was plotted with flags on a huge map in the Stone Hall. Girls went to Cardiff General Station to help see evacuees on to trains to return to their families. In September 1944 the fire-watchers were discharged and the Governors thanked all those who had been involved in voluntary duty. They asked the City Architect to arrange for the removal of the sandbags and the local authority to take down the blast walls. The old League of Nations party was replaced by a United Nations party in December, the idea originating from a request to raise money for a devastated Greek village. The girls wore national costumes or other topical fancy dress and, after processing around the Hall, they were judged by Miss Lewis. There followed tableaux representing Ancient and Modern Greece and Greek dancing before the girls split into their forms for tea, before more dancing.

It is ironic that the school remained open despite air raids, transport difficulties and other problems connected with the war, and yet an extremely heavy fall of snow forced it to close early in 1945. Relief parties of boarders were sent out to clear neighbours' paths and help to deliver bread. A shortage of coal meant that the school had to remain closed for several days, during which the boarders were occupied with a combination of lessons and dancing, while a few sixth form lessons continued at the homes of the teaching staff. That year, Howell's celebrated the academic successes of two pupils who later returned as members of staff. Dorothy Bowen gained a place at St Anne's College, Oxford, and was awarded a Glamorgan County Scholarship, a Cardiff Major Scholarship and Leaving Exhibition. Helen Richardson (later Mrs Simpkiss) won a State Scholarship to St Hugh's College, Oxford.

On VE Day, 8th May 1945, the girls were again summoned to the Hall, this time to hear Miss Lewis announce that the war in Europe was over. In the evening the boarders were allowed to wear their one non-uniform summer dress and were taken around the centre of Cardiff on the upper decks of tram cars to witness people celebrating in the streets. A few days later, a party took place in the Hall, with girls again dressed in national costumes. The end of the war in Europe was marked by a national two-day extension to half-term, with the boarders left in school hanging out flags. In the summer there was a Victory party, with pupils and staff dressed in patriotic outfits. Misses Willey and Tonkin were attired as a Back-Room Boffin and Mrs Sew-and-Sew from the *Make Do and Mend* propaganda.

Howell's had been fortunate to escape the worst horrors of war and, although there was still rationing and good quality sports equipment was lacking, it was possible to resume and develop peace-time activities. The legacy of the war was still felt, especially by those who had lost family members, but as the restrictions imposed by war and the blast walls were removed, a new era in the history of the school began. Miss Lewis had successfully united it under her leadership and had led it through difficult years – a major achievement, especially considering that she was still only thirty-five when the war ended. In Barbara Forte's words, "She was Howell's School and those of us there during her time were indeed fortunate."

The School Prayer.

O LORD our heavenly Father, who givest wisdom to all them that ask Thee, grant Thy blessing we beseech Thee, to the teachers and pupils of this school, and help us in the work Thou hast given us to do. Enable all of us to labour diligently and faithfully — not with eye-service but in singleness of heart, remembering that without Thee we can do nothing and that in Thy fear is the beginning of wisdom. Open Thou our eyes to know Thy marvellous works, to search out our own spirit and to understand the wondrous things of Thy law. Of Thy great goodness pour into our hearts the excellent gift of charity and grant that in meekness and truth and purity, we may glorify Thee the Father of Light through Jesus Christ our Lord

14

A PERIOD OF STABILITY, 1946-59

Left: Greek Dancing certificate, 1948.
Far left: Botany expedition to Peterston Bog, 1951.
Below left: Penhill Close (Kendall House).
Below right: The 1949 pageant, with Dorette and Rosalie Gould as Thomas Howell and a friend.

On 10th January 1946, the Governors heard that Howell's would continue to be recognised as one of 178 Direct Grant Schools, with appropriate modifications to come within the terms of the Butler Education Act of 1944. From this time, the Cardiff and Glamorgan Education Authorities provided 50% of the places free for girls entering at the age of eleven, instead of awarding 25% of the places as Day Scholar Scholarships to pupils from elementary schools. The two authorities each awarded an equal number of places. It was possible for aspiring Howell's pupils to enter for either the fee-payers' or the local authority examination, or both. Howell's scholarships were still awarded and the assessment for these was made for several years by Mrs Eric Evans, the wife of the Registrar of the University of Wales. There was a new scale of fees, with remission given according to parents' income. Thus Howell's continued to attract pupils of high academic calibre.

The school appears to have adapted quickly to the new peace-time conditions and opportunities, although rationing remained and the food was poor. On one memorable occasion, the cook lost her wedding ring in the suet pudding – probably made with lard – and all the girls were asked to check their portion. There was a happy ending when a pupil triumphantly exclaimed, "I've found it!" The only interruption to activities came in the severe winter of 1947, when snow and the extreme cold forced outdoor games to be abandoned and damaged the swimming pool. That year, Miss Lewis was delighted to report that every girl who hoped to gain a place at university was successful in doing so: this was a considerable achievement, especially in view of the competition for places from people coming out of the forces.

Activities and expeditions flourished in the post-war years. After school on Fridays girls spent time on hobbies and a Russian class was taken by Miss Margaret Hawkes. The Star Gymnastics class and Current News Club continued. Girls collected books to send to establish a library in a school in Nigeria and many had pen-friends in France, Belgium, Holland and the USA. Miss Fowler and Miss Tickner took a party to Holland in 1946 and the visit was reciprocated. A thriving new group was a Puppet Club, supervised by Miss Ruth Eyre and Miss Marjorie Somerscales, which by 1951 had a full-size marionette theatre. One pupil whose interest was stimulated by it was Jane Phillips, whose father, Mr Arthur Phillips, became Chairman of the Governors in 1963; she had a career as a puppeteer and created the Caricature Theatre. There was also a short-lived Guide Company, with a hut in Penhill Close. A school branch of the Barnardo's Helpers' League was formed. The new Folk Museum at St Fagans was an obvious destination for younger pupils and there were many other local expeditions. Parties also visited the International Eisteddfod. The international outlook

'No-one was permitted to be outside school unless wearing full school uniform, including hat and gloves, and coats correctly buttoned up. Any infringement of the rules would result in an Order Mark. We were required to show our clothes to our form mistress on the first day to ensure that everything was duly labelled. If you were unfortunate enough to collect two Order Marks in a week you had to go back to school on Saturday mornings at the usual time, in full uniform, to spend your time doing some unrewarding task such as tidying cupboards or helping Miss Hilda Taylor, an enthusiastic gardener, weeding or working in the potting shed.

Movement around the school had to be in silence, walking on the left of the corridors, which were often supervised by prefects. The most favoured hairstyle of the staff was the hair-scraped-back-in-a-bun or short bob. Miss Disney had a fringe and short hair and was always dressed in a tunic similar to that of the girls, worn about six inches above her knees. She wore sandals with no socks except when it snowed, when she would put on the sort of thick white socks that my father wore in the navy. She was the most forbidding of all the staff. She told us when we started that we were "less than the dust" and must always listen to our elders and betters! Diz used to stand in the Day Room directing traffic in the lunchtimes, when we all had to look at the notice board to see where we were playing games. We even played lacrosse in the snow once because the Red Indians who invented the game played in the snow! As she stood there her voice would come booming out with the same sentence every day: "Nobody but a FOOL stands in the doorway!"

There were very few visual aids, apart from the huge maps with large areas of land coloured pink for the British Empire. The Art Room was the only room that displayed pupils' work. We answered the register every morning – boarders first – by saying "Adsum". School meals were particularly dreaded. Everything on the plate had to be eaten as this was still the time of food rationing. We soon learnt to bring paper bags into the Dining Room and secretly sweep the horrors from our plates into them when the teacher was not looking. The Big Dining Room (BDR) housed the day girls and the Little Dining Room (LDR) was for the boarders. We marched into the Dining Rooms to music played by one of the pupils and sat at tables where mistresses presided. Miss Lewis was a very remote figure until we reached the sixth form. She swept around the school wearing her university gown and seemed very austere.'

Joyce Shields, née Bingham (1947-54). Written July 2009.

encouraged by Miss Trotter and perpetuated during the war was furthered by numerous excursions abroad: in 1951-2 alone, groups went to France, Germany, Switzerland, Italy and Denmark.

In the summer of 1947 the decision was reached to sell the boarding-house at 128 Cardiff Road and to purchase Penhill Close for the members of Kendall House. An attractive building, with a strong William Morris influence, it also boasted large gardens. The Hywelians seized the opportunity to buy a piece of land behind the houses in Llandaff Place, between the Penhill Close garden and the school's hockey field, as extra ground for the school. The Governors also bought an overgrown paddock next to Penhill

Close, where performances of an outdoor pageant depicting the school's origins and history, written by Miss Lewis, took place in July 1949. The new Trotter Field, as it became known, could not be used immediately as there were unexpired leases and the land contained a kitchen garden and fruit trees. Equipped with new lacrosse goalposts, it came into use in the autumn of 1950. The following summer a large-scale fair completed the Trotter Memorial Fund and provided a new Blüthner grand piano, with a substantial contribution from the Hywelian Guild. In 1953 the Guild donated five new teak garden seats and some flowering shrubs to commemorate Queen Elizabeth II's coronation.

Left: The older staff at Miss Myfanwy Williams' leaving party, 1951. Left to right: Miss Phillips (English), Miss Findlay (Secretary), Miss Thomas (Violin and Piano), Miss Disney (Physical Education), Miss Scott (Housemistress), Miss Fowler (Geography), Miss Lewis (Headmistress), Miss Tickner (Classics), Miss M Williams (History), Miss Somerscales (Art), Miss H Taylor (Second Mistress), Miss Walters (Welsh and Geography), Miss Cole (Music), Miss Bromley (English), Miss Harrison (Biology).
Second left: Prefects with Miss Myfanwy Williams, 1951.
Third left: Sunday afternoon in Oaklands, Summer Term 1949.
Bottom left: Upper IIIW, 1949-50.
Below: Lower VI Science, 1952-3.
Left to right, Back row: Thelma Dutton, Rosemary Archer, Gaye Otte, Pat Jones, Sara Plummer, Norah Hollyman. Front: Anne Phillips, Pat Hampson, Elunis Gibbs, Ruth Barraclough, Anne Williams.

The post-war years saw some notable departures and arrivals. The Cambridge Science graduates Miss Tonkin and Miss Willey retired in 1946. Ill-health forced the retirement of the carpenter Mr Window, who had done so much for the school after the fire and during the war. After thirty-five years at Howell's, Mademoiselle Rolin retired to her French homeland in 1948. In 1951 Miss Myfanwy Williams, the History mistress, left after more than thirty years. Miss Tonkin's place was taken by Miss Dilys Morgan who, after her marriage during the Christmas holiday of 1948, became known to generations of schoolgirls as Mrs Lloyd. She was one of the first married women on the staff. A former pupil, Hermione Ponting, joined the administrative staff in September 1948 and soon became Domestic Bursar. She took over the school's accounts on the retirement of Mr Pritchard, the Clerk since 1922. Miss Jean McCann was appointed in 1951 to teach History and stayed nearly twenty-four years. Two significant changes took place on the Governing Body. In recognition of the contribution of the Hywelians to the school, the Guild was invited to nominate one of its members to serve on the Board. Mrs Dorothy Wickett (née Clarke) duly took office on 31st October 1949. Alderman Mrs Rose

Davies was elected Chairman on 27th March 1950, two months before the death of Dr William Saunders, who had held that office since 1925.

Some new awards, still presented in 2010, were donated in the post-war years. On their retirement, Misses Willey and Tonkin gave £108 for a Science Leaving Prize. The parents of Jane Coffin, who tragically died in a horse-riding accident in April 1950, donated a cup to be given annually to the girl who had made the best use of her talents in Art. An early recipient was Hilary Jones, who later returned to teach the subject at Howell's for twenty-four years. The Andrews Cup for sport was donated by a family whose daughters had been at school. In 1952, Dr Parry celebrated twenty-five years as the school's doctor by giving annual prizes to boarders who had produced the most original work in their spare time.

After the new Burnham Scale was introduced in 1945, prices and teachers' salaries rose, and essential school repairs and improvements were needed. In June 1951 the Ministry of Education approved an increase in tuition fees to £40 a year and a 1d rise in the dinner fee to 9d a day. A further increase of 30 shillings a year was sanctioned for all Direct Grant Schools in 1955 to cover the cost of the first stage of the transition towards equal pay for women teachers, which was completed in six years. Women may have gained the vote partly in recognition of their efforts in the First World War, but it was not until after the Second that they started to receive salaries equal to their male counterparts.

Miss Lewis did not want to make great changes in the years after the war. She stated in her Speech Day report in July 1951, "Major operations on a corporate body are comparable to those on a human body – only justified by dire necessity." However, she acknowledged that "We must move with the times; we must keep trying to get better or we shall rapidly get worse." After the upheavals necessitated by wartime, a stable routine was probably welcome. Even the practice of the 1920s, whereby at the beginning of each term the girls were summoned to pay their fees to the Clerk of the Governors, persisted, but by then there were two aspidistra pots on the table, one for cash and one for cheques.

However, in March 1950 the Governors accepted Miss Lewis's radical proposal to close the Junior School in order to free up two form rooms for senior girls. This appeared the only solution to the problem of accommodating all the girls who needed to be admitted

'There was no central heating or other form of heating in the bedrooms unless it was frosty and then we had a small paraffin heater. We would warm up pyjamas over it until the steam was rising and go to bed wearing vests, bed-socks and dressing gowns, and double our blankets in an attempt to keep warm. Occasionally the water or drainpipes would freeze and then we would have to wash in school.

We entered school by the door on the left of the building, which led into the boarders' cloakroom. We changed into indoor shoes before going for breakfast in BDR. We ate porridge, something cooked (sausages on Sundays), and bread and butter. If it was your birthday, you were allowed golden syrup on your porridge. At break in the winter the boarders had tomato soup in mugs served in BDR but the day girls had milk. Lessons finished at 4.15 when there was a further hour of games for the boarders (we played at lunchtimes as well) – no wonder we were fit! It was possible, if you were not too keen on games, to get out of this by joining a school society such as Urdd or choir. In the dark evenings other activities were organised such as Scottish dancing in the gym or an educational film in the Hall. At about 5.30 we had high tea in BDR. Following this, boarders' Prayers took place in the Hall and then we returned to our houses. On Friday evenings shoe cleaning was compulsory in the cloakroom, and this was checked before we could return to Hazelwood.

In the house, for supper we were provided with bread and margarine or dripping and hot milk and we could have a supply of non-perishable food from home, which was kept in named pigeon-holes. We could also order a weekly supply of fresh fruit. We had to go to bed at 8pm with lights out at 9pm.

In the summer the boarders wore red and white gingham dresses on Saturdays. On Sundays we wore bright yellow dresses with brown lisle stockings. We hated this as when we were walking in a crocodile to Llandaff Cathedral, passers-by would call us "the daffodils". No ball games were allowed on Sunday, only reading, writing letters or attending to our pressed flower collections.'

Pat Parry, née Lennox (1953-60) – a boarder in Hazelwood from 1953 to 1958. Written 2001.

The blazing wreck of the plane which crashed in Pontcanna Fields.

TWO Vampire jet planes from the R.A.F. Station at Merrifield, near Ilminster, Somerset, collided at a height of 29,000 feet over Cardiff to-day.

One crashed on the roof of a house adjoining the Llandaff Hotel, Llandaff-place; the other fell in Pontcanna Fields.

Both pilots baled out—one with only minor bruises, parachuted on to Cardiff Airport; the other was picked up in a rubber dinghy in the sea near Newport by a Swedish vessel and taken to Barry.

A Llandaff North woman, Mrs. Georgina Evans, working in the house next to Howells School, was trapped in the wreckage and brought out dead.

The plane that crashed at Llandaff wrecked a house adjoining the Llandaff Hotel, after narrowly missing Howell's School for Girls.

Above and left: Report of the plane crash near the school in the South Wales Echo, 14th July 1952.
Below: Boarders from The Rise with Miss Reed in Oaklands garden, 1953.
Bottom: Bryntaf, 1956.

under the Direct Grant regulations, which stated that "those most suitable for a grammar school education" should be able to enter. The preparatory department was consequently phased out and from September 1952 the youngest pupils admitted were eleven years old. Howell's was to remain a school providing secondary education only until a Junior School was re-established in 1984. The Governors also agreed that from 1952 a maximum of two boarders who lived outside Wales could be accepted, as long as preference was given to good Welsh applicants. Another change of a quite different nature during these years was that the School Certificate and Higher School Certificate public examinations ended in 1951 and were replaced by Ordinary and Advanced Level.

There was a certain amount of unexpected excitement for the pupils in the summer of 1952. A small fire in the Science block led to the rafters smouldering and the fire brigade being summoned. More dramatically, on 14th July two RAF Vampire jet planes collided at 29,000 feet over Llandaff at 1.15pm. One fell on Llandaff Fields and the other crashed into a block of flats adjoining the Llandaff Hotel (now Churchill's), killing one person and narrowly missing the school and grounds. Some pupils saw the plane flying low and thought the school was going to be hit. After the crash they immediately went to the scene with fire extinguishers.

Two new boarding houses were purchased in the 1950s. The lease on The Rise was surrendered after thirty-five years as in 1953 a house directly opposite the school, next door to Oaklands, was put up for sale, and the Governors quickly bought it for sixth form boarders. This was Bryntaf (originally spelt Bryntaff), at 67 Cardiff Road, which was owned by Bernard Morgan, a second cousin of Miss Lewis, and his wife Mary, née Walker, a Hywelian. Bernard Morgan was the eldest grandson of the draper David Morgan of The Hayes, who had lived in Bryntaf from 1893 to 1919 and been a school Governor from 1898 to 1915. Most of the furniture for Bryntaf was transferred from The Rise and the move was made in great haste, just four days before the new term began. The girls in Bryntaf retained membership of their former houses for games and other activities.

Early in 1956 the school agreed to buy the house between school and Hazelwood, Cumberland Lodge, complete with tennis court. A former childhood home of the author Roald Dahl and his half-sister Ellen, who had been a pupil at Howell's between 1911 and 1917, it was named *Taylor House* in honour of Miss Hilda Taylor, the Senior Mistress, who had retired at the end of the summer term in 1955 after thirty-one years, twenty-two of them as Second Mistress. Nicknamed "The Bug", as opposed to her namesake, the Biology mistress known as "The Slug", Miss Taylor donated £150 for furniture for the house, and she subsequently maintained a correspondence with the housemistress and girls of Cumberland Lodge. The re-decorating costs were met from the Thomas Howell Fund, which fortunately had just received a boost of about £3,000

each year. The earlier Schemes had stated that the income of the Foundation, beyond a fixed amount to be retained for the purposes of the school, should be paid to the Glamorgan County Council. The Governors had appealed successfully in 1954 to the Council to surrender its share of the Fund.

Meanwhile, in January 1954, plans had first been discussed to build a new dining and kitchen block. A Ministry of Education inspection of the school in 1953, on the whole very favourable, drew attention to the inadequate catering accommodation as well as lack of sufficient room for Science. At that time Physics was taught in a small laboratory at the top of the back stairs. Previously the subject had been studied only for one year by the sixth form scientists, but by the 1950s universities and medical schools preferred it, with

'I started at Howell's in September 1954. I was lucky enough to be one of the girls who received a scholarship from Cardiff each year. Proud I might have been: I was following a family tradition as my mother and her two sisters and my older sister Elizabeth had all attended Howell's before me. Elizabeth was still there, in the Lower Vth as I started, but shortly before term started I discovered that my mother was returning too, as a Geography teacher, and I wasn't sure that I liked that idea.

I also disliked the uniform. We weren't very fashion-conscious in those days (rationing had only recently come to an end) but the idea of having to kneel on the gym floor on the first day of term so that those tunics could be demonstrated to be the right length (four inches above the knee for winter tunics, three inches for summer ones – no-one ever said it was logical!) was not funny – certainly not with the terrifying Miss Disney doing the measuring. Mind you, there was little incentive to want the tunics shorter when they were accompanied with those delightful khaki stockings (we used to call them bullet-proof) and a most enormous pair of navy blue knickers. As this uniform dated from the early 1920s, it was no wonder that it caused mirth among my contemporaries at other schools.

And the rules . . . well, there seemed to be a rule for everything, and woe betide you if you broke them. Some were sensible, but others seemed less logical: we could understand a no jewellery rule, but why were we not allowed to wear watches until we had been at school for several years? For some reason, we were not allowed to play tennis until we had had our fourteenth birthday. We had to tie our hair back 'if it touches your collar' – but it had to be plaited or tied centrally at the back of your head. And as for boys: they were certainly not allowed over the threshold of school and they were not to be spoken to in the street either. Some rules became so ingrained that it was years after leaving that I managed to break out of their straitjacket: even after a 'gap' year before going to University I could not be persuaded to talk or walk two abreast in a corridor. Unhelpfully, not all these rules were written down. One day, I was told that Miss Lewis wanted to see me. I was terrified: we found her very rigid, distant and stern. I had to stand in the corridor which you hoped never to have to enter and wait to be invited to go in to her office. I was told that I had been observed in the street, wearing my school hat 'like a pimple on the back of a marrow'. My prudent mother had allowed for a bit of expansion and my hat kept slipping over my eyes.'

Sue Rayner, née Davies (1954-61) – daughter of Madeline Davies, née White, Geography mistress 1954-68. Written January 2010.

Above left: The First XI hockey team, 1946-7. The team consisted of Dorothy Rees, Barbara Rees, Denise Richards (captain), Sheila Llewellyn, Jean Howell, Barbara Knight, Margaret Griffiths, Christine Hughes, Nancy Davies (vice-captain), Frances Hayward, Margaret Stewart.
Left: Cricket team, 1953.
Back row, left to right: *Camilla Smith, Rosemary Smith, Gillian Keggin, Wendy Davies, Gaye Otte.* Middle: *Margaret Hutton, Mary Gatehouse.* Front: *Elunis Gibbs, Kathleen Young, Eleanor Rogers, Margaret Turner.*

Above: Lacrosse team, 1956. Back row, left to right: *Elspeth Taylor, Yvonne Phillips, Mary Gatehouse, Judith Beynon, Susan Horrocks, Sally Thomas.* Front: *Susan Leggett, Susan Groocock, Natalie Davies, Pauline Cottam, Diana Lloyd Edwards, Frances Outhwaite.*

Biology and Chemistry, to the traditional combination of Botany, Zoology and Chemistry. Following the inspection, in 1955 a larger laboratory was created for Physics by combining the nearby room known as The Ship and Miss Disney's adjacent former bedroom. This redoubtable lady had retired in December 1954 to her primitive holiday home, a loft above a boathouse at Burnham Overy Staithe in Norfolk. She spent most of the rest of her life sailing, swimming, catching flat fish with her feet and acting as a voluntary warden. A remarkable tribute had been paid to her in the 1953 inspection report: "The complete selflessness of the teacher, who devotes all days and evenings to the preparation of pitches, courts etc., is praiseworthy… It is unlikely that any further appointment would ever give to the task the energy, vitality and industry that has been given during the past twenty years."

The enlarged Physics Laboratory was intended only as a temporary solution. The plan was to create new laboratories in what would be the former Dining Room and kitchen area. In 1955 the plans were approved but unfortunately the credit squeeze meant that the bank was unable to lend the school the necessary money. However,

a timely appeal to the Industrial Fund for the Advancement of Scientific Education in Schools resulted in a grant of £8,300 towards the cost of building the laboratories and £1,000 towards equipment in 1957. The aims behind such grants were to reinforce success in Science teaching and to produce more scientists, and as at that time only twelve girls' schools had been given money from the Fund, this was a great triumph. The plan to build a new dining and kitchen block was shelved on grounds of cost.

The two new laboratories, one for Physics and the other for Chemistry, were built in the far corner of the vegetable gardens and were in use by the end of 1958. They were formally opened on 2nd December 1958 by Sir Graham Savage, the Chief Assessor to the Industrial Fund, who was the guest speaker at Speech Day. It was the middle school girls who had their lessons in the new laboratories and the new facilities enabled Physics lessons to begin a year earlier. The sudden death on 6th December of Alderman Mrs Rose Davies, the Chairman of the Governors (and also the first female Chairman of Glamorgan County Council) led to the decision to name the laboratories after her. Her successor was Mr W E Wright.

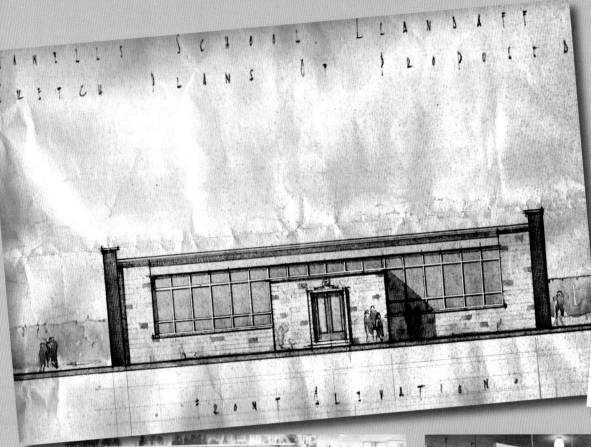

Left: Sketch plan of new Chemistry and Physics Laboratories, October 1957.
Below left: The new Science Laboratories, built in 1958.
Below: Speech Day invitation, December 1958.
Below right: The new Physics Laboratory, 1959.
Bottom left: The new Chemistry Laboratory, 1959.
Bottom right: The Preparation Room for the new Laboratories, 1959.

HOWELL'S SCHOOL, LLANDAFF

SPEECH DAY

SIR GRAHAM SAVAGE, C.B.
Chief Assessor to the Industrial Fund for the
Advancement of Scientific Education in Schools
(formerly Senior Chief Inspector, Ministry of Education
and Education Officer, L.C.C.)

will present the prizes.

THURSDAY, 4TH DECEMBER, 1958

AT 2.45 P.M.   PLEASE BRING THIS CARD.

The Staff, July 1956. Back row, left to right: *Mrs Hoffman (Housemistress), Miss Cole (Music), Miss Cossentine (Elocution), Miss Davies (Drama), Miss Findlay (Secretary), Miss McCann (History), Miss Walters (Welsh).* Fourth row: *Deaconess Allen (Scripture), Mrs Hamilton (French), Mrs Hughes (Mathematics), Mrs Mudd (Housemistress), Miss Constantine (Sports), Miss Vaughan (Piano), Mrs Lloyd (Mathematics).* Third row: *Mrs Thomas (Mathematics), Miss Lamont (Art), Miss Ewart Thomas (French), unknown, unknown, Mrs Davies (Geography), Miss Ponting (Bursar), Miss Llewellyn (Mathematics), Miss McMahon (French and German).* Second row: *Miss Eyre (Art), Matron, Miss Reed (Domestic Science), Miss Scott-Ormsby (Sports), Miss Millar (History), Miss Richards (Housemistress), Miss Jenkins (Chemistry), Miss Thomas (Violin), Mrs Evans (Physics).* Front row: *Miss Phillips (English), Miss Holland (Housekeeper), Miss Harrison (Biology), Miss Lewis (Headmistress), Miss Fowler (Geography), Miss Tickner (Classics), Miss E Taylor (Biology).*

Hywelian Guild Committee, July 1956. Back row, left to right: *Mrs Dixon, Miss Jean Houston, Miss Dorothy Sedgwick, Mrs Agnes Challenor.* Third row: *Mrs Caryll, Mrs Llewellyn, Mrs Baragwanath, Miss Joan Bowles, Miss Gwen Frewer, Mrs James Davies.* Second row: *Miss Bettie Evans, Miss Jessie Davies, Mrs Alice James, Miss Jill Birch, Mrs Mason, Mrs H Thomas, Miss Dorothy Harrison.* Front: *Miss Kathleen Campbell, Mrs Catherine Powell, Miss Hilda Taylor, Miss Lewis, Miss Knight, Mrs R Lewis, Miss Frances Stopher.*

Right: Hywelian Dramatic Society production, 1948.

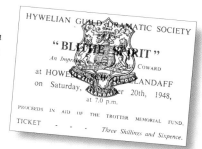

In 1954, the Hywelian Madeline Davies, née White, who had two sisters and two daughters at school, was appointed to teach Geography, and she also served as Vice-President of the Hywelian Guild from 1954 to 1957. In 1959 two more former pupils joined the staff. Joan Smith became the school's first Factor, to be in charge of all matters relating to the maintenance of the grounds and buildings, and Dorothy Bowen joined the History department.

The Hywelian Guild, having resumed its activities back in 1944, thrived in the 1950s. It created a permanent Special Fund for the school's benefit in 1951 and donated a film projector in 1952. In the same year, the London branch celebrated its twenty-fifth anniversary with a dinner, and its secretary became a member of the Guild committee. At the beginning of the decade, this was the only branch still in existence but by the end of 1956 there were groups in Brecon, Bridgend, Swansea, Bristol, the Midlands and Cornwall as well as one in Vancouver. In 1956 the Guild celebrated its fiftieth anniversary with a Jubilee Dinner and other events, including a Conversazione, attended by thirty members of staff and 151 Hywelians, which involved a variety of events in the suitably decorated Hall: a comical Ladies' Choir conducted by Miss Lewis, a Fashion Parade and a buffet supper. The Dramatic Society re-started in 1948 but sadly came to an end in 1959,

reflecting an era in which more Hywelians developed their careers and lives away from Cardiff.

The provisions for the Guild's Winny Memorial Scholarship were changed in 1953. Initially the sum of £35 had been granted annually to the same girl for three years but it was decided to make the award effectively a prize and give it to a different girl each year. At Speech Days during the late 1950s some new prizes were awarded. One, the May Chick prize, donated in memory of a Hywelian by her husband Edgar Bliault "for outstanding knowledge of anything a really good housewife should know", developed into a number of annual awards through the generosity of Mr Bliault, who left money in his own will for the endowment of more May Chick prizes.

Howell's appeared to be in a very healthy state by the time it celebrated its one hundredth birthday. The sixth form had increased to over a hundred girls, resulting in the conversion of the former resident maids' quarters on the second floor of the north wing, overlooking the tennis courts, to an Upper VI Study and a Lower VI Arts Study. The school had grown to a three form entry; academic standards were high, with the majority of pupils staying on after taking Ordinary Level examinations; and there was a splendid new science block, reflecting the increasing significance of science subjects in the school's curriculum.

1

5

2

6

3

7

8

4

***The school on the eve of the
Centenary***

1 *New Lower VI Arts Study with
   Upper VI Study beyond, 1959
   (on the second floor).*
2 *The Botany Laboratory, 1959.*
3 *The Stone Hall, 1959.*
4 *The Art Room, 1959.*

5 *The Zoology Laboratory, 1959.*
6 *The ward on the first floor of
   the Sanatorium (School House),
   1959.*
7 *The Entrance Hall, 1959.*
8 *New tennis gear, 1959.*

Activities in the 1950s
Facing page
Top: *You Never Can Tell, 1953.*
Bottom: *Joint Summer Fair with
the Cathedral School to raise
money for the new organ stop,
1954.*

Top: *Visit to Versailles, April 1954.*
Above: *Staff v. Prefects rounders
match, July 1955.*

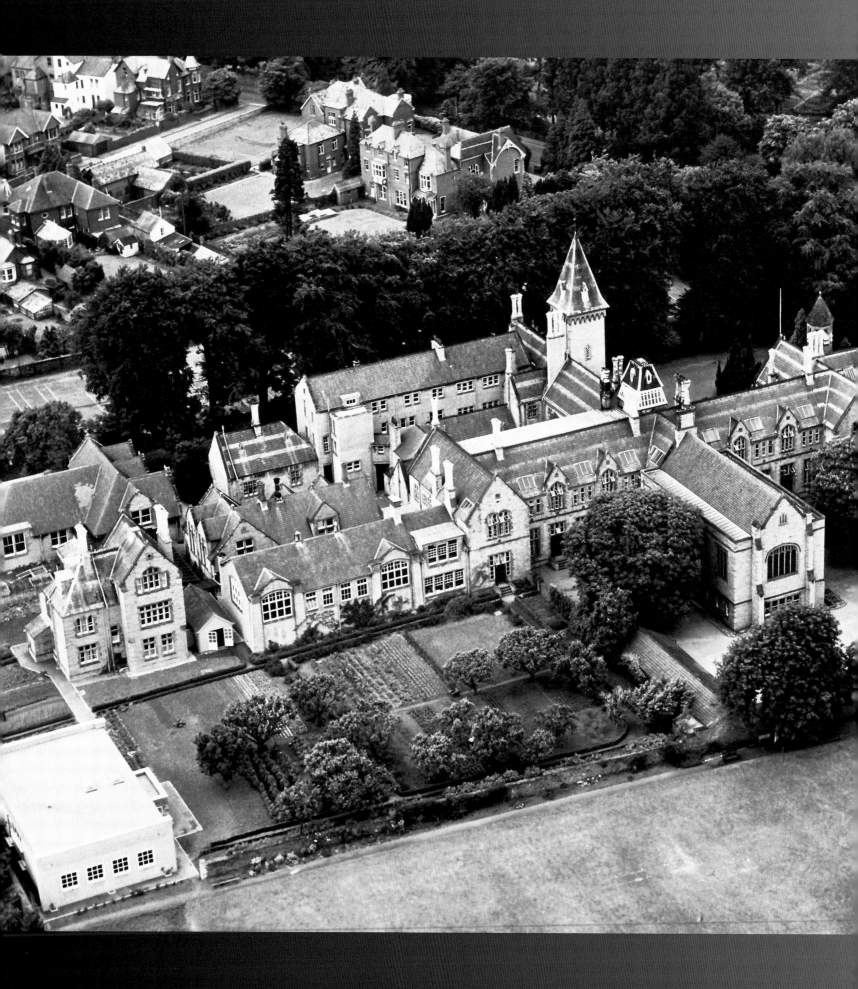

15

FROM THE CENTENARY TO THE GPDST, 1960-77

The Centenary in 1960 was marked by a series of celebrations. The major event, masterminded by Joan Smith, the Factor, was a grand garden party attended by 1,530 people on Saturday 16th July, which was selected as Centenary Day. There was also a massive exhibition indoors, to which the whole school contributed. The two formal occasions were the prize-giving, at which the Guest of Honour was Sir David Eccles, Minister of Education, and a Thanksgiving Service in Llandaff Cathedral. A building fund for a new larger Hall was launched with a gift of a thousand guineas from the Drapers' Company. The school play chosen that year was Dekker's *Shoemaker's Holiday*, with its theme about London apprentices. The exact anniversary of the opening of the school, 1st August, fell during the summer holiday, but Miss Lewis and about a dozen girls toured the original buildings and had a picnic. The Hywelians celebrated the Centenary with their own evensong in the Cathedral and a soirée, at which the main entertainment was *Thomas Howell's Dream*, a dramatisation of the history of the dowry and fortunes of the years 1860-1960. For this occasion, four old girls arrived in a horse-drawn carriage, dressed in 1860s costume.

Miss Lewis, Miss Harrison, the Head Girl (Janice Couzens) and four Hywelians also represented the school at a service in the Cathedral, attended by the Queen and the Duke of Edinburgh, to celebrate the completion of the restoration after the bombing of 1941. Since December 1957, most of the Cathedral had been back in use and the boarders had sat in the nave rather than in their traditional place in the south aisle.

An anonymous Hywelian of Miss Kendall's day donated money to purchase a statue to fit in the vacant niche over the main entrance door. Frank Roper, a local sculptor and father of a pupil, was chosen to make a bronze sculpture of St Mary of Bethlehem, patron saint of the Drapers' Company.

Top: Centenary Speech Day, February 1960.
Left: Part of the Centenary display.
Above centre left: Group of Lower Sixth in Paris, April 1960.
Left to right: *Christina Merchant, Miss Ewart Thomas, Janice Couzens, Jennifer or Judith Hill (identical twins), Susan Davies, Miss Leonard.*

Above centre right: *The Thanksgiving Service in Llandaff Cathedral with the Queen and Duke of Edinburgh.*
Above left: *The bronze statue designed by Frank Roper for the niche above the main entrance. St Mary of Bethlehem, the patron saint of the Drapers' Company, is depicted wearing a triple crown and sheltering three orphans in her skirts.*
Above right: *Easing the sculpture into position, 1961.*

HOWELL'S SCHOOL
Llandaff

CENTENARY
MAGAZINE
December 1960

Above: Centenary Year School
Magazine.
Left: Centenary Thanksgiving
Service in Llandaff Cathedral.
Below far left: Centenary
medallion, designed by Miss Eyre,
with which each girl was presented
on Centenary Day.
Below left: Centenary Thanksgiving
Service Invitation.

1860 - 1960
HOWELL'S SCHOOL, LLANDAFF

CENTENARY YEAR
Service of Thanksgiving
in LLANDAFF CATHEDRAL
on WEDNESDAY, 20th JULY, 1960 at 3.0 p.m.

(Visitors are asked to be in their seats by 2.50 p.m. at the latest)

*Please bring this ticket with you and enter the Cathedral
by the Lady Chapel Door*

HOWELL'S SCHOOL, LLANDAFF
1860-1960

Other gifts included a large television set from the independent company TWW and a new pale blue lining for the swimming pool from the Hywelians, bringing to an end the scraping of knees and feet on the previous rough surface. A new hard court surface was laid on the Cardiff Road end of the old hayfield, with an entrance to the front drive, and the school gateway was widened. At the end of the year, it was decided to approach the Ministry of Education about formally abandoning the name *Howell's Glamorgan County School*, which was still used in official correspondence, as this misleadingly suggested a Local Authority school. The formal application was made in March 1961 and the letter of approval finally received that December.

Apart from specific events, the Centenary year was marked by an announcement of a change in the indoor uniform, the first of note since the early1920s. The navy gymslip, white blouse and red girdle were replaced by a red and white striped blouse, a pleated grey terylene skirt and pinafore top (the "bib") and a grey cardigan. Unlike the old tunic, which had to be four inches above the knee when the girls were kneeling, the new skirt had to cover the knees; Miss Lewis introduced it by declaring, "Queen Victoria had no legs, and Howell's School shall have no knees!" For the first time there was a summer games tunic with a soft pleated skirt and a plunging neckline; apart from this, the girls continued to wear the old uniform for games. For travelling and attendance at the Cathedral on Sundays in winter, the boarders dressed in brown tweed suits, yellow blouses and brown shoes. In the summer they wore yellow dresses.

A new outdoor uniform followed in 1969, with a belt-less raincoat in slate blue and a pill-box hat. The next year the old scarlet scarf was replaced by a smaller one and in 1971 a new games uniform consisting of a white shirt and maroon short skirt, V-necked jersey and socks was introduced. For the first time, sixth formers had their own uniform of a pink blouse and grey skirt, and Senior Choir members wore a long scarlet skirt and white blouse for public performances. To create more hanging and storage space in the cloakrooms, in 1972 each girl was allotted a wire hanging cupboard, which also had two boot racks, instead of just one peg.

Far left: The new uniform, 1960.
Left: The termly boarders' new Sunday suits of brown tweed and a yellow blouse.
Below: Girls in outdoor uniform walking near the main entrance doorway, 17th November 1964.
Bottom left: Termly boarders entering Llandaff Cathedral wearing their new Sunday summer yellow dresses and hats with a brown band, 1960.
Bottom right: Prefects wearing the 1970s sixth form uniform, 12th July 1973.

'There was a long list of "dos" and "don'ts" concerning our appearance and deportment. Hair had to be kept clear of the eyebrows; if it touched the collar it must be tied back with a plain black ribbon, not more than one inch wide; pony-tails were not allowed; and bunches were denounced as making girls look like "Mr Rochester's first wife". Hair dyes were banned and a girl whose locks changed colour overnight had to wear her school hat indoors until the offending tint had disappeared. The hat, of course, had to be worn straight on top of the head at all times. Sixth formers were allowed to have French pleats, but wore the same uniform as the Upper Third, summer and winter. Our grey pinafore dresses had to be two inches below the knee – and this was rigorously enforced by regular checks even when miniskirts became fashionable. The nearest we got to the mini was the navy games tunic – five inches above the knee – which lost something of its style when teamed with hockey boots. There were navy blue regulation knickers, and stockings were 60 denier and in a shade only sold by Evan Roberts.'

Ruth Campbell, née Sully (1963-70). Written October 2009.

The 1960s saw no big building developments. The Sanatorium moved temporarily to a new home on the top floor of Hazelwood before relocating in 1967 to the first floor of the north wing of the main building, which had previously housed the Craft Rooms. The old Sanatorium building was renamed School House and initially accommodated some boarders before being adapted for use as classrooms. The plan to build a new Hall was reluctantly abandoned as the cost was prohibitive, although for several years the idea of building a gallery above the existing Hall was pursued. The Day Room was used as an overflow Dining Room, and the former Servants' Hall on the first floor, which had been used as a Dining Room (the food being sent up by a dumb waiter from the kitchens below), became a form room and was renamed Upper Hall. The old vegetable garden was grassed over in 1964 and became known as The Green. In 1967 the Governors approved plans to refurbish the Zoology Laboratory to cater for the new Nuffield type of experimental and practical work and the next year new large black and white tiles were laid in the Stone Hall. The kitchens were also modernised and re-equipped and the shrubbery removed from the side drive. The proceeds of two years' summer fairs enabled new stage curtains, electrical equipment for stage lighting and a new library carpet to be purchased.

In the early 1970s, the old coal store near the housekeeper's quarters was converted for use by the cleaning staff and an old air raid shelter off the Covered Way took on a new function as a stationery repository. There was one major building project this decade, which provided two new Physics Laboratories, an Optics Room, storage space and preparation rooms. These were opened in November 1974 by the Hywelian Jean McFarlane, England's first Professor of Nursing. The former "new laboratories", opened in 1958, were then both given over to Chemistry, and the former

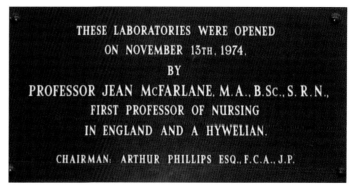

THESE LABORATORIES WERE OPENED
ON NOVEMBER 13TH, 1974,
BY
PROFESSOR JEAN McFARLANE, M.A., B.Sc., S.R.N.,
FIRST PROFESSOR OF NURSING
IN ENGLAND AND A HYWELIAN.

CHAIRMAN: ARTHUR PHILLIPS ESQ., F.C.A., J.P.

Top: Part of the old Chemistry Laboratory, which became known as Faraday.
Above: Plaque commemorating the opening of the new Physics Laboratories, 1974.
Left: Sixth form Physics pupils, 1970s.

Right: Dorothy Harrison in 1962. Far right: Staff-pupil tennis match, 1961. Left to right: Miss Ann Cossentine, Miss Dorothy Bowen, Elizabeth Phillips, Susan Williams. Below right: An interlude in the Jane Austin evening, held in honour of Miss Elsie Fowler on her retirement in 1964.

Chemistry Laboratory known as Faraday, next to the Art Room, became a form room, as did the old senior Physics Laboratory, which reverted to its earlier name of Ship. The two rooms at the top of the north wing were converted for use as Geography rooms.

From 1962, the Cardiff LEA was represented by three members on the Governing body, and Newport and Monmouthshire by one each. The Drapers' Company was delighted to be able to reclaim the portion of the income of the Thomas Howell Fund which the three authorities had been receiving (8% each). A new Scheme was drawn up, including a scholarship of £100 per year for girls from Newport and Monmouthshire in alternate years. In November 1968 Mr Arthur Phillips replaced Mr Wright as Chairman. His departure was not the only significant one outside the teaching staff. The Medical Officer Dr Parry retired in 1960 and was succeeded by her daughter, Dr Glenys Williams, until 1963, when Drs George and Hilary Lloyd took over. Miss Margaret Findlay, who had been appointed in September 1939 as secretary and in 1948 as the first female Clerk to the Governors, died suddenly in February 1961. Miss Holland retired at Easter 1968 after forty-three years as housekeeper. Always reluctant to give anyone access to her keys, she left them all on a tray, unlabelled. At about the same time, the very long-serving sewing-maid, Edith, left; she had made all the cleaners' aprons and had done Miss Lewis's mending and darning.

During the year 1962-3, there were eight Hywelians on the staff, six teachers and two administrators, Miss Ponting and the Factor, Rosemary Haigh, née Morgan, who succeeded Joan Smith. Remarkably, nine mistresses had been at school since Miss Lewis's appointment in 1941

– Misses Harrison, Phillips, Allen, Cole, Eyre, Fowler, McMahon, Tickner and Walters – as well as the housekeeper, Miss Holland, and a housemistress, Miss Richards. Most were of the generation which had seen thousands of young men killed in the First World War, thereby reducing their chances of marriage. Howell's was a school with proud traditions, high academic standards and considerable reputation, so there was little incentive to leave for a post elsewhere, especially as opportunities for promotion were extremely limited. These women therefore devoted the best part of their lives to the service of the school. However, by Christmas 1970 none of these remained. Miss Phillips, the senior English mistress, and Miss Harrison, who had succeeded Miss Taylor as Senior Mistress, both retired in 1963 after thirty-five years. Miss Phillips, a Quaker, was active in the World Disarmament Movement and lived until 1994. The organiser of numerous botany field excursions, Miss Harrison endowed prizes for fieldwork on her retirement. Following her death the next year, the staff replanted the herbaceous border that ran under the window outside the Staff Study and the Gymnasium as a memorial.

In 1964 Miss Winifred MacMahon, French and German mistress since January 1936, Miss Ann Cossentine, who taught

Far left: The fountain in the quadrangle, created by Frank Roper, 1965. It was designed by Miss Eyre, with stylised bronze leaves in a plain concrete surround, and jets rising in interlocking parabolas.
Above left: Inscription on the fountain.

Left: Nativity tableau, 1954. The background was painted by Miss Eyre and Ann Sinclair took the part of the Virgin Mary.

Diction, and Miss Fowler ("Mef") all retired. Miss Cossentine had been involved in the production of school plays; she donated to the school a Cup for public speaking, and was best remembered for teaching all girls in the Upper III to pronounce the "ah" sound properly by reciting the verse:

> *Father's car is a Jaguar and Pa drives rather fast;*
> *Castles, farms and draughty barns, we go charging past.*
> *Arthur's cart is far less smart and can't go half as far;*
> *But I'd rather ride in Arthur's cart than my Papa's fast car!*

Miss Fowler, who had taught Geography and Botany at Howell's for over forty years, had also given Oxbridge lessons on Japanese and Russian literature and was very knowledgeable about meteorology and astronomy.

In 1965 Miss Allen, Deaconess since 1961 (the first female to be ordained in Llandaff Cathedral since the Church had been disestablished some forty years earlier), left to devote herself to work in the parish. Miss Ewart Thomas ("Tommy French"), who also departed in 1965 after two years as Senior Mistress, donated the illuminated fountain in the quadrangle in memory of her mother. Like the statue placed in the niche above the main entrance four years previously, this was made by Frank Roper, and the shrubs around it were planted by the housemistress Mrs Christabel Wagstaffe. Miss Ewart Thomas's successor as Senior Mistress was Mrs Dilys Lloyd.

Miss Daisy Walters, teacher of Welsh and Geography, retired after thirty-eight years in 1966 and Miss Tickner ("Tick") in 1970, after no less than forty-seven years. The "elder statesman" in the Staff Study, where her desk was one of the original wash-stands, this formidable lady had built up a strong tradition for Classics and had led numerous school parties abroad. Sadly, she died very suddenly on 1st June 1971. She left £1,000 to the school, the interest from which was to provide an annual prize for the girl with the greatest understanding of Latin literature. Miss Cole, pianist

and harpist, also retired in 1970 after thirty years. For her, the main event of the year had been the Carol Concerts, during which the stage curtains opened to reveal one of the tableaux of the Nativity. These were designed and organised by Miss Eyre, who left to be married at Christmas 1970 after more than thirty five years as Art mistress. On Miss Cole's death in 1976 her friend Miss Phillips endowed a piano prize in her memory.

Many of the staff who left after such long service to the school were replaced by others who, in turn, stayed for long periods. These included the Hywelians Mrs Helen Simpkiss (Scripture), Miss Hilary Jones (Art) and Mrs Beulah Rowland Williams (Biology), née Blake; Mrs Katherine Howe (part-time Biology); Mrs Norma Maylin (English); Miss Catherine Barclay, later Mrs Saunders (French); Miss Christine Davies (Mathematics); Miss Margaret Jones (Physics); Mrs Nia Anthony (Classics); Mrs Joan Hamilton-Jones (English); Mrs Gaynor Howard (Music); and Mrs Elizabeth Walters. A notable way in which many of these differed from their predecessors was that they were married, reflecting a general change in society's attitudes and the aspirations of such women by this time. The family links with Howell's were continued through the daughters of no fewer than seven – Mrs Simpkiss, Mrs Howe, Mrs Saunders, Mrs Rowland Williams, Mrs Anthony, Mrs Hamilton-Jones and Mrs Howard – who also attended the school.

During the 1960s and 1970s, the curriculum saw the introduction of French using audio-visual methods, and German as an alternative to Latin. Howell's was one of only three schools in Wales to be invited to participate in the trial for Nuffield Physics A Level in September 1969, and Art and Music joined the list of A Level subjects in the early 1970s. The old air raid shelter between the Art Room and the old stables became a studio for sixth formers and the dividing walls in the Art Room were removed to make one large area. Music lessons were introduced to all younger girls in 1972 and O Level Music, previously only taken as an "extra" at lunchtime, became a timetabled option. Academic standards remained high; in Miss Lewis's final year five girls won places

Above left: Lacrosse team in action, early 1963.
Above: Carole Mort, the lacrosse captain, receiving the cup for the team's victory in the England Lacrosse Rally in London, 4th April 1963.
Left: Lacrosse team 1966-7. Left to right, Back row: Ann Morgan, Mary Foreman, Jennifer Heath-Smith, Margaret Davies, Trisha Mundy, Janet Smith, Diana Caryl. Front row: Sian Williams, Isobel Waugh, Alison Jones, Jacky Jones, Ann Tillyard.

Facing page
Top left: Girls performing the Toy Symphony, December 1972. Front row, left to right: Jane Griffiths, Maxine Altman, Rosemary Staple. Back row: Alison Fitzpatrick, Karen Beattie, Petra Cox, Ailsa Davies.
Centre left: The Senior Choir, with Mrs Gaynor Howard, on its first appearance at Llangollen, 1973.

at Oxford and one at Cambridge. Sport continued to dominate the lunchtimes and, for the boarders, the hour after school. Not surprisingly, the teams tended to do extremely well in tournaments, especially in lacrosse, for which this was the Golden Age, and many girls represented Wales. Under Miss Audrey Bates' direction, the team was victorious on a number of occasions in the All England Schools' Lacrosse Rally in London, training on Barry beach during the winter of 1963 when the school fields were covered in snow. The school acquired its first minibus in the summer of 1970, which was used primarily for the transportation of school teams.

Music developed a higher profile in the 1970s under Mrs Howard, the new Director of Music, and gained much publicity for the school. She built up senior and junior orchestras and a recorder consort, and composed the incidental music for *The Tempest*, a production directed by Mrs Catherine Powell. In 1972 some members of the Junior Orchestra were invited to perform Leopold Mozart's *Toy Symphony* at a holiday promenade concert at City Hall with members of the BBC Welsh Orchestra, marking the first occasion on which any school had participated this way with a professional orchestra. From the early 1970s, Celebrity Recitals were given each year. The Senior Choir carried on the tradition of singing a short introit in Prayers each morning, while the orchestra played the hymn on Fridays. The choir first competed at the Llangollen International Eisteddfod in 1973 and was

honoured to be chosen to represent Wales at the evening concert, alongside choirs from mainland Europe, the USA and Australia. It also regularly participated very successfully in the Mid-Somerset Music Festival, winning so many cups that the year after Miss Lewis retired, she presented a cup to the Festival from the school. Christmas 1976 marked the first year of the annual Carol Service in Llandaff Cathedral. In Miss Lewis's final year the choir was runner-up in the final round of the UK Radio Three competition for amateur choirs, *Let the People Sing*.

The Debating, Dramatic, Literary, Scientific and History societies, the Student Christian Movement (SCM) and the Urdd were among the most flourishing extracurricular groups of the 1960s and 1970s, most of them holding their meetings after school. Charity activities included Dorcas, which was organised as a house competition. In 1968, sixth formers began taking part in a voluntary community scheme, visiting elderly ladies in their spare time.

A variety of educational visits also took place. The most remarkable overseas journey occurred in 1967, in the days of the Cold War. A long and somewhat hazardous overland trip by train across the Iron Curtain to Moscow and Leningrad was led by Mrs Edith Griffith, who had joined the staff in 1966 to teach Geography. Three years later, with Mrs Helen Simpkiss, Mrs Griffith organised a visit to the Oberammergau Passion Play in Bavaria.

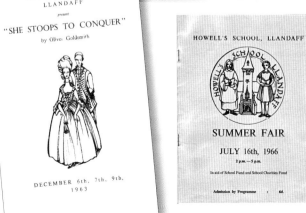

Above left: She Stoops To Conquer, *1963. Left to right:* Anna Clarke, Megan Thomas, Susan Price, Leone David *and* Judy Webb. Leone David, *as Mrs Finch, returned to teach Biology from 1991 to 2005 and became a member of the Senior Management Team.*

Far left: Programme for She Stoops To Conquer, *December 1963.*

Left: Summer Fair programme, 1966.

Top. Twelfth Night, *1976. Fourth from left in the front row is Sharon Criddle, who returned as Mrs Richards to teach English in 1986.*

Above centre: The school party leaving for Oberammergau, 1970. *Mrs Edith Griffith, Geography mistress, is kneeling on the left.*

Above: Mrs Enid Watkin Jones with George Thomas MP and girls at the Houses of Parliament, 1964.

A form of Christian worship took place in the Hall daily. As space was limited, the girls stood throughout, apart from kneeling for the prayers. The "Amens" were always sung. Any girl who was excused on religious grounds filed in at the end to hear the announcements and listen to Miss Lewis's talks on behaviour and etiquette. Jewish girls had their own assembly. During the summer, when the Hall was used for public examinations, Prayers took place on the asphalt, with the girls standing around the big horse chestnut tree. In the 1960s the piano was placed under the tree and Miss Cole used clothes pegs to secure her music. This practice, and the form of service, also continued into the 1980s.

The boarders' lives were still strictly regimented, with the fortnightly hair-washing undertaken in the upstairs cloakroom in the Tower, where there were rows of oval washbasins. The occasional six-hour leaves were eagerly awaited, together with the opportunity to replenish supplies of tuck, but anyone who arrived back late lost fifteen minutes from the next one. By the late 1960s there was an increased range of activities available at weekends, including horse-riding, shopping, cinema and theatre visits and trips to the seaside. Weekly boarding was permitted in September 1971 for the first time since the Second World War but the number of boarders was declining by 1973 to such an extent that it was decided to relinquish Penhill Close from July 1974 on account of its relatively remote situation and the cost of maintenance.

In the 1960s the Hywelians began their Biennial Winter Feasts, which were held on a grand scale. They also held wine and cheese parties from 1964, initially at the Llandaff Institute as it was deemed improper to have a social occasion with alcohol and men in school, but that notion was soon abandoned. Car treasure hunts and jumble sales were other activities of this period. Mrs Catherine Powell (née Morgan), who had taught Diction briefly during the war and founded the Bristol branch of the Guild in 1955, joined the Hywelian Committee in Centenary Year and subsequently produced one-act plays. She went on to become one of its Vice-Presidents in 1965 and taught again at school from 1970 to 1977.

In 1970, the Guild donated a glass door for the archway in the entrance Hall. Former pupils and staff have continued to benefit from the legacy of Bronwen Jacques (née Thomas), who died in November 1973. Treasurer of the Guild from 1914-20 and Secretary and Editor of the Hywelian magazine from 1920-37, she bequeathed to the Governors her house at Hewelsfield in the Forest of Dean. From the proceeds of the sale, £10,000 was given to the Cartref residential homes, on condition that each year two nominated Hywelians or former staff members should have priority of entry, and the rest was invested to provide financial support to any former pupil or staff member in financial difficulty.

The election of a Labour Government in 1964 led to momentous educational changes, which included ending the Direct Grant scheme in 1976. Strong feelings were aroused by one councillor's reference to Howell's as a "snob" school, which featured prominently in the local press late in 1964. This slight brought forth letters in its defence as well as an assurance that the Chairman of the Education Committee had stated that it was a "first class school in every way". Miss Lewis made it quite clear in 1970 that Howell's would choose to become completely independent rather than go comprehensive and that "The losers are going to be the girls who would like to have come here but whose parents have insufficient means to pay the fees themselves." In July 1971 the authority reduced by fourteen the number of scholarships but agreed to provide twenty per year to girls who had spent at least the two previous years in local state primary schools, with parental income taken into account. Three years later, the new Labour-dominated South Glamorgan County Council voted to end the scholarships completely. Fortuitously the J S Frazer Trust came forward to provide £6,000 in 1975. It was agreed with Harry Gibson, senior trustee of the Trust, that each year two scholarships would be provided annually. For September 1976, there were sufficient funds for the Frazer Scholarship and five other awards to be offered to day girls.

Boarders' lives

'Mrs Hoffman, silver hair swept up in an elegant braid, ruled [in Oaklands] with a rod of iron. One night she stood, foot-tapping, waiting for us to get into bed. Under the plank was a lump of Auntie Marj's fruit cake, some dead-fly biscuits, apples and a half-drunk bottle of Vimto. We watched nervously, praying that it would not be revealed. Food was always hidden, with no thought for refrigeration or sanitation.'

Cathy Hollowell, née Couzens (1961-8). Written 1993.

'In Kendall, in the Upper IV we did our homework, wrote letters and studied for our exams in the junior lounge, with Mrs Stephens, "Stevie", our housemistress, sitting in a chair by the fire. In the Lower V, we graduated to the senior lounge. We used to scare ourselves by taking it in turns to tell ghost stories in the dead of night and of course we had the end of term midnight feasts. Baths were taken downstairs but we could only wash our hair once a fortnight, and that was done in the main school. Stevie would use a hairdryer to dry our hair. Sunday best was a golden brown thick tweed suit with a yellow blouse, thick brown tights, brown shoes and a cream boater that refused to stay on my head. I can remember one or other of us chasing our hats down the road every Sunday. We also had to wear these suits to go home in the holidays, which of course mortified us, particularly since most of us had heavily darned tights. In the evening we could change into mufti.

Above: Lower V boarders in front of Kendall House, summer 1967. Left to right, standing: Janet Lloyd, Viv Dunn, Barbara Dowds. Seated: Rosemary Day, Ruth Roberts. Below: The Oak Room, Bryntaf, which was a replica of the Oak Tea Room in David Morgan's store.

Every morning we would walk in pairs around the edge of the playing fields over to the school, where our meals were taken. The housemistress would sit at one end and a senior prefect or the head of the House at the other. I can remember toasting bread on the very large log fire in Kendall lounge for Sunday tea. Having come from a co-ed boarding school in India where ages ranged from five to twenty-five, I was shocked by the strict segregation between years. Soon after my arrival, I created displeasure by playing snowballs with the Upper 3rd! We were not allowed to use the toilets after lights out. One night I crept along the corridor to the loo, which we believed was haunted. As I crept out, I turned to find Stevie standing directly behind me in a long white nightdress with her grey hair hanging around her face down to her waist. I nearly had a heart attack! One afternoon my friend and I were summoned by Miss Lewis. She had been contacted by the Headmaster of Llandaff Cathedral School. We had written to the boys there asking if they would like to be our pen-pals, and the letter had been intercepted!

Swimming and horse-riding became the highlights for me. Every other Saturday, a group of us would be taken by van to stables to go riding. Once when a school fête was held, the girls were allowed to spend the day with their parents. Since mine were abroad, I was allowed to ride a horse around the fields with a friend.

Life changed a lot in my last year when a friend and I moved into Bryntaff a year early. We were allowed to watch *Top of the Pops* on a Thursday night before going to bed at 8.30pm! The housemistress, Mrs Wagstaffe, was strict but fair and it was a happier atmosphere altogether. My parents returned to the UK and I left at the end of the year.'

Rosemary Lee, née Day (1965-8). Written October 2008.

With the end of the Direct Grant looming, in 1975 the school entered into negotiations with the Girls' Public Day School Trust (GPDST), which by then comprised twenty-three schools. The Governors, while welcoming the opportunity to join, needed the consent of the Charity Commissioners and the Drapers' Company, and wished to retain control of the Thomas Howell endowment. Discussions continued until finally in May 1977 it was agreed that the Council of the GPDST would be the sole Trustee but that the Governors would have delegated powers. Howell's would maintain its separate identity and complete freedom of action – the first time that the Trust had ever agreed to such a course. The benefits of being associated with such an influential body in girls' education were many: notably, it would provide financial and legal advice and administrative support, teaching staff would attend subject conferences, and pupils would participate in joint events and be eligible for Trust prizes.

After thirty-six years, Miss Lewis decided that the time had come to retire. On the recommendation of a GPDST sub-committee, a shortlist of six applicants for her post was drawn up. The interviews took place on 25th March 1977 and Miss Jill Turner was appointed. As she was unable to take up her appointment until January 1978, Miss Lewis agreed to stay on until Christmas. In her last year, the lacrosse squad travelled to the USA with Miss Bates and won every match, an achievement which delighted Miss Lewis, a former lacrosse international. It was also the Queen's Silver Jubilee year and the school lined the street to see the Queen and Prince Philip in an open carriage, accompanied by members of the household cavalry and the Metropolitan Police.

In the Jubilee Honours List that summer Miss Lewis was awarded the OBE and Miss Bates gained the Queen's Jubilee medal for services to Sport. In November, Miss Lewis went to Buckingham Palace to receive her award, a fitting end to such a long period of service to education.

A Day Girl's life

'I recall the novelty of the television in the Hall for the moon landing in 1969. It was on and if we had a prep period we could go in and watch. The new uniform looked like an air hostess uniform. The problem with the new round hats was that they lost their shape early in their life and then looked a trifle ridiculous! The best change was that from the thick, almost support-type, stockings to tights.

At lunchtime we tried to line upon the stairs to avoid sitting next to the teachers and housemistresses who presided in BDR or LDR. Miss Lewis or Mrs Lloyd sat at the head of the centre table in BDR. I remember being told by Miss Lewis that when eating soup to be sure to tip the bowl away from you and on no account to use your spoon to demonstrate the flight of aeroplanes. Depending where you sat, you had to do duties such as entertaining the head of table, clearing the plates, bringing the dessert, and wiping the table. The only safe place as I recall was fifth from the head of table.

Then there were the leavers' rituals: lining up boaters in Howell's Crescent and crushing them by driving over them or tossing them into the Taff from the number 24 bus as we went past the BBC Wales in Llandaff. The rest of my memories are a sort of jolly hockeysticks blur of compulsory games, which I for the most part enjoyed (although hockey on Llandaff Fields often required the extra, optional thick navy sweater – which I possessed well into my thirties!). I remember the long cold Covered Way and conkers from the numerous horse chestnut trees which I collected for my younger brothers. I left at the end of the Upper Fifth to study ballet in London.'

Taking a break on The Green at the end of the Summer Term, 1973.

Karen Plambeck, née Millar (1968-73). Written October 2009.

Above: The Lacrosse Squad and their American hosts in the USA, April 1977. The squad won all eight matches. Miss Audrey Bates is in the back row on the right.
Left: The Rescue Archaeology Special Merit Award for the Llandaff Cathedral Graveyard Recording project, 1977. Magnus Magnusson presented the award at the Museum of London to (left to right) Jane Lougher, Hilary Prescott, Margaret Barnes and Julie Hyett.

'When Virginia Wade won Wimbledon in 1977 we were allowed to watch it in the Board Room. We also lined Cardiff Road to wave our flags at the Queen as she rode by on her way to the Cathedral. It was very exciting; she was wearing a bright pink outfit and she was in an open state carriage, pulled by horses. They had come along Cathedral Road and then up Penhill before coming along Cardiff Road, past school. Apparently it was quite an effort for the horses to pull the carriage up the hill so when they got on to the flat part along by school, they were slowed down for them to recover so we all got a good long look and plenty of time to wave our flags and cheer!

We all did a lot of fund-raising to send the lacrosse team to America. On the fund-raising theme, the Lower Sixth Christian Aid week became more and more extreme as each successive LVI tried to outdo the previous one.

When Miss Lewis left, she gave every girl a bookmark commemorating the past Headmistresses of the school.'

Debbie Ward, née Buss, and Nicola Davies, née Salter (1973-80). Written October 2009.

'Howell's had so many rules that new girls were given a whole month to learn them. There was no mention of smoking: presumably, it was considered inconceivable that any Howell's girl would want a cigarette. Food, however, was well covered. Eating in school uniform was not allowed unless you were seated at a designated table at lunchtime. And there were unwritten rules on dining even for the girls who brought packed lunches, who could not, for example, eat oranges, which were "antisocial fruit". All pupils had instruction in table manners which varied from the sound ("Talk equally to people on either side") to the perplexing ("No aeroplane stories at the table, please") and the guilt-inspiring ("If the person sitting next to you asks for the water jug, you have failed. You should have anticipated her need."). Naturally, both talking and running in corridors were forbidden.

It was almost impossible to avoid breaking a rule or, indeed, several at a time. Detention was the ultimate deterrent as it took place on a Saturday morning and entailed travelling – probably by public transport – in full school uniform. Think of the Swinging Sixties and then imagine a teenager with no make-up, scraped back hair and wearing a long grey pinafore dress. For the same reason, few girls breached the rule that forbade them to talk to a boy when wearing a Howell's uniform.

We had to play games every lunchtime in a stipulated time and place. The weather didn't prevent these activities and we often practised lacrosse in the day room, losing balls in foot lockers. When we spent the games hour dancing in the Hall (a treat) we would tie an unsuspecting friend's girdle to her chair so that she couldn't get up to dance to Guitar Man. We knew how to make our own fun in those days.'

Ruth Campbell, née Sully (1963-70). Written October 2009.

Below: Staff farewell dinner for Miss Lewis, 17th December 1977.
Right: Miss Lewis at the time of her retirement.

HOWELL'S SCHOOL LLANDAFF

FAREWELL DINNER

IN HONOUR OF

MISS MARGARET LL. LEWIS, O.B.E.
HEADMISTRESS 1941 - 1977

17TH DECEMBER, 1977

Having begun her long tenure of office by guiding the school successfully through the war, Miss Lewis finished by initiating the process for it to join the GPDST. She had set exacting standards of scholarship and behaviour and her commanding presence had permeated all aspect of school life. From the 1960s, if not before, the majority of the girls found the numerous rules and regulations – most of which did not change in over thirty years – irksome and oppressive, and the boarders in particular hankered after a less regimented and more comfortable lifestyle. The national teenage revolution of the late 1960s, with rebellion against restrictions, tight discipline and compulsory games, had led in many schools to the slackening of rigid rules, but not at Howell's.

However, many pupils recalled individual acts of kindness and sensitivity. Miss Lewis's prize-giving speeches were a *tour de force*, lively and witty, including such inimitable comments as "This school is no Garden of Eden . . . We insist on full school uniform",

and "I do not insinuate that this is an earthly paradise – in fact, the Covered Way in cold weather can at times resemble the Anglo-Saxon idea of hell. Furthermore, some of the inhabitants can at times be insufficiently tempted by the Tree of Knowledge." Her departure, after thirty-six years, certainly marked the end of an era.

Miss Lewis began an active retirement. She particularly enjoyed a visit to the House of Lords when Professor Jean McFarlane became the first Hywelian Baroness, after being raised to the peerage in the Queen's birthday honours of 1979, and chose the title Baroness McFarlane of Llandaff to reflect her debt to Howell's. It came as a tremendous shock to everyone when Miss Lewis died suddenly on 17th October 1980 after a heart attack two days previously. An appeal was launched to raise money for a permanent memorial to her and as a result the Margaret Lewis Library and Fine Arts Collection was established.

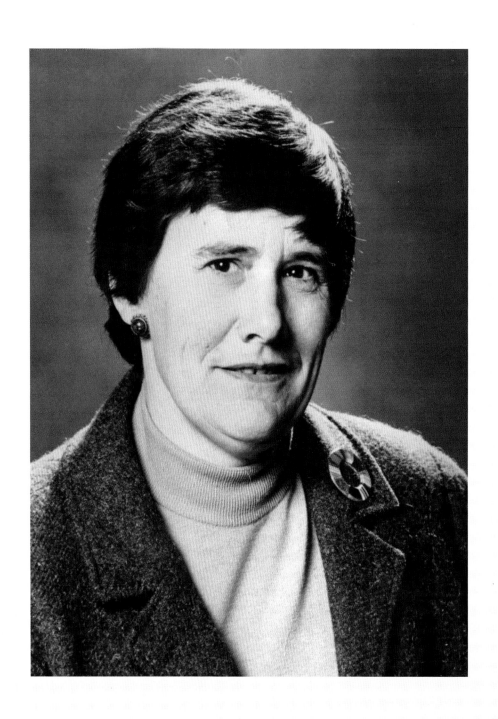

16

MISS TURNER AND THE BUILDING PROGRAMME, 1978-91

Miss Jill Patricia Turner was Headmistress of Howell's School for less than fourteen years, but the impact of her headship was out of all proportion to that relatively short period in the school's history. Born on 10th March 1931, she was educated at Guildford County School for Girls and Westfield College, London University, where she graduated in Mathematics. After gaining her teaching qualification at Cambridge, she taught at her first GPDST school, Croydon High, before working as a Government Education Officer in Kenya. On returning, she became Head of Department and, later, Deputy Headmistress at South Hampstead High School. Prior to her appointment at Howell's, she had spent eight years as Headmistress of Brighton and Hove High School, so she had had extensive experience of the workings of the GPDST. Like her predecessors, she lived in the school, but she had a self-contained flat created on the first floor, overlooking the front entrance, and she spent the weekends at her cottage in the Brecon Beacons. She soon acquired a labrador, Meg, as a companion in the building, where she was the only person at night as there were no longer any resident maids.

At her first Governors' meeting, it was agreed that long-serving staff should be given a period of extended leave at the end of the summer term, as was the GPDST's policy, and many benefited from this in future years. Miss Ponting, the Bursar, who had managed the school's finances and played an influential part in the running of the school, retired in the summer of 1978 after thirty years. The Trust then took over more accounting responsibilities and from the beginning of Miss Turner's headship, it was represented on the Governing Body. On 25th January 1980, the Governors completed the formalities involved in setting up the partnership between Howell's and the GPDST. The Council of the Trust became the Managing Trustees of the school. As Mr Arthur Phillips, the Chairman, remarked, this was "a very special occasion in the school's history". From this time, four Trust Scholarships for the sixth form were awarded annually. To mark its formal association with the Trust, Howell's donated a new prize – the Dame Kitty Anderson History Prize. Howell's initially remained legally and financially independent of the Trust but in 1984 that body took over the administration and accounting of the Thomas Howell Fund. Howell's retained its connection with the Drapers' Company, which in 1988 made a gift of two substantial leaving scholarships.

It was obvious to Miss Turner that substantial additions and refurbishments to the existing building were needed in order to bring the facilities up to the standard required in modern teaching practice. Although delightful when created after the fire of 1932, the Library could only seat about fifty girls and its use was restricted to senior pupils. The books – most of which were out of date – were kept in locked glass-fronted cabinets. There was no librarian or catalogue system and, since sections were managed by departments, there were no books of general interest. The Botany and Zoology Laboratories were some distance apart and had no preparation room. Music facilities also needed to be updated. The form rooms had old, heavy furniture and the girls remained there for most of their lessons, so there was little scope for providing specialised subject equipment or visual aids. The staff were still based in the small original Study, created in 1906, with old desks and no area for relaxation. The sixth formers had no common room and were subject to almost the same regulations as the rest of the school. The boarding facilities needed to be improved and the obligation for almost all pupils to spend every lunch-time playing games severely limited other extracurricular activities during school hours.

The purchasing of some careers literature and the setting-up of a Junior Reference Library for boarders were the first steps taken. Soon the four grass tennis courts acquired a tarmac surface and the large ward in the Sanatorium was converted into a classroom, which became the History department's base. Miss Turner was eager for the sixth formers to become more independent. During

Left: Sixth form Common Room, 1986. Left to right: Rhian Beck, Siân David, Samantha Chiles, Ceri Jackson, Lisa Mildon, Helena Clark, Suzy Bruton.

Facing page
Top left: School House and Staff Cloakroom in 1981, shortly before their demolition.
Top right: The buildings around the Urn Court, 1981: the Zoology Laboratory, the Gymnasium, the Staff Cloakroom and School House.
Centre left: The old Gymnasium.
Centre right: The New Building under construction, 1981.
Bottom: The New Building, 1982.

the summer holidays of 1979, a sixth form complex was created on the first floor of the east wing, with study rooms, a prefects' room and a large common room, complete with tea and coffee-making facilities, radio and cassette player; the girls themselves planned the decoration and furnishing. From September 1979, they were not required to wear uniform, although there were certain restrictions. Miss Turner instituted a staff-sixth form tea party in September each year to mark their new status, and a School Council, chaired by the Head Girl, was created in 1980. Not only was it the sixth formers who acquired a common room: the classroom adjacent to the Study was adapted for use by the staff. Miss Turner was also eager to improve communications with parents. In her second year, she instituted a Parents' Committee, which provided valuable help in ways such as providing refreshments at rallies, selling second-hand uniform and contributing to the programme of careers talks.

Meanwhile, representatives from the Trust had visited the school early in 1979 to assess its needs. It was agreed that there should be two new laboratories for Biology as well as one for General Science, together with six or seven new classrooms, an extension to the Library and improvements to the staff and sixth form accommodation. Following the consideration of several possible plans, it was decided to create a new building at the end of the Covered Way. This involved demolishing School House and a few smaller structures nearby. A major task of renovating and replacing existing stonework was also needed on the south-east side of the building and massive repair work required to the lantern. The total cost of the work was estimated to be in the region of £550,000. Of this, approximately £400,000 came from the Thomas Howell Fund. For the rest, it was decided to launch a public appeal, *Into the 80s*, using professional fundraisers. Mr James McGuinness was appointed as Appeals Director and Sir Cennydd Traherne KG, Lord Lieutenant of Glamorgan, became the President of the Appeal. An Appeal Committee was formed, with Miss Lewis as a Vice-President and Miss Ponting the Treasurer. Miss Turner, often accompanied by Miss Lewis, spoke at twenty-one meetings during the summer term of 1980 but sadly, Miss Lewis did not live to see the scheme completed. The

appeal was very successful: it passed its target in January 1981, the Hywelians alone contributing over £30,000.

The New Building was built of pink-grey brick to tone in with the existing buildings and had a pitched slate roof with dormer windows. There were nine new classrooms, enabling the Mathematics and Modern Languages departments to have their own bases, and new cloakrooms for staff and girls. In order for all Science lessons to take place in laboratories, three new ones were built: one for General Science and two for Biology, complete with a preparation room, flanking the old Urn Court. The urn mysteriously vanished but a new Biology pool took its place. The Gymnasium was extended and included an alcove for the storing of apparatus, and the two former air raid shelters off the Covered Way were designated as changing rooms. During the building programme, many lessons took place in *Elliotts*, temporary classrooms which were located on the staff car park. A crucial role in the whole process was played by the Factor, Mrs Elizabeth Jones, whose practical efficiency expedited the whole process

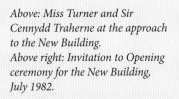

Above: Miss Turner and Sir Cennydd Traherne at the approach to the New Building.
Above right: Invitation to Opening ceremony for the New Building, July 1982.

Top right: Luncheon in the Hall on the day of the Opening of the New Building.
Right: Wall at the approach to the New Building.

By September 1981, ahead of schedule, one of the laboratories and eight of the classrooms were already in use. The next phase involved the extension of the Library and the conversion of the old Zoology Laboratory into cloakrooms (the "Zoo Loos"). The New Building, which was blessed and dedicated by the Bishop of Llandaff, was formally opened on 2nd July 1982 by Sir Cennydd Traherne. Lunch, entertainment, tea and tours were provided over two days.

The extended Library, which was more than double the size of its predecessor, was created from the former classrooms West I and II, the adjacent corridor and the existing Library. The Gallery form room was converted to a librarians' office and an area large enough to provide instruction to groups. From the fund set up by the Hywelian Guild for the Margaret Lewis Memorial Library and Fine Art Collection, the first painting was commissioned in

1984; named *The Year of the Bee*, it was painted by a Hywelian, Fiona Owen (née Davies). The Library was declared open on 20th September 1985 in the presence of Miss Win Lewis, Miss Lewis's sister. In 1987 it was equipped with new tables from the fund. Since 1979 the books had been classified, with the assistance of some parents, and in 1988 a major computerised system for cataloguing, classifying and borrowing books was introduced.

Meanwhile, in 1981, improvements had also been made to the Hall, financed by the investment from the money raised in the appeal launched at the Centenary in 1960. A pair of double doors created a side exit to the asphalt and there was a new floor of Danish oak. Its whole appearance was lightened by the professional cleaning of the panels and the Shakespeare murals as well as the addition of strong lights.

In September 1984, a new Junior School, catering for pupils aged seven to eleven, opened in Hazelwood with two classes of eight and nine-year olds, named Junior II and Junior III. The house was not needed for boarders as the number was continuing to fall. In charge was Mrs Gillian Barber, with initially only one assistant teacher, but the following September there were two additional forms, making the full complement, and consequently more staff. The old billiard room became a Hall and the tennis court was extended to provide a substantial hard area on which the girls could play tennis and netball. The girls wore a pink and white checked blouse but otherwise their uniform was identical to that of the senior girls. It was not until 14th March 1986 that the Junior School was formally opened by Miss Win Lewis, who unveiled a plaque in the Library. Earlier that day, all the pupils had been involved in its first major production, *The Snow Queen*. Having established the Junior School, Mrs Barber retired in December 1988 and was succeeded by Miss Elaine Woon, who became Mrs Thomas after her marriage in the summer of 1989.

In 1984, a major overhaul of the catering facilities was also announced and January 1985 saw the introduction of a self-service cafeteria, offering much greater flexibility than the formal meals in BDR and LDR. The new kitchens were sited conveniently for deliveries near the school entrance, in place of the former cloakrooms, and the Day Room and Schoolrooms A and B were

converted into new Dining Rooms. The old kitchen and stores area housed cloakrooms, a reprographics area and a tuck shop. LDR became the Day Room and BDR was converted into two classrooms.

The swimming pool was insulated fully against heating loss in 1986 and relined to make it suitable for use all year. In the same year, the front drive, lawns and flowerbeds had a facelift. The grounds were further improved through the efforts of the gardener Miss

Jill Connolly, who won a Lord Mayor's Civic Award in 1988 for her conservation scheme for a strip of wooded land bordering on Cardiff Road, which included a footpath, pond and seating area.

The Art department was the next beneficiary of the refurbishment programme, In 1987 a pottery, linked to the Art Room, was created on the ground floor of the old stables, and a new external staircase gave access to the first floor, which was refurbished as a

Top: The Conservation Area, c.1987. Miss Jill Connolly, who created the area, is on the left at the back.
Above: Hazelwood opens as Howell's Junior School, 1984.
Far left: The re-opening of the swimming pool after its refurbishment, 1986. On the left are Mrs Jean Hartley, Head of PE, and Mr Neville Sims.
Left: Miss Win Lewis officially opens Hazelwood as Howell's Junior School, 14th March 1986.
Bottom left: The first summer at the Junior School, 1985.
Below: The new cafeteria, 1985.

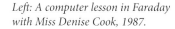

Above left: Rhian Murfin in refurbished study bedroom, Oaklands, 1991.
Above: Boarders outside Oaklands, 1987. Left to right: Rachel Smith, Ines Moncada Monadero, Laura Lougher, Shweta Singh, Sharon Finlay, Rachel Curran.

Above: Fifth form boarders, 1990. Left to right, Back row: Jessica Poole, Rhian Murfin, Joanna Reynolds, Harriet Sansom. Front row: Shweta Singh, Katy Marshall (not a boarder), Sharon Finlay, Katy Webster, Christine Masters, Laura Lougher.

Left: A computer lesson in Faraday with Miss Denise Cook, 1987.

painting and drawing studio for the sixth form. The whole area was further extended by the conversion of the former Botany Laboratory, known as Linnaeus, to a Design Studio, which could provide courses in Craft Design Technology (CDT) or Art and Design. The adjoining former Chemistry Laboratory, known as Faraday, became the home of a new fourteen-station network of Research Machine Nimbus micro-computers.

Conditions in the boarding houses were also addressed. Interior painting and new flooring soon improved the appearance of the boarding houses, and some relaxation of the rules made the boarders' lives less regimented. The brown Sunday suits with yellow blouses, previously worn by termly boarders, were abandoned, and for these girls there was a wider variety of weekend activities and trips. However, it was some time before significant changes were made to the facilities.

The idea of bringing boarding to an end, first raised in the 1970s, was considered. In common with all independent schools in the 1980s, the number of boarders continued to decline. However, the Inspection Report in 1987 commented that the boarding community made an enormous contribution to the school, so it was decided to try to maintain it by more vigorous advertising and by improving the facilities. In September 1987, Cumberland Lodge (Taylor) was taken over, initially on a trial basis, by the

Music department, and all the boarders were accommodated in Bryntaf and Oaklands, the seniors in the former and the younger ones in the latter. During the summer of 1988 Bryntaf underwent a complete renovation, including the creation of a large kitchen and plenty of showers. The next summer Oaklands was refurbished to create single and double study bedrooms. Much advertising of the enhanced facilities took place, especially in Dyfed and Powys, and boarding bursaries were offered from September 1989.

Meanwhile, in 1988 the Governors had agreed to the refurbishment of the Staff Study and Common Room, improved seating for the Hall and a sound intercom system for drama. Money for other improvements was raised from summer fairs, such as those held in 1988 and 1990, which raised over £2,000 to buy video equipment and £1,500 for lockable lockers.

The new Technology Centre, built in the old Laundry (which was re-sited in Oaklands) was built on two floors, with heavy equipment on the ground floor, and electronics and computer-aided design on the first floor. The Cookery School was redesigned for GCSE courses in Food Technology in the summer of 1990 and had a microwave, fridge-freezer and a resource area with a computer. The big communal tables and cooking facilities around the edge of the room were replaced by eight mini-kitchens, each fully-equipped with a sink, cooker and modern appliances.

'We were allowed a maximum of three inches of bathwater. There were no showers and we had to wash our hair in a washing-up bowl. We had to make hospital corners on our beds and were only allowed two items on our chest of drawers, one of which had to be a sewing basket. The only T.V. programme we were allowed to watch was Top of the Pops, from 7-7.30pm, on a black and white portable set. The oldest girls sat nearest the front and the youngest on hard seats at the back. School uniform had to be laid over the back of the chair next to our beds. Slippers couldn't be worn downstairs.

Left to right: *Julia Llewellyn, Susannah Playle, Sophie Jones, Rachel Jones, Helena Clark, Ruth Price, Victoria Morgan, at the Hywelian lunch, July 2009.*

We did have some fun, though. We had midnight feasts but if we got caught, the punishment was a week's washing-up. We also made apple pie beds. Termly boarders were allowed to go into town on Saturday afternoon, after we had done homework in school in the morning, but we were not allowed to eat in the street. Girls from other years used to throw toilet rolls over the bath cubicles and then we tried to dry out the wet rolls in the drawers. Gossip in the tuck room was the highlight at the end of the day.'

Julia Llewellyn, Susannah Playle, Sophie Jones, Rachel Jones, Helena Clark, Ruth Price, Victoria Morgan (boarders 1980-5). Written July 2009.

Right: The old Laundry, c.1988.
Below: The Cookery School before modernisation, with Mrs Pamela Rayer.
Far right: The Cookery School after refurbishment.

Overleaf
Background image: Junior boarders cross the road after school, 1985.

Life as a Boarder

'I joined Howell's as an excited eleven year-old weekly boarder in September 1985, keen to experience the fun and adventures that I'd read about in Enid Blyton's boarding school stories. In reality, boarding life surpassed even those high expectations: I met and befriended a gang of wonderful girls with whom I shared the next seven years, working and playing hard, sharing intimacies and planning our futures.

With hindsight, the tough living conditions of the boarding house were a great initial unifier. The conditions of the houses were spartan: we had institutional metal beds, one shared washbasin in each dorm, two toilets and baths between thirty girls, cracks in the glass of the windows which we stuffed with tissue paper to keep out the draughts, peeling paintwork and cold wooden floors. Mrs Emerson, our housemistress, was very tall and very thin, never seen without her trademark stiletto heels, long red fingernails and a glowing cigarette. She barked commands at us, refused all phone calls from parents and relished her reputation as the Cruella de Vil of Oaklands. She clearly had a strong view, probably correctly, that teenage girls were an accident waiting to happen, and she favoured strict discipline over pastoral care.

The food was worse, with damp toast and grey sausages for breakfast, and whatever meat dish featured on the lunch menu that day was recycled into Hungarian goulash or curry dishes for our tea. The custard had a thick coating of cold skin on top, and during the apple season we were given baked windfalls most evenings complete with bruises and wriggling fauna. We survived with the help of rapidly depleting tuck boxes and by raiding bread from the kitchens, which we toasted on our tepid radiators at night.

Those were the trials of the early years; after the 1989 Children Act, when we were in the fourth form, the renovation works to the houses improved conditions considerably, and we were provided with multiple toilets and showers, rugs on the floor, a colour television, and even allowed posters on the walls and a pay phone on the landing, which we could use to ring home.

When I first started I shared a dorm with four other new first form girls, out of a boarding intake that year of thirteen. Our bedtime in Chestnut Dorm was 7.00pm, with lights out at 7.30pm, which left us with ample hours ahead for pillow fights, somersaults over the metal beds and the opportunity to dash across the landing from room to room to see our other friends without getting caught by 'Emmy'. Fortunately for us her high heels click clacking on the wooden floors usually gave enough notice of impending peril, although on one memorable occasion she changed into soft slippers and so did catch us dangling a care bear on a dressing-gown cord over the staircase, for which we had our tuck confiscated.

As less innocent fourth formers, we mastered the art of undetected night-time prowling and used to climb out of the sash windows at the top of the house, leap across a small but lethal gap and climb down the fire escape into the gardens at the back. We held séances, told ghost stories about the Blue Lady who haunted Oaklands and hosted magnificent midnight feasts.

A typical boarding day would start at 7am when 'Emmy' would march up and down the stairs of Oaklands ringing a loud handbell to wake us. By 7.45am we would be crossing the road heading for the dining hall and breakfast, often passing Miss Turner and her labrador Meg on their morning walk of the grounds. We joined our 'day bug' friends in our classrooms for the school day, and usually met up again as a gang at the end of lessons at 4.10pm. For the hour before tea we had great fun, occasionally torturing a musical instrument, sometimes scrumping apples from the gardens, usually playing lacrosse on School Field. The percentage of boarders in the school teams was always high, no doubt as a direct result of all the practising we fitted in after school . . .

By the start of the sixth form, and under the more relaxed eye of housemistress Miss Pierson, we were awarded considerably more responsibility, sharing double study bedrooms and managing our own free time, and we were finally allowed the privilege of walking up to Llandaff village after school. We were also allowed out in Cardiff on a Thursday and Friday night, as long as we were back by 11pm. We often met up with the 'day bugs' for a drink in The Philly. I have clear memories of running back along the never-ending Cathedral Road at about 10.50pm after an excellent evening's entertainment, and seeing the bus sail past us, convinced that we wouldn't make it in time.

Weekly boarding was fantastic, all the fun and independence of being away with friends during the week, but going home to family at the weekends. Without a doubt, it was a wonderful preparation for life at university and beyond, and the sense of fun and self-motivation it instilled in us has indisputably paid dividends throughout our careers and family lives. We worked, we played, we talked endlessly and we occasionally quarrelled, but usually we laughed and laughed, and for that I am forever grateful.'

Fifth formers Laura Lougher and Katy Webster in Bryntaf, 1989.

Katy Chantrey, née Webster (1985-92). Written October 2009.

Below: Cumberland Lodge, summer 1989.
Bottom: The Edwardian garden, Cumberland Lodge, summer 1989.
Below right: Hazelwood and Cumberland Lodge before the Hall and Octagon were added, summer 1989.

Below right, centre: The Lord Mayor, Councillor Beti Jones, lays the foundation stone for the new development as Mr Neville Sims, Chairman, Miss Turner and girls look on, 29th January 1990.
Bottom right: The Octagon under construction, summer 1990.

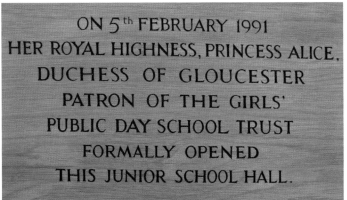

ON 5th FEBRUARY 1991
HER ROYAL HIGHNESS, PRINCESS ALICE,
DUCHESS OF GLOUCESTER
PATRON OF THE GIRLS'
PUBLIC DAY SCHOOL TRUST
FORMALLY OPENED
THIS JUNIOR SCHOOL HALL.

*Top left: Princess Alice opens
the new Junior School Hall,
5th February 1991.
Left: The plaque unveiled by
Princess Alice.
Below left: Princess Alice with her
Lady-in-Waiting and Mrs Elaine
Thomas, Head of the Junior School,
5th February 1991.
Above: Members of the Senior
Choir in the new Octagon, 1991.
Right: The new Junior School Hall
and Dining Room, 1991.*

In October that year, the builders moved in to construct a two-storey building between Hazelwood and Cumberland Lodge, which had proved successful as a music building. The new project involved the creation of a Junior School Hall on the ground floor and an orchestral and choir rehearsal studio upstairs. The new Hall incorporated facilities for dining, which obviated the need for the girls to use the Senior School cafeteria each day. Cumberland Lodge itself was completely refurbished; apart from the rehearsal room, which came to be known as the Octagon, it contained an Electronics Studio, a Control Room, a Computer Room and a wing of practice rooms. On 29th January 1990, the Deputy Chairman of the Governors, Councillor Beti Jones, who was Lord Mayor that year, laid the foundation stone and, on the same occasion, she declared open the newly renovated boarding houses.

The crowning event of this remarkable building programme was the opening of the new Junior School and Music School by HRH Princess Alice, Duchess of Gloucester, the Patron of the GPDST, on 5th February 1991. The visit had significant implications for security and protocol and the preparations were severely handicapped by two inches of snow the preceding two days, together with a major outbreak of flu and a gastric germ, resulting in the absence of almost half the pupils. Mrs Howard had retired in December 1990 and her successor, Mrs Elizabeth Phillips, had the task of organising a programme of entertainment in all the rooms in Cumberland Lodge. The occasion set the seal on Miss Turner's achievement in completely transforming the facilities of the school. Yet it was not only the buildings which changed during these thirteen years. Within the walls, the life of the school also altered significantly.

17

CURRICULAR DEVELOPMENTS AND THE EXPANSION OF ACTIVITIES, 1978-91

Facing page
The school c.1985.

Left: Julia Full, new entrant 1981.

Concurrently with the alterations to the premises, Miss Turner introduced major changes to the school's organisation, curriculum and activities. The appointment of men as full-time members of the teaching staff led to form mistresses being renamed form *tutors*, and from September 1984 the Senior School forms were labelled Years I to V. Initially from the Lower IV upwards the girls were still divided into three streams, known as H, S and L, but these were replaced in the mid-1980s by a top stream and two parallel streams. By 1991 the streaming had come to an end, girls being placed in sets for Mathematics only. The names of the houses, which had existed since the 1920s, also changed. The larger proportion of day girls to boarders led briefly to the creation of a new house, Kendall, for the former in 1980. Two years later, however, it was decided to divide the whole school into four large houses, which were given the surnames of the longest-serving former Headmistresses: Baldwin, Kendall, Trotter and Lewis.

Miss Turner at once arranged to have a guest of honour for Junior Prize-giving, a marked improvement on the previous practice of listening to a tape-recording of the speaker – sometimes accompanied by extraneous noises – at the senior occasion. The ceremonies, which included tea afterwards, were masterminded with military precision by Mrs Lloyd, who ensured that every word of the school song was known and clearly enunciated. For those girls who had just left from the Upper Sixth, Miss Turner organised a more informal evening early in the Autumn Term at which they received their certificates and prizes. New awards included the Enid Watkin Jones prize for French; the Jane Griffiths Mathematics prize; the Braddy Memorial Cup for achievement in the First Year, the Mollie Lane-Nott prize for Needlework, the T M Evans Prize for Physics; the Dean Williams prize, the Pembroke College Oxford prize; the Wynne Lloyd prize for Welsh and several music awards. On her retirement in December 1990, Mrs Howard donated a prize for a pupil going on to study Music.

Early in 1980 the school applied successfully to join the new Conservative Government's Assisted Places scheme, which effectively restored the former benefit of the Direct Grant by enabling able pupils, whose parents would not have been able to afford the fees, to attend. The Open Day that November saw twice the usual number of visitors. Howell's had a generous allocation of forty places for entry at eleven plus and five for the sixth form, and hundreds of girls benefited from the scheme. The academic level rose and the former wide social mix of pupils was restored. In 1982, the A Level pass rate was 94%, the best ever achieved, and Sally Broughton gained the highest mark awarded by the WJEC in Biology at A Level. In 1987 Sarah Charles was the top performer of 13,000 candidates in Nuffield Physics O Level (Midlands Examining Group). In Miss Turner's final year, a record eight girls gained places at Oxford and Cambridge and at GCSE 95.4% of the results were grades A to C, with fifteen girls gaining nine As. There were other successes, notably in GPDST competitions and the Evan Morgan Scholarship examinations for Aberystwyth. In 1986 Liane Saunders won a trip to Athens for an essay on international understanding; later, having gained a DPhil at Oxford, she went into the diplomatic service, and received the OBE in 2004.

To broaden the sixth formers' educational experience, there was a programme of minority studies once a week, which included at different times subjects such as Spanish, Italian, Russian, Astronomy and World Development. Another option was community service in schools, hospitals, conservation areas and riding stables for the disabled. Economics joined the list of A Level subjects. For younger pupils, a General Studies

Left: Kate Richards, Shalini Narayan and Elizabeth Hughes at the Summer Fair, 1984.
Below: Fifth formers with Mrs Nia Anthony and a younger girl, summer 1985. Left to right: Rebecca Hains, Bethan Jones, Sarah E Percy, Lucy Higginson, Helen Burrows, Sandra Harwood, Amanda Tucker.

Left: Miss M Seager in the Careers
Room, mid-1980s.
Above: Julia Haworth, Fay Roberts
and Satwinder Palia reached
the National Final of the BAYS
Mastermind Competition, 1986.

programme evolved, incorporating the cross-curricular themes of Economic Awareness, Health Education, Careers Education and Technological Awareness. For the first time, issues relating to pastoral care and guidance on general matters were considered in a weekly period designated as form time. The school had to adapt to major educational changes imposed by the government, including the introduction of GCSE courses in 1986, with the consequent demise of O Level, and optional Advanced Supplementary (AS) levels designed as two year courses in as much depth as full A Level subjects but with half the content. The 1988 Education Reform Act imposed the National Curriculum on maintained schools and departments' Schemes of Work were adapted to accommodate it, although they were not constrained by it. A new departure in the summer term of 1987, after examinations, was a Projects Week, during which the usual timetable was suspended to allow extended blocks of time for visits and other activities. This was a forerunner of the Challenges Week which evolved later.

The work of the new Careers department expanded steadily with the growth of the Careers Library, Careers Conventions, links with the South Glamorgan Careers Service, visiting speakers, work shadowing and mock university interviews. Spoken English, previously known as Private Diction, grew significantly. In Miss Turner's first year, a mere nine girls opted for lessons and were not examined. In 1989, more than a hundred girls sat examinations of the English Speaking Board and London Academy of Music and Dramatic Art examinations, with great success at all levels.

The school's first microcomputer, a Research Machines 380Z, arrived on 14th May 1982 and set in train the growth of the most significant piece of technology in the school's history. The number and the role of computers steadily increased so that by the time of Miss Turner's retirement, they were established as a vital tool. During the 1980s, the emphasis in teaching shifted from programming to familiarity with microcomputers and a City and Guilds course entitled *Basic Competence in Information Technology* was introduced in 1987. Fortunately a handsome surplus of income had accrued, partly as a result of a growth in pupil numbers but largely because of an increase in the Endowment Fund. The expansion of technology in various forms was a main feature of the academic year 1989-90. Information Technology appeared on the timetables of girls in the first, second and third years. The first GCSE course in Craft Design Technology (CDT) also began, having been taught since 1986 to younger pupils. The Home Economics GCSE course previously known as Cookery was renamed Food Technology in 1990.

The reduction in the amount of compulsory lunchtime games had two major effects. First, no longer could many teachers count on "free" lunchtimes, as supervisory duties were required. To some long-established staff, albeit excellent subject practitioners, this initially came as unwelcome development, but the majority soon recognised that changes were desirable. Second, there was now time during school hours for a variety of new clubs to emerge, some of which staff supervised, although a number were organised by sixth form girls for younger members of the school. These included Conservation, British Association of Young Scientists (BAYS), Computing and Crafts. The Senior Dramatic Society, established in 1981, was very active and in addition sixth formers directed at least three annual productions for younger girls. The driving force was Mrs Julie Williams, a Chemistry teacher, who during her time at school (1979-93) oversaw no fewer than twenty-two productions. The Urdd continued to flourish, with girls annually attending camps at Llangranog and Glan Llyn and gaining success in the National Eisteddfod Welsh Choral Speaking class on three occasions from 1988.

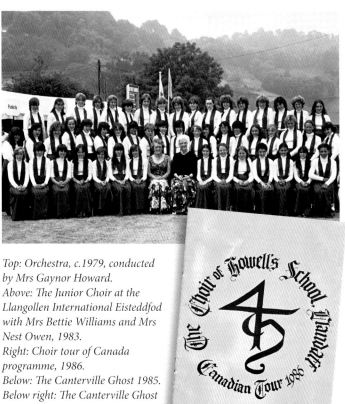

Top: Orchestra, c.1979, conducted by Mrs Gaynor Howard.
Above: The Junior Choir at the Llangollen International Eisteddfod with Mrs Bettie Williams and Mrs Nest Owen, 1983.
Right: Choir tour of Canada programme, 1986.
Below: The Canterville Ghost 1985.
Below right: The Canterville Ghost programme, 1985.

Musical activities increased, with increasing numbers of individual instrumental lessons each week given by peripatetic tutors. At Christmas 1978, the Senior Choir produced a record of carols. Five girls were founder members of the new South Glamorgan Youth Choir in 1979 and many were involved in South Glamorgan orchestral activities.

During the academic year 1980-1 the Senior Choir made its television début, singing three songs for the Welsh programme *Hamdden*, while the Junior Choir made the school's first musical appearance in London, singing at the Festival Hall in the Schools' Music Association's annual concert. Musicians of different ages returned from the Mid-Somerset Festival after a few years' absence with nothing less than first class certificates. At the international festival at Llangollen, in 1979 the Senior Choir was placed third in the Youth Choir section and in July 1983 it was invited to perform in the International Concert. Following a visit from a choir of the Fine Arts Core Education School of Montreal the previous year, in March 1986, the Senior Choir toured Canada and New York, performing at many venues.

May 1989 saw the first Thomas Howell Foundation Concert, with a performance given by the New Chamber Ensemble of Wales. In celebration of its fifth birthday in 1990, the Junior School commissioned *Baba Yaga*, a Russian fairy tale, composed by Mervyn Burtch, which was funded by the Welsh Arts Council. Five years previously, to celebrate the school's 125th anniversary, the Welsh Arts Council had funded two commissioned works. The first, an opera, *The Canterville Ghost*, also composed by Mervyn Burtch, was the school's contribution to British Opera in Retrospect, which was part of European Music Year. At a 125th Anniversary concert in Llandaff Cathedral a choral work, *Anthem for a Modern Generation, The Song of Courage* was performed, the music composed by David Nevens (whose wife Mary was the Junior School's first music specialist) and the words by a Hywelian, Elizabeth Heaven.

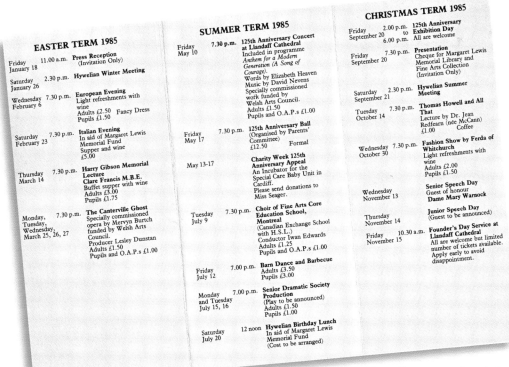

EASTER TERM 1985

Friday January 18, 11.00 a.m. **Press Reception** (Invitation Only)

Saturday January 26, 2.30 p.m. **Hywelian Winter Meeting**

Wednesday February 6, 7.30 p.m. **European Evening** Light refreshments with wine Adults £2.50 Fancy Dress Pupils £1.50

Saturday February 23, 7.30 p.m. **Italian Evening** In aid of Margaret Lewis Memorial Fund Supper and wine £5.00

Thursday March 14, 7.30 p.m. **Harry Gibson Memorial Lecture Clare Francis M.B.E.** Buffet supper with wine Adults £3.00 Pupils £1.75

Monday, Tuesday, Wednesday, March 25, 26, 27, 7.30 p.m. **The Canterville Ghost** Specially commissioned opera by Mervyn Burch funded by Welsh Arts Council. Producer Lesley Dunstan Adults £1.50 Pupils and O.A.P.s £1.00

SUMMER TERM 1985

Friday May 10, 7.30 p.m. **125th Anniversary Concert at Llandaff Cathedral** Included in programme *Anthem for a Modern Generation (A Song of Courage).* Words by Elizabeth Heaven Music by David Nevens Specially commissioned work funded by Welsh Arts Council. Adults £1.50 Pupils and O.A.P.s £1.00

Friday May 17, 7.30 p.m. **125th Anniversary Ball** (Organised by Parents' Committee) £12.50 Formal

May 13-17 **Charity Week 125th Anniversary Appeal** An Incubator for the Special Care Baby Unit in Cardiff. Please send donations to Miss Seager.

Tuesday July 9, 7.30 p.m. **Choir of Fine Arts Core Education School, Montreal** (Canadian Exchange School with H.S.L.) Conductor Iwan Edwards Adults £1.25 Pupils and O.A.P.s £1.00

Friday July 12, 7.00 p.m. **Barn Dance and Barbecue** Adults £3.50 Pupils £3.00

Monday and Tuesday July 15, 16, 7.00 p.m. **Senior Dramatic Society Production** (Play to be announced) Adults £1.50 Pupils £1.00

Saturday July 20, 12 noon **Hywelian Birthday Lunch** In aid of Margaret Lewis Memorial Fund (Cost to be arranged)

CHRISTMAS TERM 1985

Friday September 20, 2.00 p.m. to 6.00 p.m. **125th Anniversary Exhibition Day** All are welcome

Friday September 20, 7.30 p.m. **Presentation** Cheque for Margaret Lewis Memorial Library and Fine Arts Collection (Invitation Only)

Saturday September 21, 2.30 p.m. **Hywelian Summer Meeting**

Tuesday October 14, 7.30 p.m. **Thomas Howell and All That** Lecture by Dr. Jean Redfearn (née McCann) £1.00 Coffee

Wednesday October 30, 7.30 p.m. **Fashion Show by Ferda of Whitchurch** Light refreshments with wine Adults £2.00 Pupils £1.50

Wednesday November 13 **Senior Speech Day** Guest of honour **Dame Mary Warnock**

Thursday November 14 **Junior Speech Day** (Guest to be announced)

Friday November 15, 10.30 a.m. **Founder's Day Service at Llandaff Cathedral** All are welcome but limited number of tickets available. Apply early to avoid disappointment.

Above: Programme of events for the 125th anniversary.
Left: The Green on the day of the press reception and former Head Girls' visit, January 1985.
Bottom left: Former Head Girls with Cathryn McGahey, Head Girl 1984-5, third from left in the back row, January 1985.

Top right: Natalie Kondora and Rosalind Excell at the European Evening, February 1985.
Second right: Chemistry demonstration on Exhibition Day, September 1985.
Third right: Girls waiting for prize-giving outside the Cardiff Students' Union building, November 1985.
Right: Programme for service of Dedication and Thanksgiving, November 1985.

The 125th anniversary celebrations also included a visit of former Head Girls (on a January day of heavy snow), an Anniversary Ball organised by the Parents' Association, an Exhibition Day, a European Evening and a Founder's Day Service in Llandaff Cathedral. The School Council decided to bury a "time capsule" containing a collection of items representative of 1985, to be dug up in 2110 when the school is 250 years old. For prize-giving, the whole school was taken to the Great Hall of the Students' Union building in Park Place for a single occasion, at which the guest speaker was Dame Mary Warnock.

In the following year, 1986, designated Industry Year, everyone took part in an industrial visit. The Lower Sixth established three Young Enterprise activities, heralding a scheme which endured well into the twenty-first century. The links with industry expanded during the next few years, with a number of work placements and, in Miss Turner's final year, the first European Work Experience in France for sixth form girls.

Outdoor pursuits holiday in Snowdonia, August 1985.

Facing page
Top: *Junior School girls' Victorian Day at St Fagans, 1987.*
Centre: *Visit of the Lady Mayoress of London, Lady Rowe-Ham, to Hazelwood, March 1987. Girls (left to right): Rebecca Roberts, Jenny Bell, Jane Baker, Sarah Bibby.*
Bottom: *Junior School girls plant a commemorative tree in Bute Park arboretum, c.1990.*

Sports teams continued to enjoy success, notably at GPDST rallies. From 1979 some sixth formers spent sessions at the National Sports Centre, participating in activities such as archery and squash. Swimmers gained many awards and were successful at the Welsh championships. Girls represented Wales in sports as diverse as judo, lacrosse and sailing. In the 1980s groups spent weekends canoeing on the River Wye and enjoyed outdoor pursuits holidays in Snowdonia.

A new venture, beginning in the spring of 1981, was an annual visit by a large group of Lower IV girls to Normandy, where they stayed in a château, experiencing French culture and practising the language. Following the appointment of Miss Anne Eddy as Head of German in 1985, an exchange involving girls in the first year of their GCSE German course was established with the Couven Gymnasium in Aachen, which was repeated for many years. There were other study trips overseas to places as diverse as the Soviet Union, Crete, Italy and the Baltic.

Charitable activities abounded, though Dorcas activities came to an end in the mid 1980s. An annual Harvest Festival was instituted in 1978. For the 125th anniversary there was a particular appeal for the Special Care Baby Unit at the Heath Hospital. The Lower VI regularly raised substantial sums for Christian Aid Week in a variety of ingenious ways. Their first May Ball, held in City Hall in 1988, produced over £1,000. Much further afield, through the organisation *Dolen Cymru* and the efforts of Miss Margaret Seager, the school formed a link with St Catherine's Girls' School in Lesotho, southern Africa. The connection with this country was to be developed in the future.

Howell's benefited enormously from the generosity of Harry Gibson who had been Managing Director at the Frazer Ship Chandlery in Bute Street, and whose daughter Susan (Mrs Reardon Smith) had attended the school. As Senior Trustee of The Frazer Trust, Harry Gibson made donations to many causes. It was he who had instigated the Frazer Scholarships in the mid 1970s. After his death in 1981 the Trustees donated a sum of £2,000 to be invested in order to finance an annual Harry Gibson Memorial Lecture and Literary Competition, the first occasion being a poetry reading by Philip Madoc in February 1983.

From the time the Junior School was established, it had an active Parents' Committee, and a number of traditions were quickly established – for Hallowe'en, Harvest, Christmas and St David's Day. Girls in the Lower VI provided assistance and parents accompanied educational visits, which featured prominently from the early days. Clubs were soon begun for activities including swimming, patchwork, gymnastics and computing. In 1985 its orchestra gave its first performances and girls went on residential trips to London and to the Urdd camp at Llangranog.

A full-scale inspection by the Welsh Inspectorate in March 1987 resulted in a glowing report. The concluding sentence read,

"*Strong leadership and a committed staff play an important part in maintaining a school where academic goals and broader aspirations are well combined in a lively community where courtesy and mutual respect prevail.*" The inspectors recommended that posts of responsibility immediately below those of Deputy Headmistress should be created, and the incentive allowances enabled Miss Turner to create three Heads of Section in the Senior School in 1988: for Years I to III, IV and V, and the sixth form.

These years saw the retirement of some loyal staff and Governors. The family connections of most of these with the school are striking. After twenty-five years of full-time teaching, Miss Bates, former pupil and one of Wales' most distinguished sportswomen, left in 1982, having added to her Queen's Jubilee medal of 1977 a Medal of Honour for services to lacrosse from the Sports Council of Wales, which she had played a key role in establishing. In her younger days she had represented Wales in lacrosse, tennis (and also played in both singles and doubles matches at Wimbledon), table-tennis and squash, declining the invitation to play hockey at international level through lack of time. Her three sisters were also Hywelians. One, Margaret (Mrs Taylor), had been the school housekeeper and another, Betty (Mrs Noel), had helped with games.

The Hywelian Mrs Rowland Williams (Beulah Blake), whose daughter Jill was also a former pupil, retired in 1982 after teaching Biology full-time for twenty years. The next year saw the departure of Mrs Lloyd, the Deputy Headmistress, whose association with the school went back to 1946. Renowned as a strict disciplinarian, she had promoted A Level Mathematics and a strong Welsh ethos, had organised numerous public occasions and her daughter Elinor had also attended Howell's. Her successor was the highly efficient Miss Glynis Owen. The Physics mistress and, latterly, the Head of Science, Mrs Evans, left in 1984 after thirty-five years' continuous service, during which she had introduced the Nuffield Physics course and had been in charge of School Fund, playing a key role in school fund-raising and meticulously keeping the accounts.

Above: Miss Glynis Owen, Deputy Headmistress 1983-1992.

Miss Bowen, Head of the History department, retired in 1986. Known affectionately as "Dotty", she had first set foot inside the door as a pupil in 1940. A staunch Hywelian, in September 1987 she was elected as Vice-President of the Guild. She had acted as the School Liaison Officer for the Hywelian magazine for about twenty years, and for several years she had been its editor. Christmas 1990 saw the departure of Mrs Howard, Director of Music since 1970, whose daughter Eleanor had also been a pupil. Under her leadership, musical activities had multiplied. The majority of girls had become involved in learning an instrument and the subject had become one of the mainstream public examination courses.

Mrs Anne Williams retired as Secretary and Clerk to the Governors at the end of September 1980 after nearly twenty years. The Hywelian and last Factor, Mrs Elizabeth Jones, who left in 1983, had been responsible for the maintenance and decoration of the school and the boarding houses for the previous sixteen years. The retirement of Mr Phillips as Chairman of the Governors in 1981, after eighteen years, brought to an end a very long family connection with the school. One of his mother's cousins had been an orphan boarder in the early days of Miss Kendall. His sister Nest had been Head Girl under Miss Trotter and Mr Phillips had even taken part in Hywelian Dramatic Society productions. His father, John, became a Governor as a nominee of the Drapers' Company in the 1920s and served until 1953. Mr Phillips' daughter Jane also attended Howell's, as did Heather and Caroline, the two daughters of his successor, Mr Neville Sims. Mr Sims had become a Governor in June 1978 and his wife, Jennifer Warwick, was also an old girl.

The longest-serving Governor, Mrs Dorothy Wickett, the first Hywelian Guild representative, retired in June 1987 after thirty-eight years. As Dorothy Clarke, she had started at school with Nest Phillips in 1920, at the same time as Miss Trotter, and since leaving she had made an enormous contribution to both the Hywelian Guild and the Governing Body. Her family's connections with

'I joined the Hywelian Guild as a Life Member upon leaving School in 1928. I became its treasurer from 1936-9 at quite a young age and then secretary from 1939-51, taking over from Bronwen Thomas, mainly because no-one else would take it on! We worked very hard over those years to raise funds for the swimming pool, which was a memorial to Miss Kendall. This was achieved eventually, with the Hywelians paying for the building and the Governors paying for the roof. Garden parties were held every summer, I remember, among other events. I was the first Hywelian to be appointed as their representative to the Board of Governors in 1949. When I eventually retired as Secretary in 1951, I was asked to join the Board in my own right. I was delighted to be able to continue to be involved and remained a Governor for very many years, even after moving to Cornwall, retiring in June 1987. From 1951-54, I was also Vice-President of the Guild.'

Dorothy Wickett, née Clarke (1920-8). Interviewed August 2009, aged 98.

Above left: Hywelian Committee on the 80th anniversary of the Guild, 1986. Back row, left to right: Judith Mackie (Mrs Williams), Susan Orchard (Mrs Thomas), Shelagh Pontin (Mrs Hughes), Barbara Vernon (Mrs Phillips). Middle row: Dorothy Bowen, Carol Rees (Mrs Southwell), Veronica Davies (Mrs Smith), Bettie Evans, Margaret Auckland (Mrs Maton), Adrienne Timothy, Elizabeth Pipe (Mrs Lewis), Betty Jeanes (Mrs

Dixon) Mary Foxall (Mrs Watkins) Catherine Raymond (Mrs Clarke). Front row: Eryl Howe (Mrs Hicks), Heather Kelly (Mrs Robertson), Barbara Mealing (Mrs Forte), Jessie Davies, Mrs Dilys Lloyd, Miss J P Turner, Helen Griffiths (Mrs Richards), Susan Childs (Mrs Greening), Deborah Buss (Mrs Ward), Rosemary Gregory-Jones. Left: Junior School girls say goodbye to Miss Turner, July 1991. Above: Form 1Z, July 1989.

Howell's were also extensive. Her two sisters, Joan and Isabel, her daughter Christine, daughter-in-law Siân (née Williams) and her sister-in-law Lorna Clarke (née Williams) were also pupils, as were her great-nieces, Alice and Sally Clarke. Her sister-in-law Christabel Wagstaffe (née Wickett), a professional artist, had been Housemistress in Bryntaf in the 1960s and early 1970s and responsible for all the school flower arrangements.

The Hywelian Guild continued to flourish. In the summer of 1980 it initiated the practice of *Generation Calls*, with the aim of particularly attracting to meetings those who had left during a particular period. It also organised a wine and cheese party for sixth form leavers and their parents, to introduce them to the Guild. By 1990 it had some 3,000 members. At the beginning of that year, Jessie Davies, who was also a school Governor, retired as its Secretary; she had been a committee member since 1938 and had also served as Treasurer.

Miss Turner's energy seemed to know no limits; thus her announcement that she intended to retire in the summer of 1991 was greeted with some incredulity. As a result of the interviews at Trust headquarters on 21st November 1990, Mrs Jane Fitz was appointed as Howell's eighth Headmistress. The final major musical event of Miss Turner's headship, the 120th anniversary concert of

the GPDST, took place at the Royal Festival Hall on 19th March 1991. About thirty girls represented the school and Sara Trickey, a remarkably talented violinist, aged just fifteen, was chosen as the leader of the Trust orchestra. That year also saw the inaugural concert in the new Octagon in Cumberland Lodge.

Miss Turner retired to her cottage in the Brecon Beacons. It would be no exaggeration to say that the school had undergone a revolution under her leadership. By the time she left, it was at the forefront of educational practices, with enviable facilities. Teaching and learning resources, extracurricular activities, opportunities for community involvement: all these and others increased enormously. The girls had been given more opportunities to develop qualities of self-reliance, leadership and independence. Archaic rules and the practice of holding detentions on Saturday mornings had been abolished, though some traditional practices, such as Dorcas, the wearing of hats and separate indoor and outdoor shoes, holding Prayers outside during the summer examinations and a separate Jewish Prayers had been retained. The involvement with the GPDST had brought many benefits for staff and pupils. Miss Turner had also served as President of the Hywelian Guild and Chairman of the Bronwen Jacques Fund. Soon after her departure, the school was delighted to receive a donation for an annual musical event, reflecting her own love of music.

'Miss Turner was a formidable character: an old-school Headmistress, dressed in practical tweeds and brogues, she held high expectations of hard work and impeccable behaviour. Her deputy, Miss Owen, super-organised and with an occasional twinkle in her eye, was probably even more fearsome; and between them they ran the school throughout the late 1980s with military efficiency and strict discipline.

Howell's resembled a traditional grammar school, with a highly competitive entrance exam at eleven and the streaming of year groups. There were ninety girls in my year, split into classes of 30. All teachers expected our full commitment; woe betide any girl who produced shoddy work. My messy primary school handwriting was soon given an overhaul and I learnt to study quickly and efficiently. And boy, did we work hard! The school exams, taken twice a year by each class, were, as the school's official results proved, an excellent preparation for the formal GCSE and A Levels, and honed our exam technique at a tender age. I recall us huddled over our desks that first December in Hampden, hoping desperately that when the results came out, our names wouldn't be too far down the list. To my knowledge, no one ever received 100% in those school exam papers and marks in the 90s were rare; in comparison, sitting the GCSEs seemed much less stressful.

I was lucky enough to have some of the oldest and quirkiest form rooms, with access up twisting staircases, nooks and crannies for hiding, and views across the school grounds. In the older classrooms we sat at aged wooden desks with hinged lids and long-abandoned inkwells. For first years, the science labs were very exciting, with high stools, Bunsen burner gas taps, glass boxes of stick insects and the prospect of dissecting a yellowed rat in a bag. The spotless white science overalls, which drowned us when we first arrived, became more and more colourful with friends' autographs and cartoon characters as we progressed up the school and finally grew into them.

There were some real characters on the teaching staff: Mrs Maylin, Head of English, terrified us all into submission, scolding us for the inappropriate use of the subjunctive or a misused semi-colon, and tormenting us with endless recitations of *The Rime of the Ancient Mariner*. Miss Withey, a Maths teacher, was equally old-school; a stickler for cleanly scrubbed faces and immaculate dress, she would call regular uniform inspections to ensure that our grey woollen socks were pulled up to the knees and our faces devoid of make-up. Mr Belton, the Physics teacher, used to roar like a lion and throw wooden board rubbers at fidgety pupils; and 'Diddy Williams', who taught Chemistry and took Drama, could spot the illicit chewing of gum at two hundred metres, and petrified all those who crossed her, despite her diminutive size.

Physical exercise played a large part in the life of the school, with weekly lessons in lacrosse, hockey, netball, swimming, gym and dance, as well as lunchtime and after school clubs and team training sessions. Happily for me, I loved sport and didn't mind getting soaked and mud-splattered, but for others the relentless changing for games in 'the cages' and the competitiveness on the Sports Field must have been purgatory. In the Games section of her end of year report, one friend memorably received the comment, 'She tries to the best of her ability: D minus', to her initial mortification, but subsequent amusement. The games kit was a striking maroon, with short skirt, loathed gym 'bags', socks and tracksuit, and a white aertex shirt, which had to be embroidered in maroon thread

The victorious Under 15 Lacrosse team, 1989.

with the full name of each girl across the chest. The older the games kit, the better, so we ransacked the annual second-hand clothing sale for the most faded tracksuits and tried to look as dishevelled as possible. Lacrosse was the main sport and the teams, under the tutelage of Head of PE Mrs Hartley and Welsh international Mrs Parker, flourished. Our U15 Colts team were unbeaten throughout the winter season, winning shields at tournaments across the South and South West at Monmouth, Badminton and the annual GPDST Rally in London.

Music, particularly singing, was also taken seriously, and the words to the interminable school song *Land of our Birth* will be forever etched into our memories. We enjoyed singing a series of favourite hymns every morning at assembly and performing at the end of term Christmas Service in the Cathedral.

Whilst rules and discipline were tight in the lower half of the school, by the time we reached the sixth form we were awarded considerable leniency and even given responsibilities over the younger girls. We could put aside the grey tunics and candy striped shirts to wear our own clothes, and for the most part swapped one uniform for another one, of denim. Lessons were relaxed, and I recall trying *escargots* and listening to Jacques Brel songs with Miss Beattie, playing Trivial Pursuit in German with Frau Davies-Schöneck, and watching the fall of the Berlin Wall on television with Miss Eddy. When not in lessons, we spent our time on the sofas in the Sixth Form Centre, drinking coffee, eating biscuits and endlessly chatting, good preparation for the next stage of our life as university students...

I had seven wonderful years at school, made countless good friends and learnt an enormous amount. Miss Turner's down to earth attitude and focus on discipline ensured that we went out into the world with a thorough academic grounding, a strong work ethic, self-confidence and a respect for others, which has no doubt stood us in good stead. I am grateful for an exceptional education, fun and fantastic memories.'

Katy Chantrey, née Webster (1985-92). Written October 2009.

Distinguished Visitors
Left: Lady Rowe-Ham, Lady Mayoress of London, her Lady-in-Waiting and the Lady Mayoress of Cardiff visit a Welsh class, 1987. Mr Neville Sims, Chairman of the Governors is on the right.
Right: George Thomas, Viscount Tonypandy, former Speaker of the House of Commons, at the Junior School to receive a cheque for the National Children's Homes, November 1990.
Below right: Visit of Peter Walker MP, the Secretary of State for Wales, November 1990.

18

MRS FITZ AND FURTHER MODERNISATION, 1991-2007

Facing page
Mrs Jane Fitz, 1991-2007.

Above: The Upper Sixth, 1991-2.
The Head Girl, Anna Bicarregui, is
fifth from left in the front row.

The eighth Headmistress of Howell's School differed from her predecessors in some notable respects. Cheryl Jane Fitz was the first not to have been born and bred in Britain; she came from Tasmania, where she gained a degree in Biological Sciences and taught in Hobart. By the time she was appointed to the headship of Howell's, at the age of forty-four, she was very familiar with the workings of the GPDST, having been employed in three of its schools since moving to London. She became Head of the Chemistry Department at Bromley and then taught at South Hampstead, gaining another degree, in Chemistry with First Class Honours, through studying at Birkbeck College while teaching. After holding several positions of responsibility, including that of Second Mistress, at South Hampstead, she was appointed to the headship of Notting Hill and Ealing High School in 1983. Mrs Fitz also had the distinction of being Howell's first married Headmistress, a reflection of the fact that by the late twentieth century it was recognised that such women were capable of holding highly responsible positions in the workplace. Moreover she had a daughter, Emily. Not surprisingly, unlike her predecessors, she did not live in school, which enabled rooms on the first floor of the east wing to be opened up to provide teaching and office accommodation.

Like Miss Turner, Mrs Fitz was determined that Howell's should be a school at the forefront of educational practices and facilities. She also took over at a time when, nationally, educational practices were being subjected to great scrutiny by the Government and also, increasingly, by parents. The former involved itself in education through frequent new edicts concerning the curriculum and the way schools were run, including extensive Health and Safety legislation. The formalisation of procedures was essential in the business-orientated environment of the time. The consumer culture led to many fee-paying parents having high expectations, a determination that they should receive value for money and a preparedness to question aspects of school practices. As independent education became more and more competitive, their views could not be ignored. Neither could the controversial league tables, which were published from 1993. Government legislation and trends in society therefore had a considerable impact on the running of the school.

As in all institutions at this time, there was consequently an increasing amount of bureaucracy, with staff and departmental handbooks, Action Plans, Strategic Development Plans, monitoring, staff appraisals and regular departmental and section meetings. Policy documents on every aspect of school administration were written, and management issues featured prominently. A new post of School Administrator, the first in the GPDST, was created early in 1993, to which Mrs Fitz's secretary and Domestic Bursar, Mrs Diane Reilly, was appointed. As the Trust's first Health and Safety Officer, she created the policy which was subsequently adopted by other member schools. There were

also more formal procedures for the letting of school facilities, for which there was an increasing demand. It was largely as a result of the efforts of Miss Jean Ballinger, who became the Deputy School Administrator, that the school was opened up for public use; not only did she make all the arrangements but she also made herself available at all weekend functions, including Hywelian reunions. One of Mrs Fitz's early measures was to amalgamate the two Parents' Committees and establish a new one with a constitution. The goodwill of parents enabled a Careers Sub-committee and

Top: Staff group outside the Staff Study, 1993.
Above: Prefects' Christmas party, 1991.
Left: The last Howell's boarders, September 1993.

Facing page
Top: New Senior School uniform, 1994.
Below: Mrs Marissa Davis with Juniors wearing new uniform, 2003.

a Social and Fund-raising Committee to come into being, and groups of parents operated a monthly second-hand uniform shop. A newsletter for parents was introduced, which was named *The Golden Ducat* from the Autumn Term of 1993. In the competitive environment of the time, marketing became a more important thrust of the school's concerns, with more eye-catching brochures, a house style and Open Days seen as a major opportunity to display its strengths. The first Sixth Form Fair was held in the autumn of 1991 and ten years later a part-time Marketing Officer was appointed. When Mrs Reilly (by then called Mrs Cox) retired at Christmas 2000 she was succeeded by Mr Stuart Williams, who was later termed the School Business Manager. He was a member of the Senior Management Team, which also included Mrs Fitz, the Deputy Headmistress, the Head of the Junior School and two Senior Teachers.

Alongside these administrative developments, other aspects of school life were undergoing considerable change. At the beginning of Mrs Fitz's second year several key events took place, including the arrival of Mrs Sally Davis as Deputy Headmistress, Miss Owen having left in the summer. September 1992 also saw the admission to the Junior School of the first pupils aged four and five, including Emily Fitz. By September 1993 there was a Reception class for four-year-olds as well as separate classes for girls aged five and six. The forms were re-named according to the terminology of the National Curriculum so that, after the Reception class, girls entered Year 1 of the Junior School and the Senior School ended with Year 13, although the use of the term *sixth form* persisted. This expansion in the Junior School necessitated new furnishings on the ground floor of Cumberland Lodge, where rooms were used to accommodate them. Another change that term was that the three separate prize-givings were replaced by a single evening event, concentrating largely on the achievements of the Year 13 leavers. Until 1997 this was held in the Assembly Room of City Hall. The school song was abolished, on the grounds that Kipling's words extolling the virtues of loyalty to the British Empire were no longer appropriate, but the occasion remained formal, with staff continuing to wear academic dress. The role of the prefects also soon changed. No longer did they patrol the corridors at break and lunchtime. Their new tasks initially included organising the Eisteddfod and a Christmas party for the Year 7 girls. Later they were all assigned specific responsibilities as well as undertaking more general duties.

Perhaps the most momentous change announced at the beginning of Mrs Fitz's second year was the decision to bring boarding to an end. Despite the upgrading of the facilities and extensive publicity, the number of boarders had continued to decline, in line with a national trend; there were fewer than fifty in the early 1990s, so they constituted a small minority. A Working Party recommended in May 1992 that the last boarders should be admitted in

September of that year, with boarding ceasing in July 1994. A sub-committee of Governors recommended converting the boarding houses for use by the sixth form. Bryntaf was adapted as a base for the girls in Year 13 from September 1993, with the Billiard Room initially becoming a Common Room and the Oak Room equipped with individual study carrels. The remaining boarders, together with the housemistresses, Mrs Ruth Emerson and Miss Ros Pierson, were accommodated in Oaklands for their last year. Those who wished to remain at Howell's either travelled from home or lodged with family friends.

Attention to individual needs was given a high priority. In response to changing patterns of family life, from the Autumn Term of 1993 a system of After School Care was set up, and later Before School Care was also provided. The recognition of dyslexia and the number of foreign students for whom English was not the first language led to greater attention being paid to Special Educational Needs by the end of the century. A member of staff (the Special Educational Needs Coordinator or SENCO) was designated to coordinate the arrangements. In 1998, for the first time, fifty-two girls in the sixth form were trained in Peer-led Drugs Education and as counsellors for *Childline*, in partnership with *Youthlink Wales*.

The abolition of hats as an item of uniform came as a relief to both pupils and staff, who were aware that the girls removed them as soon as they were out of eyesight. In September 1994 the Senior School uniform, virtually unchanged since 1960, was replaced by a plain navy kilt and a navy jumper with the Thomas Howell logo in Welsh red. The new shoes were black, and worn with navy short socks or tights. The blazer and the red and white blouse were unchanged except that the latter could now be worn with long sleeves. In 2005 it was replaced by a blue blouse, at the girls' request. Meanwhile, in 2003 the Junior School acquired a distinctive uniform with a new Welsh tartan; the younger girls wore a pinafore with a light blue shirt, while the older girls could wear a blouse and tartan skirt.

'I started at Howell's in the year that Mrs Fitz became Headmistress and we were baptised into Miss Turner's era in terms of traditions and dress. We wore all the old uniform, which had been unchanged for years – grey tunics, grey jumper and socks pulled up to the knee, brown shoes, red and white striped blouses, blue macs and blazers, boaters and winter hats. These varied colours bore absolutely no resemblance to the games uniform – maroon gym skirts, gym knickers with "go-faster stripes", Dunlop green flash and Aertex blouses with our names embroidered on the front. Nobody had a blue hat that hadn't been squashed entirely out of shape by the second week of term as they were consigned to the bottoms of lockers, only seeing daylight when we were forced to wear them to the Carol Service.

Thankfully we shortly dropped the hats, exchanged the grey socks for black tights and eventually dropped the grey altogether and switched to a much more sensible navy blue. Whilst the new uniform made so much better sense aesthetically, I did feel a tinge of sadness as the old one gradually disappeared.

The new uniform was symbolic of the other changes that occurred. When I joined, we had stone in the Stone Hall, flip-top desks with ink-wells, iron cages for "lockers" at the foot of the stairs near Hampden, a fully functioning tuck shop selling junk (not health) food, compulsory games at lunchtime, and a finish time of 4:10pm. Science was taught as three separate subjects, we had a lesson called Religious Education, and a Senior Dramatic Society (boasting some very fine talent) was in place. When I left, all of these things had disappeared.'

Eira Smith, née Jones (1991-1998, Head Girl 1997-8). Written November 2009.

By 1993 the number of girls on Assisted Places had been reduced to twenty-eight a year, but even so, a third still received financial support. Concern about the likely end of the scheme prompted the

Above: Girls ready for the GPDST's 125th anniversary concert at the Royal Albert Hall, 1997.

GPDST to set up the Minerva Fund in 1994 in the hope of raising a large sum for investment, the income from which would provide bursaries for deserving pupils. The Trust's 125th anniversary concert in the Royal Albert Hall in March 1997, the year the scheme came to an end, raised £50,000, and at Howell's, the launch of the Minerva Campaign in the Autumn Term that year was marked by several appeal meetings. Thanks to the Thomas Howell and Minerva Bursary Funds, over sixty girls had bursaries in Year 7-9 in September 2001. Although the Minerva Campaign did not produce as much revenue as had been hoped, on the positive side, a Minerva Network of former and sixth form pupils in Trust schools developed, which provided careers advice, a work experience directory and extensive networking opportunities. Sixth formers also benefited from Minerva seminars on "life skills" topics.

The long-standing tradition of academic distinction continued. Early in Mrs Fitz's first year the Science Department, under the leadership of Mrs Angela Jackson, was the first in South Wales to win an award for excellence from the British Association for the Advancement of Science. Howell's scored highly in the league tables and was regularly recognised as Wales' leading independent school. From September 1994 Year 7 girls took Cognitive Ability Tests on entry to the Senior School in order to assess the value added academically by the time they took their GCSE examinations, which

Above: Staff, 1998.
Left: Girls celebrate A Level results, 1999. Left to right: Priyanka Nayan, Rebecca Shellard, Isabelle de Montét Guerin, Julia Kim, Elizabeth Brennan.
Below left: Successful Oxbridge candidates, 2000. Left to right, back row: Claire Dancer (Natural Sciences), Rosie Bolton (Geography), Mathilda Davidson (English), Hannah Robinson (Medicine). Front row: Angharad Ferris (Classics), Helen Brinson (Physics), Lucy Wilkins (History), Rachel Borysiewicz (Mathematics), Helen Tarbet (Classics).
Bottom left: 140th year birthday cake. The youngest infant, Tess Chandler, is with the Head Girl, Dionne Antrobus.

was subsequently shown to be considerable. In 1997, 41.8% of the GCSE results were grade A* (the new top grade introduced in 1994), a percentage bettered by only six schools in England and Wales. The 21st century, and the school's 140th anniversary, began on a high note, with the news of nine successful Oxbridge candidates. The new Curriculum 2000 introduced an A Level examination in two parts, the AS (Advanced Subsidiary) in the first year followed by A2 in Year 13. The vast majority of girls embarked on four subjects at AS Level, leaving less time in school for private study. In 2004, when the last girls on Assisted Places left, the school celebrated the best A Level results so far, with 64 % of all results at grade A, 87% A or B and more than a third of the year group gaining three or more grade A passes.

There were also notable individual successes, with girls gaining national awards for achieving the highest public examination results in several A level and GCSE subjects. Two Upper VI girls, Elisabeth Slater and Nejra Ćehić, won the Trust's prestigious Frederica Lord Scholarship to spend time studying at the College of William and Mary in Virginia, thanks to the generosity of Mr Christopher Fildes, a member of the Council of the Trust and its representative on the school's Governing Body, who endowed it in memory of his wife. Other leavers gained Trust Scholarships for travel and university study. In 2005, Imperial College awarded Khushboo Sinha, the Head Girl, an Academic Scholarship for six years to study Medicine, and Angharad Thomas qualified for the British Mathematical Olympiad.

Mrs Fitz's era saw major curriculum innovations. One subject which changed its character considerably was Religious Education, renamed Religious Studies under Mrs Susan Evans, who was Head of Department from 1992 to 2007. The syllabus was broadened to include studies of the world's major religions, in part reflecting the increasing ethnic mix in school and in British society, and Ethics formed a component of the A Level course. At GCSE all girls took the Double Science Award from 1993 until 2006, after which they took Biology, Chemistry and Physics as separate sciences. Information and Communication Technology (ICT), Drama and Design Technology (DT) were introduced for all in the Senior School and as options at GCSE and A Level, while Food Technology disappeared. Towards the end of Mrs Fitz's headship, in 2006, the Cookery School was converted into an extra DT workshop. At A Level, Business Studies replaced Economics in 1997, and Critical Thinking (at AS Level) and Government and Politics were additional options by 2007. From 1993 to 2000, all sixth formers followed a popular skills-based course, known as the Diploma of Achievement, to complement their A Level studies, Howell's being the first Welsh school to run it. Everyone became computer literate and an increasing amount of schoolwork began to be word-processed. Girls undertook module tests for the European Computer Driving Licence qualification and a number of the teaching staff followed the same course.

Careers Education and Guidance continued to expand. The school's enrolment in the Independent Schools' Careers Organisation (ISCO) brought many benefits, including the services of the organisation's staff and access to careers courses. From 1997, all girls in Year 11 took ISCO's Morrisby test, which gave an indication of aptitudes, with guidance on suitable A Level courses and possible careers. There were industrial visits, biennial Careers Conventions and seminars, Careers Question Times from 2004, *Take Your Daughter to Work* days, work experience weeks after GCSE, university mock interviews and work shadowing. In 1997, the Careers Sub-committee was renamed the Careers Development Committee, with the aim of forging more links with business and industry. That November, the new well-stocked Careers Library was officially opened in the room colloquially known as the Horsebox. In 2006, Howell's became the only Welsh independent school to gain the *Careers Wales* Quality Award, which was presented to Mrs Elizabeth Pexton, the Careers Coordinator from 1996, by Welsh Assembly Minister Jane Davidson.

A resounding endorsement of the school's practices and standards came in 2000. A major inspection by the Independent Schools' Inspectorate from 27th to 31st March resulted in a glowing report. The summary stated: *Howell's School is a very good school. Firm and decisive leadership provides the school with clear educational direction. . . . Standards of achievement are consistently high with strong performance in relation to girls' ages and capabilities in both* the Junior and Senior Schools. *Pupils work hard, they are strongly motivated to do well. . . . They gain considerable benefit from the high quality of the teaching. Systems of welfare and support respond to pupils' individual needs. Behaviour and attitudes are excellent. Teaching and learning are supported well by effective resources and facilities, and by the support and administration staff.* In their oral feedback the inspectors made the comment that the Junior School was "a place where childhood is celebrated", a fitting tribute to the leadership of Mrs Marissa Davis. The new Welsh Inspectorate, Estyn, subsequently conducted successful one-day inspections in the Summer Term of 2001 and in February 2004.

Top: *Design Technology workshop, 2005.*
Above: *Careers Convention, 2003.*
Left: *Careers Library, 2005.*
Left to right: *Helena Asprou, Olivia Webb, Hannah Marriott.*

Unusual distractions occasionally added interest to the normal business of the school day. Twice the fire brigade was called to Oaklands, once to deal with an exploding skip and once to douse smouldering rafters in a garage after a squirrel chewed through the wires. It was also summoned to the Junior School and, on the last day of term in 1999, its services were required to free a sixth former whose fingers were trapped in a chair. Earlier that year, police ran through the grounds as helicopters whirred overhead, in pursuit of two wanted men, and the whole school lined Cardiff Road to see the Queen and the Duke of Edinburgh pass by after opening the Welsh National Assembly.

Alongside all the curriculum changes, improvements to the facilities continued almost uninterrupted. On the departure of the boarders, Year 12 girls moved into Oaklands after it had been suitably equipped. The staff then moved from the old Study, where their predecessors had been since 1906, and the adjoining Common Room, to the much more spacious area on the first floor vacated by the sixth formers. With so many lessons taught in Bryntaf and Oaklands, there was space available in the main school for a large Drama area (in the former BDR, which had been divided to create two classrooms), another IT room and a Laboratory in the room known as A1.

The Chemistry Laboratories were completely refurbished during the summer of 1992 and during the next academic year the area under the Hall became a base for relaxation for Years 10 and 11. Over the years every room and corridor was carpeted. Young trees were planted outside Cumberland Lodge in memory of Miss Hilda Taylor, the former Second Mistress. In 1994 two large oak Honours Boards were provided, thanks to the generosity of The Friends of the GPDST and the Hywelian Guild, to record the names of the Head Girls and the Drapers' Leaving Scholarship winners respectively. The swimming pool was refurbished in the summer of 1994 and a display marked its official re-opening in May 1995.

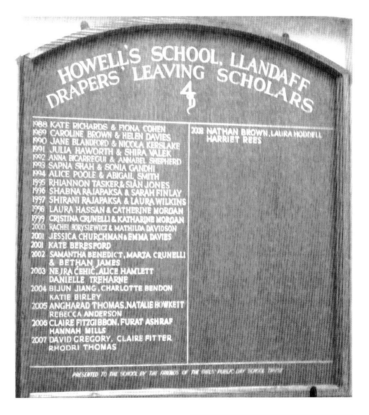

Top left: The Queen and Duke of Edinburgh pass school after the Welsh National Assembly opening ceremony, 26th May 1999.
Top right: Hannah O'Connell and a hair-raising experiment, 1992.
Above: Drapers' Leaving Scholars Honours Board
Right: Mr Neville Sims and Mr Bryn Williams, Director of the Welsh Swimming Association, at the Opening Ceremony for the refurbished swimming pool, 1995.

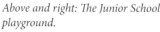

Top left: The Nursery playground on The Green, adjacent to the new Sports Hall, autumn 1997.
Left: The Nursery, housed in the former Staff Study and Study form room (later Staff Common Room), 2001.
Above and right: The Junior School playground.

In keeping with the age, the need to increase security was also addressed. Cumberland Lodge was the first building to be fitted with a digital locking system, early in 1994, and during the next few years all external doors were similarly equipped. A gate, locked during the day, was also erected at the end of the lane near Howell's Crescent at the end of 1996, and all visitors to school were required to sign in and wear a badge.

To celebrate the tenth anniversary of the opening of the Junior School, the back garden was developed in 1995. The result was a greater hard surface area, with games painted on the tarmac, brightly-coloured Wendy houses, tables and benches, and new flowering shrubs. A reception class for four-year-olds was introduced that year. The Junior School expanded further in September 1997, with the opening of a Nursery for three-year-olds, which was housed in the former staff area on the ground floor of the main building, with a self-contained play area outside. Among the new entrants were Angharad Phillips and Hannah Southern, daughters of staff members Mrs Elizabeth Phillips and Dr Sara Southern, who were therefore the first to have the opportunity to be educated at Howell's from the age of three to eighteen. In 2002 the Nursery received high praise in an Estyn Inspection report.

The major building project of the 1990s was a new Sports Hall. There were lengthy discussions about its location but the decision was taken in 1995 to extend the existing Gymnasium southwards, on the site of the old kitchen garden. The new Sports Complex included not only a Hall, with facilities for gymnastics and suitable courts for volleyball, badminton and basketball, but also a Fitness Suite, changing-rooms, an equipment store and a staff room on

the ground floor and a viewing gallery (complete with piano), lounge, catering area and activity space above. The total cost was approximately £900,000, of which the Parents' Association raised the magnificent sum of £10,000 and the girls contributed £2,277 from a sponsored sports week.

The new complex, designed by the Trust's architect Mrs Pauline Farrow, was ready for use by the end of May 1997 and was officially opened by the Paralympian Tanni Grey in a grand ceremony on 16th October. From that time onwards, the annual prize-giving was held there, with a reception held afterwards for the leavers and their parents in the Great Hall, as the Senior School Hall then became known. As well as being rented out in the evenings and for Sports Camps during the holidays, the Sports Hall came to be used for many other purposes such as Senior School assemblies, public examinations, large-scale concerts, Careers Conventions and the house choir performances on Eisteddfod Day.

The technological revolution begun under Miss Turner also gained pace. A second dedicated Computer Room, with the latest equipment, was opened in the autumn of 1994, and the administrative computer system was updated to link with the Trust Head Office. Two years later, the first part of the building was networked and in 1997 the school was connected to the internet. In 1998 a second large room, part of the former Sanatorium on the first floor, was converted for use as an ICT room. The following year, a small room on the east wing of the first floor became an ICT suite for A Level students and staff, and the Junior School was fully networked, with the existing computers updated. Two years later, the school began to develop its own website.

Left: The Sports Hall under construction.
Below and bottom left: The new Sports Hall, 1997.

Right: Programme cover for the opening of the Sports Complex, October 1997.
Above right: Sports Complex Opening Ceremony.
Far right: Paralympic athlete Tanni Grey with girls after the opening of the Sports Complex.

The Strategic Development Plan of 2000 assessed the main requirements for the next few years as the refurbishment of the Great Hall, to include a sound and lighting box and stackable chairs; an eighth Science Laboratory, Preparation Room and storage space; an astroturf pitch; and the possible enlargement of the Junior School. The Junior School received new bright playground equipment in 2001. In the Easter holidays of 2002 work began on creating the new Laboratory between the existing Physics and Chemistry blocks, with a Science staff room and a covered glass walkway. By the end of September the whole new area was ready for occupation. The new Laboratory, for Chemistry, was equipped with the school's first interactive whiteboard. Such was the pace of change that by the time of Mrs Fitz's retirement, virtually every teaching room had one.

In the same year, Mrs Fitz had the idea of enlarging the Junior School to a two-form entry in 2004 and 2005. The plans for the astroturf pitch and the refurbishment of the Great Hall were consequently shelved, although the Great Hall did acquire new stage curtains and lighting in 2003 through the fund-raising efforts of the Parents' Association. The main development was an S-shaped building situated near to Cumberland Lodge, to house the classes from Reception to Year 3. Like the Sports Hall, this was designed by

Above: The new Chemistry Laboratory, 2003.

Below left: Design for the new Junior School expansion, November 2002.
Bottom left: Tŷ Hapus under construction, 2003.
Below right: The opening of Tŷ Hapus, 2006.

Pauline Farrow. Work began in September 2003 and girls helped to create the new circular stained glass windows. The music practice wing attached to Cumberland Lodge gained an additional storey, providing a new Music Room, Library and Computer Suite, and the Junior School Hall was extended. There was also a new room for Art, Design and Technology in Hazelwood and a large area for the Nursery girls, who then vacated the rooms on the main school site. These developments necessitated additional parking facilities, so a new car park was created at the Pencisely Road side of the playing fields. The extended Junior School provided places for the girls from the nearby Elm Tree House School, which closed in the summer of 2004. The new building, named *Tŷ Hapus* (Happy House), was formally opened by Mr Sims on 5th May 2006, at the end of a special Creativity Week involving thirteen different activities undertaken in mixed age groups.

The final momentous development during Mrs Fitz's headship was the decision to admit boys to the sixth form. The idea of co-educational sixth forms in otherwise single-sex schools was nothing new, Marlborough College for boys having first admitted girls back in 1969, and since then the practice had become quite widespread. In October 2003 the Governors gave their unanimous support to the idea. All interested parties were asked for their views during a consultation period. The vast majority were positive about the plans, which gained the backing of the Council of the Trust. Under the terms of the Education Act of 2002, the Welsh Assembly Government was required to give its consent for the change to the school's educational status. It was also necessary, under the Sex Discrimination Act of 1975, to apply for a variation in the Trust Deed in order to admit boys. Howell's became the first school in Wales to apply to the Welsh Assembly for such an order.

The new coeducational sixth form was named Howell's College, with Mrs Natalie Chyba as its Head, and the first twenty-seven boys entered Year 12 in September 2005. The opening ceremony was performed by Mrs Elisabeth Elias, a former Governor and the Chairman of the Council of the Trust. From this time onwards, Mrs Fitz was termed Principal and Mrs Davis Deputy Principal, the other main positions of responsibility in the academic hierarchy being those of Head of College, Head of Senior School (Years 7 to 11) and Head of Junior School (Nursery to Year 6). Those who attended the College were called students rather than pupils, though in fact this term had been introduced earlier for younger girls as well. The form tutors became known as personal tutors and the Head Girls' team was renamed the Head Students' team. In the Summer Term of 2006, Will Docking became the school's first Deputy Head Boy.

The College was promoted as offering "a balance between a supportive environment and a university-style education, promoting independent learning as well as academic rigour". In addition to the facilities in Oaklands and Bryntaf, which were

Top: *The Sixth Form College Opening Ceremony, July 2005. Left to right: Mrs J Fitz, Mrs Natalie Chyba, Mrs Elisabeth Elias (Chairman of the GDST), Mrs Barbara Harrison (GDST Education Officer), Mrs Rosemary Smith (Deputy Chairman).*

Above: *The first boys in the Sixth Form College with Mr David Thomas, College tutor and teacher of Music (right, second row). Bottom right is Will Docking, the first Deputy Head Boy.*

appropriately updated, a new common room was created in an area above the Fitness Suite in the main school, primarily to cater for the students whose lessons took place in the laboratories nearby. A new Secretary was appointed to serve the College and deal with the great demand for places. The establishment of the College spawned several new clubs and societies, such as those for Politics and Debating, and a College Choir. Rugby coaching was provided, which marked the beginning of several sporting activities for the boys. In March 2006, the first musical, *Oh! What a Lovely War* took place. There were occasional lectures by guest speakers on subjects of general importance. A final new initiative under Mrs Fitz was the introduction of the Open University's Young Applicants in Schools and Colleges Scheme (YASS) so that able students could study undergraduate modules alongside their A Level courses. All the signs in 2007 were that the College was going to prosper.

19

CLUBS, CULTURE AND COMMUNITY CONNECTIONS, 1991-2007

Facing page
Top: *The Astronomy Club and some junior girls watching the Transit of Venus, 8th June 2004.* Below: *Tasneem Khatib and Keely Howard, winners of a trip to NASA, February 2001.*

Left: *Mock election candidates, April 1992. Left to right:* Natasha Thomas, Judith Richards-Clarke, Sadia Salam, Sarah Breckenridge, Wijhdan Abusrewil.

During Mrs Fitz's headship, the already extensive opportunities for students to broaden their range of experiences through trips and involvement in charity work, clubs, societies and other enterprises increased further. At lunchtimes the school was always buzzing with activity, with younger girls in particular proffering passes which allowed them to go into the Dining Room early in order to rush off to a club or other event. Seniors were known to by-pass the Dining Room altogether, surreptitiously munching sandwiches between, or even during, activities.

By 2007, there were about forty different clubs and societies, catering for all tastes. The History Club began to enter the Welsh Heritage Schools' Initiative Competition, gaining a prize each year. In two consecutive years, 2001 and 2002, four members of the Astronomy Club won a trip to visit NASA sites in Houston and Florida in a *Science in Space* competition organised by the International Space School Education Trust.

The Young Enterprise scheme continued, with enthusiastic participation each year by many Year 12 students. In 1996 Anna Castledine won a holiday in the USA for being placed in the top nine of 22,000 candidates in the scheme's examination. The Managing Director of the company *Jive*, Natasha Francis, won the Young Achiever in Wales section of the Women in Wales Award in 2007. In 1997-8, Year 12 Physicists took part in the Welsh Schools' Engineering in Education Awards, producing a project in response to a problem set by a company, and this became an annual undertaking, often culminating in gaining awards.

Book Week, first organised in October 1996 by Mrs Pat Williams, the school librarian, became an annual fixture. It included quizzes, visits from theatre companies and speakers and a variety of activities relating to literature. With Mrs Joy Guy, Mrs Williams initiated a Reading and Reviewing Club, the Carnegie Shadowing Day and a *Kids' Lit Quiz*, which involved other Cardiff schools. The year 2001-2 marked the launch of activity weeks focussing on particular areas of the curriculum such as Languages, Science and Geography. During the Summer Term of 1996 a week-long Arts Festival included a poet-in-residence and saw the transformation of the Day Room and part of the Stone Hall into an art gallery. The Hywelian Miss Hilary Jones, who had overseen the expansion of the Art department, had retired in 1995, and under her successor, Mr Robert McPartland, students' work was regularly on display in those areas and on the walls of the Dining Rooms. In June 2003 a Creativity Week took place and this developed into an annual Challenges Week for the whole school.

The emphasis on oral work in English GCSE promoted a great interest in public speaking and debating, encouraged by Mrs Maylin, the Head of Department, and the 1990s heralded the beginning of major successes. The Year 10 team were runners-up in the National Final of the Observer English Speaking Union competition in 1996. Following the death of the Trust's Legal

Adviser, Chrystall Carter, a public speaking competition for the member schools was initiated and the first winner, in 2002, was a Howell's girl, Biyun Jiang. The following year, in the Welsh final of the English Speaking Union Public Speaking competition, Maybo Fung won the prize for the best speaker. Successes continued under Mrs Rachel Gregory, the Head of Department from 2005. In 2006, the junior team of Katie James, Sidi Bai and Emily Davies won the Welsh title of the Rotary *Youth Speaks* Competition and came third in the UK final and David Gregory and Claire Fitter (Year 13) won the final of the Welsh Debating Championships. At the Urdd International Eisteddfod girls more than once won individual and group recitations.

Reflecting social concerns of the new Millennium, two sixth formers, Lizzie Cooke and Hannah Coakley, were chosen as members of the UNICEF UK Youth Advisers' team, the only two from Welsh schools, to raise awareness of children's rights. A Building Bridges Committee was set up in 2000 to increase links with the local community and with those further afield. Already for some years the prefects had organised an annual Christmas party

Left: Biyun Jiang, the first winner of the Chrystall Carter competition, 2002.
Below: Claire Fitter and David Gregory, Welsh Schools' Debating Champions, 2007.
Bottom: Visitors from Lesotho, including Patrick Mojarane, with Mrs Ceri Elmes, 2005.

Top: The Library, 1993. Lisa Thomas is in the foreground.
Above: Book Week 1997.
Left to right: Catherine Slater, Melissa Ng, Emma Jones, Shirley Mukisa, Ceri Vokes, authoress Jean Ure, Louisa Oliver, Amanda Benedict, Amy Baxter, Emma Edwards, librarian Mrs Pat Williams.
Right: A level Artwork in the Stone Hall, 2003.

Facing page
Top: The Young Enterprise group which won three prizes in the Welsh Final, 2003. Lydia Gibbs, Philippa Morgan, Eleanor Scaglioni Georgina Wilson, Hannah Tillyard.
Below: The Engineering Team, 2004, which won the Royal Navy prize for the best team performance. Left to right: Natalie Bowkett, Holly Hansen, Lizzie Cooke, Bethan Jones-Mathias, Alice Clarke, Catherine Hodge, Helen Yung.

Above: Fair Trade stall in the Stone Hall, 2003. Elizabeth Cowie, Deputy Head Girl 2002-3 and Jade Charles, Deputy Head Girl 2003-4.
Below: Coins collected for Children in Need, 2000.
Bottom: Anna Bicarregui, Joanna Lewis and Kathryn Haggett

enjoying a picnic with Mrs Davies-Schöneck and Miss Eddy, 1992.
Right: Cheque for the Children's Hospital in Wales presented to cricketer Ian Botham by the Charity prefects Lizzie Webster and Charlotte Cooke, 2000.
Far right: Red Nose Day, 2007.

for the children of Tŷ Gwyn Special School. The most noteworthy new development was the revival of the connection with Lesotho. In 2003-4 the school began fund-raising to build a Science Laboratory for Likhakeng High School. That summer profits from the very successful Leavers' Ball, held at school, contributed £500 and by July 2005 more than £8,000 had been raised. Miss Mari Brewer, the Head of French, paid two visits to Lesotho, and Likhakeng's Deputy Head, Mr Patrick Mojarane, spent several days at Howell's in October 2004, inspiring everyone by his presence.

Girls also became involved in activities relating to globalisation, recycling, Fair Trade, homelessness and safer routes to school as part of the Envision scheme, especially during *Make a Difference Week*. In September 2005, Jane Davidson, Welsh Assembly Minister, presented the Envision team with an Impetus human rights award for raising awareness of the issues. The team of 2005-6 launched a *Make a Difference* (MAD) magazine and at the Envision Ceremony in London in June 2006 received several awards. Meanwhile, Mrs Sally Davis was particularly involved in the local *Sustrans* initiative for Safer Routes to School, which in 2004 gained an award of £270,000 for bicycle sheds and lockers for participating schools, and Howell's won a Secondary Schools' Road Safety Award under her leadership early in 2006.

Continuing the school's long-standing charity efforts, each year large sums were raised in a number of imaginative ways. Members of staff were often involved, undertaking such antics as donning silly hats, dressing up to play sports matches and even, in one case, having a beard shaved off in public. Indeed, under Mrs Fitz, staff and students joined in a number of events together, including the house choirs and the Christmas pantomime, in which the staff were directed by the prefects. There was always a sense of unity on these occasions, which further helped to foster positive staff-student relations. These were often very warm and were based on mutual respect, with everyone together to achieve the best results, whether in academic or other areas.

Expeditions, whether local trips or extended overseas visits, now required far more planning and paperwork in advance to comply with Health and Safety requirements, but they were recognised as forming a vital part of each student's educational experience and were organised regularly by all departments, with many residential ones taking place during the holidays. Closer links with Europe, improved

Above left: Alison Yates on European Work Experience in the Vendée, 1994.
Left: The German exchange group in City Hall, celebrating the tenth year of the exchange with the Aachen Couven Gymnasium, April 1997. Miss Anne Eddy, Head of German, is third from the left in the front row.
Above: Girls at the Pushkin Summer Palace in St Petersburg, October 1991.
Right: China tour group in Beijing, 1995.
Below: Girls at Burg Eltz, Rhineland, 2003.
Bottom: Year 10 girls at Mametz Wood memorial, July 2004.

transport networks and the growing number of travel companies specialising in various sorts of school expeditions all played their part in increasing the opportunities for cultural and language visits abroad. Notable among these were European Work Experience during the 1990s in Aachen, Germany, and in the Vendée region of France. The participants stayed with host families on a reciprocal exchange scheme and spent the weekdays in various business enterprises, gaining self-confidence and independence as well as enhancing their linguistic skills. Year 10 girls regularly took part in an exchange with pupils from the Couven Gymnasium in Aachen.

The first long-distance excursion during Mrs Fitz's headship took place to Moscow and St Petersburg, in the autumn of 1991, which gave the participants a glimpse of life in a country experiencing the after-effects of the collapse of Communism. In March 1995, a party went even further with the school's first trip to Hong Kong and China. The summer of 1998 saw the first annual History GCSE study tour to the First World War battlefields in Belgium and Northern France. In addition, trips took place to Normandy, where the girls were surprised to stay in a château with carpets on the walls rather than the floor, Paris, the Rhineland, Kenya, Greece and the USA, all visited in connection with academic studies. In the summer of 2000 a group of Year 11 girls represented Wales at the Second World Water Forum in The Hague, having won the Welsh round of the Water Aid Youth Challenge.

Right: Lacrosse, 1992.
Left to right: Annabel Shepherd, *Wijhdan Abusrewil, Katy Webster, Melissa Davies, Sarah Giles.*
Below: Year 8 caving group in the Peak District, 1993.
Left to right: Navjinder Palia, *Charlotte Clayton, Laura Hassan, Joanne Chinnock, Natalie Eddins, Tanusree Nath, Elinor Carter.*
Bottom: The Under 18 Welsh hockey champions, 2000.
Back row, left to right: Rachel Guy, Victoria Howell-Richardson, *Elinor Jenkins, Sarah Clarke, Isabelle Greaves, Laura Warren, Elen Richards. Front: Josie Brown, Hannah Fisher, Zoe Phillips, Bethan Fisher, Lucy Lougher.*

An annual skiing trip for younger pupils in the Senior School was initiated in February 1995 by Mrs Wendy Moyle. In 2000, as a new enterprise to mark the millennium, eighteen girls and two staff undertook a four-week summer trip to Bolivia, where they trekked and undertook voluntary work. Following this successful World Challenge trip, in each subsequent year the opportunity was given either to sixth formers to undertake a similar expedition or to Year 9 pupils to participate in a shorter First Challenge. There were expeditions to Poland, Ecuador, Costa Rica, Morocco and Zambia, all serving to promote teamwork and leadership skills as well as requiring a high level of fitness.

Concurrently with these activities, the Physical Education Department became involved in new initiatives, first under Mrs Jean Hartley and then her successor, Mrs Carol Jones. Some girls took fencing lessons from 1991 and that year the school began its involvement in the Duke of Edinburgh's Award Scheme. Sixth formers were able to attend regular sessions at Llandaff Rowing Club and the Welsh Institute of Sport. In Mrs Hartley's final year, 1993-4, Howell's once again won the Royal Life Saving Society's trophy for the East Wales area. Other outdoor pursuits, not run by the department, were organised in the early 1990s, such as weekend caving, canoeing and rock-climbing expeditions for sixth formers and a week's residential activity course in the Peak District for members of Year 8.

Under Mrs Jones, from 1995 girls took part in cross-country events and in the first year the Middle School team emerged as the county champions. She organised the training of a rapidly increasing number of girls (and, later, boys) for the expedition section of the Duke of Edinburgh's Award Scheme, necessitating frequent excursions at weekends in all weathers. Occasional map-reading errors, resulting in longer walks than anticipated, erecting and dismantling tents in gale-force winds (one once disappeared into a reservoir) and camping in the snow one May all provided memorable experiences, as well as being character-building. There were annual Sports Days, the infants and juniors having their own separate events, a Sports Presentation at the end of each Summer Term for seniors and, from 1997, a sixth form ski trip. The senior ski team won the Welsh Schools' championships at Llangranog for three years in succession from 2003-5. Meanwhile, success in traditional team games continued, with victories in Trust rallies and Welsh championships. Kirsty Thomas was the Under 14 and Under 16 Welsh singles champion in 1995 and the Welsh tennis player of the year; she was selected to represent Great Britain. In 1996, Ruth Verrier-Jones and Rebecca Matloubi were named the Welsh Young Sailors of the Year after becoming the Welsh Schools' and Youth Sailing champions. Hannah Mills became the Girls' World Optimist Sailing Champion in August 2003 and three years later, when in Year 13, she won the International 420 Ladies' World Championships with her sailing partner. Many other

Far left: Kirsty Thomas, Welsh Under 14 and Under 16 tennis champion in 1995.
Left: Hannah Mills, Girls' World Optimist Sailing Champion in 2003.
Below left: Infants performing in Toby's Ark for the Millennium celebrations, 2000.
Right: Music Hall Extravaganza programme, 2000.
Below right: Orchestral rehearsal in the Octagon, 2005.
Bottom: Senior Choir outside the Wales Millennium Centre, 2005.

students performed at international level: in 1999 thirty-one girls represented Wales in twelve different sports.

Under Mrs Phillips, Music went from strength to strength. Girls performed at the Mid Somerset Festival, Drapers' Hall, the Elgar Choral Festival in Worcester, the Miners' Eisteddfod in Porthcawl and the Royal Festival Hall, gaining prizes in competitions. The annual Jill Turner concert involved girls and professional musicians, and several other concerts were performed annually in school, often demonstrating remarkable talent. At the colourful and lively Middle School Concert at the end of the Summer Term, members of staff sometimes also provided some entertainment in costume. The arrival of Charlotte Church in September 1998, with her extraordinary singing voice, resulted in two television companies filming the Middle School Choir shortly before she signed a major deal with Sony and released her first album. In 2000 the school was able to purchase a Bösendorfer grand piano, which was first used publicly when over four hundred girls and a number of staff were involved in the musical shows at the end of the Summer Term to mark the Millennium. Orchestra rehearsals in the Octagon were remembered for such comments from the conductor as: "I am not a tree. I do not enjoy standing here with my arms out", "*pp* means very quiet, not pretty powerful" and "*ff* means very loud, not fairly feeble."

At Christmas 2001 the Senior Choir performed with the BBC Singers in a Radio 3 broadcast entitled *Christmas Presence*. A major event was the Senior Choir's performance at the Wales Millennium Centre on 4th December 2004, the second Saturday after it opened, in a *Christmas Presence* concert with Sir Willard White, Owain Arwel Hughes and the Royal Philharmonic Orchestra, at which it sang *Celebro*, a specially-commissioned work by Karl Jenkins. This was the first of several consecutive Christmas performances there; the girls having the privilege of appearing with the flautists Sir James and Lady Galway in 2006 and with the singer Hayley Westenra in 2007. On the latter occasion, a group of girls from the Junior School also participated.

'The staff, who were simply fantastic, were what I believe made school the most wonderful experience. The lengths they would go to are the stuff of legend. Miss Eddy once jumped repeatedly in and out of a waste paper bin to demonstrate the difference between the German dative and accusative. Mrs Sully took on a drunk old man who was attacking some of our class on a school trip. The teachers accompanied endless trips, braving hiking, caving, skiing in all weathers and climates as well as accompanying us in other countries on work experience. And they were all absolutely brilliant teachers who would do anything to help you.

Whilst we were bound by a strict schedule of lessons and games, we had great times having fun too – hours in the music practice wing composing (mostly awful) pop songs, summer term on the tennis courts after school or in the pool, debating, the school mock General Election of 1997, to name but a few. For me, however, the musical experience at school really stood out. I sang all the way through the school, taking part in concerts, singing in the Capitol Centre, and of course, in the Carol Service. The candlelit entrance of the choir, singing "O Come, O Come, Emmanuel" was always simply electric. I had watched my sister do it and desperately wanted to emulate her. I just loved singing then – we sang until we were hoarse. We sang Britten, Fauré's *Requiem*, Haydn's *Creation* and plenty of Holst. We sang in countless competitions and even in the Royal Albert Hall.

I'll always treasure my memories of school – it couldn't have been a better experience.'

Eira Smith, née Jones (1991-1998, Head Girl 1997-8). Written November 2009.

Left: Cast of Annie *which performed in St David's Hall, 2003.*
Right: Lucy James, Anita Aggarwal and Alys Dewey in Daisy Pulls It Off, *November 2004.*
Below right: House Captains at the 2003 Eisteddfod: Emily-Jane Thomas (Trotter), Zoe Jones (Lewis), Jenine Abdo (Baldwin) and Victoria Morley (Kendall), with the bard, Flora McKay.
Below: The Welsh cakes competition at the Eisteddfod 1993. Left to right: *Sally Clarke, Ellie Griffiths, Sara Castledine, Sherianne Woodward, Anjuli Davies, Catherine Evans.*

Top left: Head of the Junior School, Mrs Elaine Thomas, cutting the cake for the Junior School's tenth birthday, 1994.
Top centre: Year 5 trip to London, 1995.
Above far left: Junior girls at the Millennium Stadium, November 2004.
Above left: Visit of Michael Morpurgo, the Children's Laureate, for the Harry Gibson lecture, 2005.

Bottom far left: The Welsh Guards' visit, 2003.
Bottom left: Junior School Eisteddfod, 2006.
Above: Alice Donnelly, Sophie Thomas, Amice Du-Feu and Rosheen Fehily in the Reception class, who worked with Year 4 to produce a Fashion Show in the first Creativity Week in June 2003. They designed and made all their own clothes.

In October 2002 fifty-four girls took part in a performance of *Annie* in the first Cardiff International Music Theatre Festival in St David's Hall, a joint enterprise between the Music and Drama departments. In its own right, the latter department was active under the lively direction of Mrs Maggie Fletcher and then Mrs Alyson Rees. Events included a biennial Drama Festival for Years 7, 8 and 9, organised by sixth formers, an annual *Showcase of Talent* and productions such as *Under Milk Wood* in 1997, the first sixth form play, *Dr Faustus*, in March 2002 and, later, an annual performance by sixth formers at the end of Challenges Week after just one week of rehearsals. Great house rivalry and community spirit was evident in the annual Eisteddfod, which culminated in an atmosphere of great excitement in the afternoon, with a house drama competition, increasingly elaborately choreographed house choir performances and the Chairing of the Bard ceremony. The wearing of house colours and large house banners added to the occasion.

The Head of the Junior School, Mrs Elaine Thomas, left at Easter 1997 after seeing it through a period of vigorous expansion, and was succeeded by Mrs Marissa Davis, who took up her post one term before the opening of the school Nursery. A system of houses – Dewi, Glyndwr, Hywel and Llywelyn – was introduced. The older girls were given more responsibilities, the range of extracurricular activities increased further and parents were invited to evening curriculum meetings and workshops. Musical activities and shows, all produced as a result of a team effort, expanded particularly through the commitment of Mr Ian Beckett, the musical director. By 1999, there was a Junior School orchestra, an infants' band and girls were participating in GDST events (the word *Public* was dropped from the name in 1998) and inter-school matches. There were Creativity Weeks and annual visits to Storey Arms Outdoors Centre as well as many other trips. In 2003, girls in Year 6 spent two days at the BBC studios in Llandaff recording the backing vocals for a new musical adaptation of *Peter Pan*, broadcast in January 2004, and they performed the musical for their parents with the support of professional musicians and staging and lighting engineers beforehand. The Junior School's first skiing holiday, to Austria, took place in 2006 and in the same year a Junior School Olympic Club was launched, incorporating dance, gymnastics and movement. That summer Mrs Davis and her deputy, Mrs Marion Dunstan, who had been a member of the Junior School staff almost from its beginning, both left and were succeeded by Mrs Judith Ashill and Mrs Barbara Ludlam.

Above left: Hywelian Centenary cake, 2006.
Left: Hywelian Centenary lunch in the Sports Hall, 1st July 2006.
Above: Concert for the Hywelians after the Guild's Centenary lunch, 2006.
Right: Mrs Dorothy Wickett, pupil 1920-8 and later a Governor, at the Centenary lunch, with Mrs J Fitz.

Between late 1999 and 2001 the Hywelian Guild lost three very loyal and hard-working members who had dominated its administration for at least thirty years: the Treasurer Margaret Maton (Hilda Auckland), the Secretary Jessie Davies (who had also been a School Governor since 1971), and the magazine editor Bettie Evans. Jessie Davies left money for a prize which was used for a Travel Scholarship. Two of the most distinguished Hywelians received more honours in 2003. Professor Rosalie David, a pupil from 1957-64, the first woman to hold a Chair in Egyptology (from 2000), was awarded the OBE for her services to Egyptology and was given the world's first Chair of Biomedical Egyptology at the new Centre at Manchester University. Jane Crowley (née Rosser), a former Head Girl, who held the distinction of becoming Wales' first female QC in 1999, won the Western Mail's Welsh Law Award for Leading Counsel in November. She was one of four Hywelians on the Governing Body by January 2005, the others being Linda Quinn, Professor Vivienne Harpwood (née Robinson) and Lady Sue Reardon Smith, Harry Gibson's daughter. In that year the former Deputy Headmistress, Mrs Dilys Lloyd, who was a Vice-President Extraordinary of the Guild, died and the Hywelians launched a fund to buy a harp in her memory.

Several celebratory festivities occurred to mark the Guild's Centenary in 2006. The major events took place over the weekend of 30th June-1st July, notably a Thanksgiving Service in Llandaff Cathedral and a grand lunch in the Sports Hall, followed by a display of some archive material and a concert, recitations and a play performed by members of the school. In November, twenty-eight Hywelians enjoyed a visit to Seville, exploring the city where Thomas Howell spent part of his life, and the trip was so successful that it spawned a Hywelian Travel Club.

Two long-serving members of the English department retired during this period. Mrs Maylin left in 1997 after thirty-six years. The next year saw the departure of her colleague Mrs Joan Hamilton-Jones, who had had taught English since 1970 and held the post of Head of Libraries since 1979, when the facilities were enlarged. Other staff who left after at least twenty years included Mrs Saunders (Head of French and, later, Modern Languages), Miss Margaret Jones (Physics and Examinations Officer), Mrs Carol Davies (Head of Welsh), Mrs Elizabeth Walters (Geography and, latterly, a Senior Teacher responsible for administration, pastoral care and public relations) and Miss Eddy (Head of German and then Modern Languages). The appointment of the Hywelian Mari Brewer to succeed Mrs Saunders meant that three members of the French Department were old girls, the others being Mrs Barton (Elizabeth Brien) and Mrs Gaskell (Rowena Case).

Below: Eisteddfod Trophy, donated
by Mrs Carol Davies in 2000.
Bottom: Howell's first musical:
My Fair Lady, *February 2007.*

Miss Margaret Jones and Mrs Walters donated prizes when they left, for Physics and Geography respectively, and Mrs Carol Davies gave a trophy depicting the Welsh dragon for the winning house in the Eisteddfod. The value of the prestigious Drapers' Leaving Scholarships rose to £350 each in 1999 and from 2000 three were awarded annually. In addition to other prizes awarded for a limited number of years, the Leeke prize for Welsh was donated by the parents of three former students; Sir Donald (a Governor) and Lady Walters gave prizes for Commitment and Achievement; the husband of a former member of staff donated the Dorothy Thomas prize for Biology; and the Nurse M Joan Martin prize was endowed by a Hywelian at school from 1945-52. On his retirement as Chairman of the Governors in 2006, Mr Neville Sims also donated a prize, for Care and Compassion.

There were also three new memorials to girls who, tragically, lost their lives. A prize for a student intending to study Law was inaugurated in memory of Nadia Pearce, who was killed in a car accident shortly after finishing her A Level examinations in the summer of 1991. A special garden was created in Oaklands to commemorate Rachel Harper, who died of Hodgkin's Disease in March 2001 when in Year 12, and a tree was planted in the main quadrangle in memory of Alison Kemble who, having played an exceptionally active role in school life despite suffering from lupus, died in 2006, a year after leaving.

The school doctors since 1962, the husband and wife team Doctors George and Hilary Lloyd, departed in 1995. Howell's stayed with the same practice, which included their daughter, Dr Fiona Morgan, a Hywelian. The nurse Mrs Barbara Budd, who had been associated with Howell's since 1974 as a relief house-mistress and assistant nurse, left in 2003. On Mr Sims' retirement as Chairman of the Governors after twenty-five years in August 2006 (the longest-serving of all the Trust Schools' Chairmen), he was invited to become an Honorary associate of the GDST.

'Obviously exams, important events, school traditions and occasions such as the Eisteddfod and Sports Day will always be remembered, but I also have more light-hearted recollections of my time at Howell's. Year 7 meant stepping into the established rivalries between the girls in forms H, S and L. Still to this day, I remain a proud 'H'. These rivalries were exacerbated in the 'Decorate a Christmas tree' competition and the Drama Festivals. I will never forget the lacrosse lessons first thing on a Monday morning, come rain, wind, snow or injuries. Having said that, an ability to soldier on and brave all conditions was certainly fostered in our first term of Year 7. Christmas at Howell's was like no other: decorations, competitions, Christmas lunch and of course, the pantomime. Each year the brave teachers would put on a pantomime, dressing up as ridiculous characters which left the girls in the crammed Great Hall in raucous laughter. Mr Evans' award-winning performances as the damsel in distress, Mrs Sully's animal depictions and Mrs Fitz's debut as Dumbledore never failed to amuse us. One of my fondest memories is summer lunch times when we would organise mass games of rounders on the field, attempting to eat sandwiches whilst bowling. Small things like the dreaded 'blue slips', standing up in assembly as Mrs Fitz walked in, our awful (as we considered them) candy striped shirts and pleated skirts and the weekly humiliation of dropping one's tray at lunch-time seemed so important at the time, yet looking back were quite insignificant. However, Howell's would not have been the same without them.'

Lydia Lewis (2001-8, Head Student 2007-8). Written December 2009.

Staff pantomime.
Left to right: *Mrs C Jones, Mrs J Baker, Mrs H Smith, Dr G Everett, Mr D Evans, Mrs J Sully.*

Facing page
The cover of the first magazine in colour, 1997.

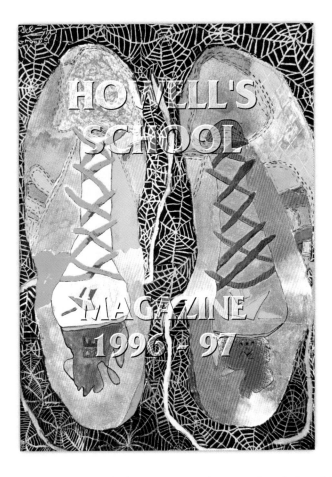

He was succeeded by Mrs Anne Campbell, a mother of a former student, Sarah. In the same month, Lady Reardon Smith retired as a Governor after twenty-five years, her association with the school having begun when she was admitted at the age of nine in 1950. Finally, Mrs Fitz herself retired at the end of the Spring Term in 2007 after almost sixteen years. After a lengthy selection process, her Deputy, Mrs Davis, was announced as her successor. Mrs Fitz's last term saw the school's very successful first full-length musical, *My Fair Lady*, a joint enterprise between the Music and Drama departments. On her retirement, she made a generous donation towards equipping the Science Laboratory a the school in Lesotho and paid for a plaque commemorating Cumberland Lodge as a childhood home of Roald Dahl.

In addition to her demanding role as Headmistress and then Principal, Mrs Fitz had served on various committees of the GDST and the Girls' School Association. She served as Chairman of the Trust's Headmistresses' Standing Committee in 1994-5. For many years she was also an inspector for the Independent Schools' Council. After the establishment of Estyn and the Welsh Assembly she helped to set up a new body for all the independent schools in Wales, named the Welsh Independent Schools' Council. She was also a committee member of the Universities and Colleges Admissions Service (UCAS) in Wales and a member of the Council of Cardiff University. From 1995 she worked for *Save the Children* on the Women in Wales Luncheon Committee, during which time she was Chairman and Vice-Chairman, and she continued her involvement after retirement.

Under Mrs Fitz, links with the Drapers' Company had also become closer. A welcome gift had been its endowment of a Millennium Bursary for an entrant to Year 7 in September 2000, which paid the full fees for her seven years at school. In honour of Mrs Fitz's work at Howell's and her contribution to education in general, in February 2004 she had been invited by the Court of the Drapers' Company to become an Honorary Freeman and the ceremony had taken place in the magnificent surroundings of Drapers' Hall. In her final month at school, on 15th March, she was presented with the Livery of the Company. Howell's School had gone from strength to strength under her direction. She had been extremely hard-working and had shown great vision, driving the school forward and ensuring that it maintained its reputation. Academic achievement went hand in hand with superb facilities, increased extracurricular activities and opportunities for leadership, confidence-building and serving the wider community. Assemblies had gradually become more multicultural and inclusive. Sixth formers relished the extra freedom, being able to drive cars to school and enjoying splendid Leavers' Balls. At both ends of the school there had been a huge increase in numbers: the Junior School had grown from four to sixteen classes and the sixth form had expanded, particularly as a result of the creation of the co-educational College. Attention to the needs of the individual had been given a high priority. By any standards, Howell's was a forward-looking, successful and very well-equipped school by 2007.

20

MRS DAVIS AND A SCHOOL FOR THE TWENTY-FIRST CENTURY, 2007-10

Facing page
Mrs Sally Davis, appointed in 2007.

Left: Junior School girls at ease with computers.

When Mrs Sally Anne Davis succeeded Mrs Fitz in the Summer Term of 2007, she became the second person appointed to the headship from within the school, Miss Ewing having been the first back in 1872, and also, after Miss Lewis, the second of Welsh birth. Born on 2nd July 1959, Mrs Davis became Head Girl at Bassaleg School in Newport before studying Geology at London University's Bedford College. She taught at two London state schools, becoming Head of Department, and subsequently held the post of Director of Studies at Harris City Technology College in Croydon. Unlike her two predecessors, therefore, she was firmly rooted in the state school tradition when she arrived at Howell's as Deputy Headmistress in 1992, and she brought many fresh ideas and a new perspective. On the other hand, she quickly assimilated and appreciated the values of Howell's. Dynamic, creative and open, she reflected the lively, friendly and more informal ethos of the school which existed by the early twenty-first century. Her main priorities were to develop the school along the lines most suited to the modern world, with the growth of the internet, better telecommunications systems and more affordable travel. Thus she aimed to extend the IT provision, increase the range of foreign languages taught and extend the international dimension of the school's activities. She was well trained, too, for her new role: in the

school year 1997-8 she had been one of the first in the UK to gain the new National Professional Qualification for headship.

During her first term as Principal, Mrs Davis worked without a Deputy. Mrs Michelle Gosney, another geographer, joined the staff as Deputy Principal in September 2007 and quickly became valued for her calm efficiency and excellent managerial skills. The Senior Management Team was re-named the Leadership Team and the College Management Team the College Leadership Team. Staff and students returned from the summer holiday of 2007 to find the main Reception Office refurbished, with a new entrance and reception desk just inside the main door. Celebration teas were introduced to acknowledge those who achieved particular success in any field. Another early change related to prize-giving. The main occasion became a function for the previous year's leavers only, and while still retaining a degree of formality, the atmosphere was more one of a lively celebration of their achievements.

In pursuit of Mrs Davis's aims, technological advances continued. The school's video-conferencing facilities enabled her to hold discussions with Heads of other GDST schools, Junior girls to communicate with their counterparts at Bromley High School, and the ICT department to deliver an AS Level course to sixth formers at the Royal High School, Bath. The Trust's portal, developed at the end of Mrs Fitz's headship, meant that students and staff could gain access to their school files and e-mails from home. The development of *SchoolComms* made it possible for all parents to be e-mailed at the touch of a button, and they could also receive text messages on their mobile phones. Staff began to be equipped with laptop computers to take to their lessons and the Geography and Biology departments were supplied with hand-held Personal Digital Assistants (PDAs) which the students could use for fieldwork. The Hywelian Guild also adopted modern technology, with copies of the magazine sent to the younger former pupils in Portable Document Format and communication made with members on *Facebook*. Following an extensive external assessment, in February 2010 the school was awarded the prestigious ICT mark by *Becta*, the government-funded body responsible for promoting the use of ICT in educational establishments.

Mrs Davis was also quick to extend the range of foreign languages available. Spanish was introduced to the curriculum, with girls in Year 6 learning the rudiments of French, German and Spanish. In the Autumn Term of 2009, Year 7 girls were able to choose two modern languages from French, German, Spanish and Welsh, and Spanish was introduced at AS Level. Senior School and College students were able to take a fast-track German course after school and Ancient Greek was added to the choice of A Level options. Extracurricular languages clubs flourished in both Senior and Junior Schools and included French, German, Spanish, Russian, Ancient Greek, Turkish, Japanese, Mandarin and *Minimus*, a Latin Club for girls in the Junior School, which had begun in Mrs Fitz's time.

Above: Nursery girls celebrate the Chinese New Year, January 2009.
Right: Sixth Form College students in Washington, October 2008.

Facing page
Top left: First Challenge group in Croatia, July 2007. Mrs C Jones, Head of PE, is on the left.
Top right: First Challenge expedition in Iceland, 2009.

The development of the international aspect of the school's activities was seen in the Junior School's participation in the *Join Up Global Campaign for Education* in the summer of 2007 and the newly-formed College Interactors group (part of the youth section of the Rotary Club) led by Mrs Helen Davies, which regularly raised money for projects at home and overseas. Three girls from Year 10 went abroad to help with project work relating to water supplies in Tanzanian villages, having won the *WaterAid* competition for schools. Some students featured on the international stage. Hannah Coakley, who had been involved with UNICEF since 2006, held the position of Youth Champion for the UK and in 2009 was selected as one of two Youth Advisers to the Board of Trustees of UNICEF UK. The previous summer, she and three other Year 12 students, Rose Stuart, Harry Brooks and Jasper Warner, had the honour of being selected to represent the UK at the Junior 8 summit in Tokyo, which ran parallel to the G8 summit, and which provided a platform for young people to make their voices heard on global problems. The Head Girl for 2007-8, Lydia Lewis, was a UK Youth Ambassador for *Save the Children* and also chaired the Global Young Leaders' Conference in Washington and New York in July 2008, in which four other Howell's sixth formers participated.

New European links were fostered by the introduction of a sixth form work experience exchange with a school in Landivisiau, Brittany, and pen-friend links with schools in Brest, Germany and Switzerland, which resulted in meetings between the correspondents in many cases. Howell's received young people undertaking teacher training from Germany and there was a visit from a group of Danish school students. Overseas educational visits abounded: in the first seven terms of Mrs Davis's headship there were trips to Paris, the Rhineland, Berlin, Krakow, Barcelona, the USA, the Black Forest and the First World War Battlefields. For the more physically active, there were skiing holidays, a hockey tournament in Holland and First Challenge expeditions to Croatia in 2007 and Iceland in the summer of 2009.

Left: The Junior School in the Send a Friend to School Global Campaign for Education, April 2007.
Above: Howell's representatives at the Global Young leaders' Conference in the USA, 2008. Left to right: Lydia Lewis (Head Girl 2007-8), Niamh Baker-Loughlin, Astrid Grindlay, Eman Baig, Melissa Sim.

In the autumn half-term of 2009, following months of planning, forty students and six members of staff went to China for a cultural and choir concert tour, during which girls from the Senior Choir performed at the Forbidden City Concert Hall in Beijing, where they were thrilled to receive a standing ovation.

The relationship with Likhakeng School in Lesotho also continued, to the benefit of both institutions. Howell's had raised £10,000 for it to build a Science Laboratory, Mrs Fitz had contributed towards its equipment and Miss Brewer, who became a Trustee of *Dolen Cymru*, raised money to buy a generator. Miss Rhian Chard spent time at the school in the autumn of 2007 and its Head of Agriculture and a Science teacher, Mrs Justine Ramollo, returned the visit the following April. During the summer holiday of 2009, a group of sixth formers and two staff flew out to the school and spent time in lessons, exchanging information about the two countries and going on visits. They donated equipment to develop the school's music department.

Mrs Davis had long been interested in teaching young people how to think and work, using their multiple intelligences, and had introduced ideas such as mind-mapping and "Buzz Your Brain". In the Junior School, Mrs Anna Parry-Hearn was a great exponent of the development of thinking skills, and "Exploration" group activities involving different year groups promoted logical, creative, analytical and critical thought. Revision breakfasts for Year 11 girls prior to GCSE provided exercises in "brain gym" and mind-mapping activities.

Top: School party in Beijing, October 2009.
Right: Programme for the Senior Girls' Choir at the Forbidden City Concert Hall in Beijing, 19th October 2009.
Above: The choir in the Forbidden City Concert Hall, Beijing.
Below: Group at Likhakeng High School, Lesotho, summer 2009.
Below right: Junior School children of different ages work together: Charlotte Wheeler and Isobel Thomas carry out an Explorations activity.

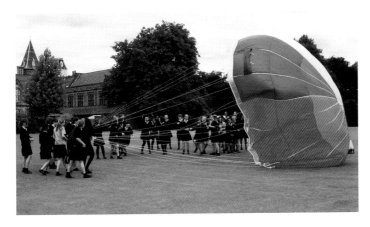

In the early years of Mrs Davis's headship, other aspects of school life continued much as before. Clubs and societies, competitions, sports, numerous day and residential visits, Christmas festivities, grand concerts, the Eisteddfod, Drama Festivals, Challenges Week and the weeks devoted to particular areas of the curriculum: all these engendered palpable feelings of purposeful activity. In the autumn of 2007, as part of Book Week, the plaque donated by Mrs Fitz was unveiled on the wall of Cumberland Lodge commemorating Roald Dahl's childhood home, in the presence of his widow, Mrs Felicity Dahl, with an information panel nearby.

Above: Challenges Week, 2008: Year 9 try to launch a parachute.
Left: Felicity Dahl meets "Mr Fox", Alex Ryan, at the unveiling of the plaque to Roald Dahl on the wall of Cumberland Lodge, his childhood home, 2007.
Below: The Junior School outside Cumberland Lodge in their Roald Dahl costumes, 2007.

Cumberland Lodge

Roald Dahl
Author
lived here 1921-1927

Presented by
Jane Fitz

Principal 1991-2007

In April that year, in readiness for Christmas, the Senior Girls' Choir recorded six songs for a CD entitled *Let's Celebrate Christmas* with the Royal Philharmonic Orchestra, the proceeds going to UNICEF and the GDST Bursary Fund. Once again the choir performed at the Millennium Stadium *Christmas Presence* concert, on that occasion with the soprano Lesley Garrett. Each year, all the Junior School girls took part in well-rehearsed, lively productions at school at Christmas or in the summer. The Music and Drama departments collaborated to present the musical *Oliver!* in February 2009, performed to a packed Sports Hall on four nights and involving pupils from the Junior School through to the College. All these activities served to bring different groups of students together and the involvement bred more self-confidence.

Top: The cast of Robin Hood, *Years 5 and 6, June 2009.*
Left: Senior Concert, Llandaff Cathedral, April 2008.

Above left: Junior School music percussion session, April 2008.
Above: Juniors in Ocean Commotion, *December 2008.*
Below: Oliver! *February 2009.*

'The current Principal of Howell's is Mrs Davis, a very warm and friendly person who seems to have a wonderful relationship with all the pupils and staff. I enjoy taking part in the concerts, especially the Summer Concert, because there's a really good atmosphere. Mrs Phillips is always so enthusiastic and everyone works hard to produce a great show. In the Eisteddfod I love taking part in the house competitions, when everyone pulls together. Howell's has a very strong family atmosphere. Sport and music play a huge part in the activities on offer as well as modern and classical language clubs and creative activities such as photography and drama. I love the facilities such as the swimming pool and tennis courts.

Howell's is a great school in which we can flourish and gain skills for later life. In the classroom there's a good working environment, with everyone trying to achieve their best. Any young person lucky enough to a part of Howell's past and present has, I am sure, one of the best starts in life. The school today, in 2010, is at its best and that is thanks to everyone who has been a part of its history.'

Lydia Phillips, aged 13. Written January 2010.

This was particularly seen in the area of competitive debating and public speaking. In May 2007, the CEWC Cymru Debating Champions, Claire Fitter and David Gregory, represented Wales in the International Schools' Mace Debating UK final in the House of Lords. In speaking first Claire made history as the first commoner to speak in the House of Lords in peace-time. During the summer holiday, David went to Seoul to participate in the World Debating Championships as part of the Welsh debating team; eighteen months later, Jasper Warner was ranked as the world's seventh best speaker in the Championships in Athens. Emily Davies, Katie James and Sidi Bai (Year 9) became the Rotary Club National *Youth Speaks* Champions in 2007 and in the following year won the Welsh final of the English Speaking Union's Debating competition. In the autumn of 2009, Sophie Jenkins (Year 10) came first in the national final of the LAMDA performance awards in London, with two other Howell's girls placed in the top five.

The Junior School's chess team had tremendous success at the central South Wales Schools' Championships in 2009, with three girls also qualifying for the British Gigafinal in Manchester. In March of the same year, Eirys Morley Jones (grand-daughter of former English teacher Mrs Hamilton-Jones) and Kristy-Ann Wilson were chosen to represent Wales at Downing Street for the BBC's Schools Report. Both these girls had other successes in 2009: Kristy-Ann was one of four girls who came in the top ten in a national Anne Frank writing competition, and Eirys was part of the Year 8 team which won the Welsh Final of the *Kids' Lit* quiz, thereby qualifying for the UK final in Edinburgh in August 2010.

Above: Katie James, Sidi Bai and Emily Davies: the National Youth Speaks champions in 2007.
Left: Eirys Morley Jones and Kristy-Ann Wilson representing Wales at 10 Downing Street for the BBC School Report, April 2008.

Left: Year 7 and 8 cross-country team 2007-8. Back row, left to right: Laura Woods, Cerys Broad, Libby Jegou, Sophia Pauley, Alex Shaw, Jasmine Lenton, Alice Derby. Front: Michaela Melia, Katie Collins, Elinor Thomas, Claire Jenkins, Grace Barningham, Tara James, Izzy Lewis.
Below far left: The Under 15 netball team which won the County Championships, 2009. Back row, left to right: Naomi Benjamin, Sophie Kosinski, Isabel Jenkins, Viraja Kadaba. Front row: Manon Davies, Megan Fairclough, Olivia

Westmacott, Caroline Lakin.
Below left: Rugby on the school field, March 2009.
Below third left: Junior School group in the Brecon Beacons, July 2008. Left to right: Emily Bowden, Faith Madsen, Gabriella Engelhardt, Izzy Shaw, Harriet Elliott, Sarah Davies.
Bottom left: Junior School Olympic Club.

Below: Celebrating A Level results, 2009.

Successes continued in the traditional sports, with players wearing smart new navy and white kit, and teams began to compete also in golf and football. The Junior School ski team won the Central and South East Wales Championships in 2009 for the fourth year in succession and in November 2009 Sam Maurice, daughter of Biology teacher Mrs Janet Maurice and the chief Science technician Mr Phillip Maurice, was the top placed Welsh girl skier at the British Championships. In 2008 Imogen Pauley, in Year 6, set new GDST records in the Under 11 butterfly and front crawl events. Large numbers continued to participate in the Duke of Edinburgh's Award Scheme.

A resounding seal of approval was given to the school by a team of Estyn inspectors, who spent a whole week scrutinising all aspects of teaching and learning in November 2008. From this, Howell's emerged with the highest grade (1) in each of the seven key categories, and by early 2010 was still the only Welsh independent school to have achieved this feat. Among the inspectors' comments were: *Pupils display outstanding features in their work including extensive knowledge, recall and application of skills and techniques and skills in the subjects they study. Pupils of all ages are highly motivated, apply themselves conscientiously to their work and work together effectively. Working relationships between staff and pupils are outstanding. The school has extensive resources and facilities of high quality. The school provides an outstanding programme of extra-curricular clubs and societies. The school is very successful in promoting tolerance, mutual respect and understanding from pupils of diverse backgrounds.* For Mrs Davis and Mrs Gosney came the accolade: *The Principal and her Deputy provide outstanding leadership. They work well together and give the school a strong sense of purpose and direction.* As the school approached its 150th birthday, it could not have had a better endorsement.

Top left: Anna Selway, Ffion Bending and Gwen Smith meet HRH Princess Anne at the Save the Children luncheon in City Hall, 2007.
Above: Mrs Roswitha Davies-Schöneck with Howell's Fairtrade certificate, September 2008.

Above right: Nursery children raise money for Children in Need, November 2008.
Above: Harriet Elliott, a UK Environmental Ambassador.

The inspection week coincided with the annual *Children in Need* appeal, for which the school raised over £1,200. Charity and sustainability efforts featured prominently, encouraged particularly by Mrs Davies-Schöneck, Miss Brewer and Mrs Helen Smith. Over £6,000 was raised for charity in 2007-0 in the Senior School and College, with the Junior School organising its own novel fund-raising efforts for charities such as Save the Children, with which Mrs Fitz and Mrs Davis were actively involved. During the latter's first full year as Principal, the school worked towards gaining Eco status and, as part of that effort, the Year 12 Eco team made a DVD for the Trust Sustainability Challenge, which won the award for the best overall entry. The school gained *Fairtrade* status in the summer of 2008, and Harriet Elliott (Year 7) won a place as a UK Environmental Ambassador in 2009. Linked to the charity efforts, under Mrs Davis there was a drive to ensure that the school undertook as many activities as possible for the public benefit. Links with several local junior schools were established, with children being invited to Howell's for events such as *Be a Doctor for a Day*, a Languages Day and Schools' Council Days, the first of which was attended by Rhodri Morgan, the First Minister of the Welsh Assembly. Closer connections with Howell's Junior School were also developed with English, Maths and Science link days.

The early years of Mrs Davis's headship saw the retirement of a number of staff who had been at Howell's for at least twenty years, continuing the tradition of long service: Mrs Susan Evans (1986 to 2007), Religious Studies; Mrs Pat Williams (1987 to 2007), a member of the Junior School support staff and then Senior School Librarian; Mrs Elizabeth Pexton (part-time from 1982 to 2009), Domestic Science and then Careers Coordinator; the Hywelian Mrs Elizabeth Barton (1985 to 2009), French; and Mrs Davies-Schöneck (1986 to 2010), German. Those teachers remaining who had been at school the longest were Mrs Janet Maurice and Mrs Sue Marusza, both Biologists, who had arrived in 1978 and 1980 respectively, and Miss Denise Cook (Mathematics), who joined in 1982. Also serving for at least a quarter-century were two of the Laboratory technicians, Mrs Gill Stevens and Mr Phill Maurice who, like many of the staff, contributed to a variety of aspects of school life.

Mrs Davis faced the challenging task of leading the school at a time of economic recession but the school continued to flourish, with particularly large numbers of applications for the sixth form College. An Apple Mac suite of computers was purchased for the Art Department from funds donated by friends of the school, a school uniform shop was opened at the end of the lane leading to Howell's Crescent, and a *Stay and Play* scheme once a week for

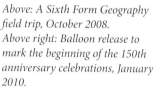

Above: A Sixth Form Geography field trip, October 2008.
Above right: Balloon release to mark the beginning of the 150th anniversary celebrations, January 2010.
Right: Caitlin Trow, Year 10, designer of the 150 logo.
Far right: The Governors, 2009.

Below: Plaque on wall of Bryntaf, 2010.

toddlers and their parents was introduced. On 29th January 2010 a ceremony marked the presentation of a blue plaque for Bryntaf by the family of its famous former resident, the draper David Morgan, whose great-great-great-grandson Tom Sutton was a student in the Sixth Form College from 2008 to 2010. Those driving past the school from late January saw a new crossing, and separate entrances from Cardiff Road for vehicles and pedestrians were planned; for the first time in the school's history, the students would no longer enter on foot through the main gates.

As the 150th anniversary – the Sesquicentenary – approached, the school remained a thriving and vibrant community, with an enviable range of extracurricular opportunities and a strong system of pastoral care as well as superb facilities. The wealth of activities did not detract from the academic standards, which remained high. In GCSE English and Geography, Howell's girls gained the examinations boards' highest mark in successive years, and the Geography department gained its association's Secondary Geography Quality Mark. In the public examinations of 2009, at A Level the 109 members of Year 13 achieved a 100% pass rate, with 36 students gaining three or four grade As. At GCSE, more than half the girls gained A* or A in every subject and thirteen girls achieved ten or more passes at A*. As a result of Oxbridge interviews at the end of the Autumn Term in 2009, nine students were offered conditional places.

In true Howell's style, a host of events was planned to mark the landmark year 2010, including a celebratory concert in St David's Hall in March, a large-scale Open Afternoon, with departmental displays and activities in June, and a Thanksgiving Service in Llandaff Cathedral in November. Plans for major future additional facilities included an Astroturf pitch and a Theatre. Time will tell what other developments lie ahead. One thing that *is* certain is that under Mrs Davis the school will be at the forefront of educational practice and will adapt to meet the requirements of the future, just as it has always done in the past.

'*Amo amas amat: I love, you love, he loves.* A routine yet determined chant of pupils through the ages. It has tripped from the lips of students for many decades – fifteen, I should imagine – and yet in the 150th year of Howell's still holds a little magic which beautifully sums up my time at school.

The Head Students, 2009-10: Ellen Brookes, Bronwen Warner (Head Girl), Rashmi D'Souza, Priyantha Kulatilake.

The Howell's of everyday life rumbles along contentedly and with consummate grace. Each day comprises a hundred laughs, coincidences, close shaves and proud moments. We're in it together, and intend to make the most of every giggle and every toe edged over the line. In the soft security and pleasant order of our classes, we soak up a splendid variety of subjects, which will provide the building blocks of not only good grades but an excellent education. It is routine, yes, but immensely satisfying.

But in a world where everyday life is syntax, and grammar the tricks of the trade pulling you through, it is the intrinsic meaning which adds spark to routine and triumph to endeavour. Special occasions at Howell's are truly thrilling, and surely never forgotten. In my fourteen years the Carol Services, Middle School Concerts, Eisteddfods, Sports Days, Christmas Pantomimes and productions of *Oliver!* and *My Fair Lady* have been quite wonderful. Working tirelessly and passionately with hundreds of other people for a really great result creates an excitement impossible to match.

Howell's really is a wonderful school; surely as bright and happy now as one hundred and fifty years ago. Yet today the school holds both well-learned lessons of the past and keys to an exciting future. We might add another verb to that chant, and relish truly its meaning as well as the fond reminiscence of a cosy classroom. *Amabimus: we will love* – for all our lives.'

Bronwen Warner, Head Girl 2009-2010. Written March 2010.

'The sheer number of girls was both attractive and intimidating, which originally made me wary of Howell's, but now I couldn't see it being any other way, nor would I have wanted it to be any other way. Coming here has introduced me to some amazing people who I'll never lose touch with: the type of people you would want backing your corner and to be around when you feel like being alone. It's really not the buildings, the age, the name or the prestige that defines Howell's for me. What defines this school are the people I spend my time with every day.

Howell's has given me memories I will always remember: the times where I have laughed to the point of tears with both my friends and teachers, and the ten-minute basketball games between lessons with some of the boys. However it hasn't been all fun and games. My time here has shown me that life can throw some unexpected curveballs at you; but what I have learnt as a result is that you should never lose sight of the goals you set yourself. It's all about dusting yourself off when you don't succeed and learning from the mistakes you make. I feel these are the most important things I've learnt at Howell's which I'll never forget.

Lastly, may I take this opportunity to say thank you to everyone here. If it weren't for you, I wouldn't be who I am today. Happy Birthday, HSL!'

Priyantha Kulatilake, Deputy Head Boy 2009-2010. Written March 2010.

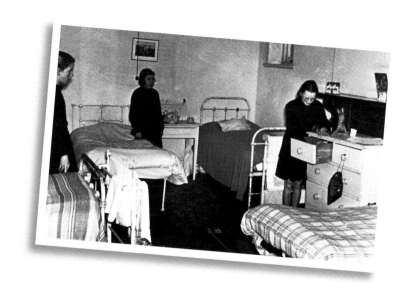

EPILOGUE:
CHANGE AND CONTINUITY

Facing page
Top: *The school field in snow,
8th January 2010.*
Bottom: *Languages Week, 2008.*

*Above: Dormitory in Hazelwood,
early 1950s.*
Left: *Ancient and modern: Eirys
Morley Jones wears the uniform of
the 1870s and Hannah Loyns the
uniform of the early 21st century.*

233

During the course of its long history, almost everything about Howell's School, Llandaff, has changed, as one would expect. The curriculum, teaching methods, age range of pupils, facilities, public examinations, discipline, uniform, extracurricular activities, its management: none bears much, if any, resemblance in 2010 to those of 1860. With the emphasis today on discussion and debate, pupils are now much more self-assured and encouraged to express individual opinions; the old emphasis on conformity has disappeared. So has the distant relationship between staff and pupils; an atmosphere of mutual respect prevails, and two sets of visitors in 2009 were particularly struck by the warmth of the relationship. The school has evolved from one exclusively for boarders to one for day pupils alone, though for all but seventeen years of its first 150 years it had both. The admission of boys to the sixth form in 2005 marked a break with its long tradition of being solely concerned with the education of girls. It has developed very differently from its sister school. Howell's School, Denbigh, was administered by the Drapers' Company until 1997 and then, through a new Charity Commission scheme, its management was undertaken by Howell's 2000 Limited, with a group of parents as directors and trustees. The Drapers' Company subsequently established the Thomas Howell Educational Trust Fund for North Wales to make money available for educational purposes. In recent years, the Llandaff school has regained closer links with the Company and one of its senior members still sits on the School Governing Board.

Despite the many obvious changes, a girl who started at Howell's School, Llandaff, one hundred and fifty years ago would still recognise the main building and, despite the momentous changes in all aspects of life since then, not to mention the physical development of the surrounding area, much of the learning and recreation still take place on the same site. Moreover, many of the

essential features of the school and school life have not changed significantly. Dorothy Fleming, née Oppenheimer, a pupil in the late 1930s and 1940s, wrote in 2001 that she recognised many enduring characteristics of the school, such as "the international and multi-cultural and tolerant philosophy" and the "drive to aim for the highest". She continued, "Typical is the strong feel for news and current affairs; the encouragement towards charity and caring for others and the balanced view of all aspects of life. This is demonstrated by the emphasis not only on educational achievements but also on sports and games, literature and the arts, travel and international events, politics and economics, faith and beliefs and the environment. In all cases active participation is clearly valued." A first-rate education and highly accomplished teachers, favourable inspection reports, extracurricular opportunities, charitable activities and a recognition that the school should serve the wider community, the development of a sense of responsibility and leadership skills, an international outlook, links with the Cathedral – reinforced in 2007 with the appointment of Canon Graham Holcombe as a Governor – and an

emphasis on good manners and respect for others: all these have been features of the school throughout its history. Loyalty to the school is shown by the number of multi-generation families and the continuation of the thriving Hywelian Guild, with its regional and overseas branches.

Howell's has been extremely fortunate in its Headmistresses, all women of vision, and it is quite remarkable that the current Principal is only the ninth in the school's history. The only two to have served for less than ten years, Miss Ewing and Miss Knight, began promisingly and were unfortunate to face adverse circumstances. The two with the longest tenure, Miss Kendall and Miss Lewis, restored stability after taking over at difficult times and showed enormous dedication. Miss Baldwin, Miss Trotter, Miss Turner and Mrs Fitz, while facing very different situations, all strove ceaselessly and most effectively to improve the school's facilities and to enhance its reputation nationally. Mrs Davis resembles Miss Trotter in her love of large-scale occasions, seemingly boundless energy and ideas for driving the school forward. No-one can possibly know what the next one hundred and fifty years will bring but Howell's has stood the test of time, responding to changing circumstances and rising to overcome challenges and problems. No doubt it will continue to do so. In addition, numerous Hywelians have had tremendous achievements in all walks of life. Thomas Howell could not possibly have foreseen what his legacy would achieve but he would surely have considered that it had been well fulfilled.

Facing page
Above: Lewis House on Sports Day 2009.

Left: The school in August 1860.
Below: The school in April 2009.

Three generations of the same family compare their experiences of Howell's School: **Mary Lister** (née Williams), her daughter **Sharon Spackman** (née Pritchard) and her granddaughter **Claire Spackman**. Interviewed April 2009.

Mary Lister, Claire Spackman and Sharon Spackman: three generations of a family of Hywelians, April 2009.

ML: I was a pupil at Howell's from 1947 to 1953, a few years after Miss Lewis had started.

SS: I was also there under Miss Lewis, from 1970 to 1977!

CS: I was in the Junior School, so I've been there from 1995 until 2009, under Mrs Fitz and now Mrs Davis.

CURRICULUM

ML: Apart from sport, generally speaking our subjects were academic, except Cookery, Needlework and Home Management. We were taught how to lay a table. We had Diction as an option and we had some choice of subjects further up the school.

SS: We weren't taught how to lay a table but we had Needlework. There was a choice of languages but not a wide choice. We also had Diction as an option. There was a certain amount of choice at O Level.

CS: It's a lot more varied now. There's a much wider range of options, like Drama, IT and DT. I started French and Welsh in the Junior School.

ML: We all worked exceptionally hard but as our peers were doing the same we didn't realise how hard we were working. When you went to College and compared with others, you realised how hard you'd worked and how much homework you'd had.

A class in West 1, early 1950s. This room became part of the extended Library in the early 1980s.

The Art Room, early 21st century.

SS: We had a lot of work too. I think there's a far more balanced approach now. It's a selective school so it's bound to be academic, but now there's an emphasis on other qualities as well, such as building confidence, which there wasn't in my day.

PUBLIC EXAMINATIONS

ML: Mine was the first year to take O Level, but we still called it School Certificate. For School Certificate you had to pass in a range of subjects. Then there was Higher School Certificate but there was nothing in between. For HSC you chose which subjects you took.

SS: We did nine O Levels and then three A Levels.

CS: In Year 12 we had AS levels. For A2 I'm taking French, Maths and IT.

ML: . . . a subject that was never heard of in my day!

SS: Nor in mine. When I was at school, for A Level you tended to do Arts or Sciences, but one of the changes I've seen with Claire is that there's much more of a mix.

CS: Now we do a lot of coursework for A Level. For IT there's a huge amount but then we only have to do two exams. In French, we do a project and the oral, and then there's only one exam, which I think is good.

ML: No, I don't approve!

SS: I've got mixed views. There were definitely very capable girls in my year who did not perform well in exams and got themselves very stressed.

Design Technology A Level work.

ML: You say they were capable but when you're in a career you have to cope with pressure. That's life. So I'm for exams.

CS: I had coursework for GCSE as well: a major project for IT and for Geography, and in English Lit, Maths and Physics as well.

SS: We took Nuffield Physics, and we did a project, so there was a small element of coursework.

CS: I think the results now show the effort you've put in over the year as a whole more than in the past.

PHYSICAL EDUCATION

ML: There were two lunch sittings and we had a full hour's sport either before or after lunch every single day. We also had swimming during the day and gym two or three times a week. At weekends we played in teams. We used to play on about three pitches in Llandaff Fields as well as on the school pitches, including Trotter Field.

Above: Equipment in the Fitness Suite, early 21st century.
Right: Bronze Duke of Edinburgh's Award Expedition, 2009. Left to right: Viraja Kadaba, Angharad Phillips, Sahithya Balachandran, Emily Bradbury.

SS: It was still called Trotter Field in my day. The sports arrangements were exactly the same – an hour a day at lunchtime. We had to take lacrosse tests. We were superb at lacrosse! I think Haberdashers' Aske's and Alice Ottley gave us a run for our money but they were the only ones who could touch us on the lacrosse field.

CS: Now you still have to do PE, hockey, lacrosse, netball, tennis and athletics in lesson time but you don't have to do sport at lunchtime unless you want to. In the sixth form, we can use the Fitness Suite, the Sports Hall and the swimming pool. We can also do sports like rowing. There's the Duke of Edinburgh's Award Scheme as well, which starts in Year 10.

DISCIPLINE

SS: You had to queue on the stone stairs to go into lunch and you weren't allowed to talk while you were queuing. Miss Lewis always used to come into lunch and if you ended up sitting next to her you had to make polite conversation with her, but this was good from a social point of view.

ML: It was very strict, right through the school. You were not allowed to talk or run in the corridors unless you were reporting a fire. There was no talking at all in the Library or in the Stone Hall. I had an awful lot of order marks! If you had two order marks, your name was read out in assembly and you had to go into school on Saturday and stay all morning for detention. My friends

Gardening with Miss Hilda Taylor, early 1950s.

would be off to the Kardoma in all their gear, all glammed up, and I would be on the bus wearing my uniform going to school!

SS: It was the same when I was there. If you dyed your hair, you had to wear your hat in school. Miss Lewis used to read out punishments, but would also give out praise and read any achievements.

ML: If you had to go to see Miss Lewis because you'd been misbehaving you had to stand outside her door in the corridor for at least a quarter of an hour, and that was as mortifying as going in to see her.

CS: I think the punishments are far less severe now. You still get told off for things like running in corridors and not tucking in your shirt. But now with boys in the sixth form, we get told to tidy up the common rooms very frequently!

ML: Prefects had a lot of power, giving order marks.

SS: It was the same in my day.

CS: Now they mainly help the teachers with assemblies and running clubs. They have specific jobs.

SS: You had the Head Girl, the Deputy Head Girl and Heads of Houses, so those had roles, but that's all.

ASSEMBLIES

ML: If you were a Catholic or Jewish, you would sit outside the Hall for the religious part and then come in when the notices and order marks were read out.

SS: It was still like that when I was there!

CS: When I was younger, we used to have a prayer and a hymn; I can remember this in the Junior School. In the Senior School I just remember singing hymns from the hymn

Miss Lewis taking Prayers, 19th May 1977.

book. In the sixth form, school assembly is optional but we have College meetings. We only go for occasions like the end of term assembly, when it's fun to go.

FREEDOM

ML: It's a lot more fun for them now in the sixth form. When I was in the sixth form we had to be in school from 9 o'clock until 4 o'clock, the same as the rest of the school, and the uniform was identical.

SS: We had a little more freedom in the sixth form. We were allowed to walk up to Llandaff village at lunchtime if we weren't playing games. But the school hadn't moved on very much. I enjoyed the first five years but I didn't enjoy the sixth form very much. I think we'd got to the stage where we wanted a bit more freedom and responsibility. We had two very small common rooms with a kettle and tea.

CS: Now we're allowed to go home to study. In school we have two special houses for the College students, with common rooms and kitchens.

ML: We had to go into the Library to study and, because there was nothing else to do, we used to study. There are undoubtedly more distractions now. Much more self-discipline is required.

EXTRACURRICULAR ACTIVITIES

SS: There were some after-school clubs but there wasn't much emphasis on clubs. It was very much sport and academic work. There was also quite a lot of music and we did plays as well, particularly in the Lower Sixth.

ML: In my day, the emphasis was mainly on sport and academic work.

CS: There's a wide variety of different things you can do. I used to go to the Maths Club, where we did origami, and there's a whole range of languages and other clubs. There are still lots of sporting, drama and musical activities.

SS: We had Speech Days, which were very formal occasions. We had to sit on benches, straight-backed, for what felt like about three hours! Prizes were given for the best academic results in each year.

ML: I remember Speech Days. They were about the same in my day, with results read out and prizes given.

Senior Choir members in the Octagon, c. 1994.

CS: The only prize-giving I can remember was the one where we had our GCSE certificates. There's also a special Sports Presentation awards ceremony.

BOARDING

ML: I boarded for about six months in Hazelwood, right up at the top. The main thing that sticks in my mind is that it was just after the war and food was still very short. The food was abysmal. You were expected to eat everything. There were no paper hankies in those days, of course, so if you remembered you took in toilet paper but if not you used your own hankie and you put the kippers you were given in it. So everyone knew the boarders, because they stank of kippers! It was very cold because there was no heating, so you used to get up in the morning and scrape the windows.

SS: Many of the boarders were quite outgoing and robust but there were a few more sensitive souls who found it very difficult.

ML: If you think of an eleven-year-old going in to board as it was then, leaving your family and the friends you had made at Junior School, it must have been very hard with all that discipline and fairly spartan conditions.

SS: Perhaps it was even harder for my generation, when things had moved on more outside the school. I can remember when I was first there that the boarders were only allowed to wash their hair once a fortnight.

Hazelwood boarders having lunch in LDR, early 1950s. Bottom right, left to right, facing forwards: *Maureen Richards, Jeanette Townsend and Margaret Hutton.*

CS: Ugh! That's dreadful!

SS: They used to do it at night in the dark. The boarders formed a clique. For them I suppose it was like a substitute family.

ML: Yes, they did keep themselves apart. They ate in the Little Dining Room, which was purely for boarders, and the Big Dining Room was for the day girls. But we played games together at lunch-times and in the teams.

SS: We became quite friendly with some boarders. While I was there, weekly boarding was introduced, which I think worked better.

TEACHING STAFF

ML: All the teachers were characters then: Miss Disney, Miss Bates, the two Miss Taylors, Miss Tickner. They were exceptionally strict, especially the spinsters – stricter than the married ones who had more rapport with the students than the others.

SS: There were still some of the same teachers when I was there, such as Miss Bates and Mrs Lloyd.

CS: The atmosphere is now very friendly and the staff help you quite a lot. You're encouraged to take part in activities. The teachers know you as a person and encourage you in lessons so much.

SS: I think the attitude of the younger teachers was changing when I was there. But I must say that when we left, we had a sixth form leaving party at Tito's (now Oceana), and Miss Lewis actually came and sat through a good part of an evening of blaring music!

ML: Miss Lewis knew what every student was good at, what was your special sport and so on. Of course the school was smaller then.

KEEPING IN TOUCH

ML: We made some great friends in school and in fact there are still two friends that I see every couple of weeks, which is nice.

SS: We've had a few reunions over the years, one at school. It was quite interesting as it was something like twenty-five years since we'd left. The perceptions of the day girls and boarders were very different. The day girls were quite positive about the school but a few of the boarders were coming back to lay ghosts to rest.

ML: We had a reunion a few years ago. There were people from Canada, New Zealand and America. It was fantastic!

SS: I can't see Claire losing touch with her friends. With modern technology it's so easy to keep in touch. We didn't have mobile phones and computers.

CS: Yes, I'm sure I'll keep in touch.

Top: Junior School girls enjoying Art, April 2008.
Above centre: Year 7 gymnastics team 2007-8.

Above: Junior girls practising marching, 2003, following the Welsh Guards.

'Reading the draft of this book, I realised for the first time what an amazing team of teachers there was in my day, women who gave their lives to Howell's and its pupils: Miss Disney, Miss Tickner, Miss Fowler, both Miss Taylors 'Bug' and 'Slug', Miss Harrison, Miss Phillips. Earlier Headmistresses had few means of networking with others in similar positions and it must have been quite a lonely post to hold – especially as they all lived in the school until Mrs. Fitz came. Joining the GPDST (as it then was) must have made a huge difference to the networking opportunities.

We thought we were doing pretty well in my day but it doesn't compare with some of the achievements and awards won in recent years. We competed with a small range of other schools, particularly in the traditional games of hockey and lacrosse, but otherwise there was not a lot of external contact. We didn't have the same degree of community involvement, nor were we as broadly educated. No Politics, DT, IT or Business Studies for us, no careers conventions or work experience. And I wish I could have had some of the great musical opportunities which the school's choirs have had in recent years. And all credit to the staff who have encouraged and supported students in entering (and winning) national public speaking, debating and sporting competitions and events. The list of places visited now stretches round the world, and is a great tribute to the recent and current Principals and their Deputies as well as the staff who in this day and age are willing to take parties of students on such trips.

Today's pupils and students must find it very hard to imagine life without computers (and the internet), iPods, social networking sites and all the gadgets of modern life. And they certainly will struggle to believe some of the reminiscences of former pupils, but it really was like that. The relationship between the staff and pupils and students has clearly changed radically for the better, and when I have been to events at school recently, I have been struck by how much fun it all seems to be compared with my days. But, if anything, looking at what happens at school now, it makes me even prouder than I was in 1954 that I can count myself as a Hywelian.'

A postscript by Sue Rayner, née Davies (1954-61). Written January 2010.

Far left: Howell's youngest pupil, March 2010: Daisy Burch, born 4th October 2006.
Left: The oldest known Hywelian, March 2010: Marguerite Desmond, née Milner, born 4th March 1910, pictured with her card from the Queen on her 100th birthday.

SELECTIVE BIBLIOGRAPHY

PRIMARY SOURCES

Admissions Registers

Cardiff Directory and Handbook, 1858

Censuses 1861, 1871, 1881, 1891, 1901

Court of Assistants' minutes, Drapers' Company Archives

Duncan and Ward's Cardiff Directory, 1863

George Woods' reports on his visits to school, 1865-89

Golden Ducat newsletters, 1992-2009

Governors' minutes, 1859-2009

Hywelian Guild Annual Reports and New Year's Letters 1910-22

Hywelian Guild magazines, 1923-2009

Hywelian Guild Minutes Books, 1906-75

Illustrated London News, 30th September 1961

Inspection reports

Kernick family history records

Ladies' Committee Book, 1861-3

Letter Books, 1859-1919

Letter from Annie Llewellyn, 1942

Letter from Annie Poole, 1941

Letter from Gertrude Harré, 1960

Letter from Gertrude Kathleen Robertson, 1960

Letter from Olwen Davies, née Jones, 1952

Letters in Drapers' Company Archives

Letters (various) written by Miss Kendall

Miss Baldwin's Book of Requests to the Governors, 1860-9

Miss Trotter's report to the Governors, 1923

Music reports, 1863

Prize-giving reports, 1978-91, *passim*

Prospectus of the Welsh School for Girls at Ashford, Middlesex, 1882

Rammell, T W, Report on Cardiff, HMSO, 1850

School magazines, 1924-2009

School prospectuses

Schools Inquiry Commission (Taunton Commission) report, 1870

South Wales Echo articles, various

Staff Registers

Surgeon's Journal and Medical Records, 1879-1960

Thomas Howell's will of 1536, translated from Spanish by Hare in *Reports on Charities under the Management of the Drapers Company*, PRO, Ed 27/6390

Thomas Howell's wills of 1520 and 1528, Drapers' Hall

Wakeford's Directory, 1863

Western Mail articles, various

Year Books, 1989-2005

SECONDARY SOURCES

Anon, *Howell's School Centenary booklet* (1960)

Avery, Gillian, *Best Type of Girl: History of Girls' Independent Schools* (André Deutsch and Co, 1971)

David, Lisbeth ed, *Llandaff 1860-1880, recollections of Ebenezer Moses and Clement Waldron*, (Llandaff Society Occasional Paper no. 4, 1989)

Dictionary of National Biography

Drapers' Company booklet

Evans, Leslie Wynne, *Voluntary Education in the Industrial Areas* (National Library of Wales journal 1966, winter volume XIV/4)

Evans, W Gareth, *Education and Female Emancipation, The Welsh Experience, 1847-1914* (Cardiff, University of Wales Press, 1990)

Evans, C J ed, *The Book of Cardiff* (OUP, 1937)

GPDST booklet, *A Guide to the GPDST* (1971)

Hilling, J B, *Llandaff Past and Present* (Stewart Williams, 1978)

Johns, C N, *The Castle and Manor of Llandaff* (Glamorgan History volume 10, Stewart Williams, 1974)

Johnson, Rev A H, *The History of the Most Worshipful Company of the Drapers of London*, vol II 1509-1603, and vol III 1603-1920 (Oxford, Clarendon Press, 1915 and 1924)

Jones, G E and Roderick, Gordon Wynne, *A History of Education in Wales* (University of Wales Press 2003)

Lowdon, John, *Notes* (1st October, 1923)

McCann, J E, *Thomas Howell and the School at Llandaff, 1860-1890* (D Brown and Sons Ltd, Cowbridge, 1972)

Morgan, Dennis, *The Cardiff Story* (D Brown and Sons Ltd, Cowbridge, 1991)

Tilney, Chrystal, *Llandaff 1871-82* (Glamorgan History volume 12, Stewart Williams, 1970s)

Welsh Dictionary of National Biography

SELECTIVE INDEX

... a ... for my ...
... parish ... for the ... of ... parish ...
... to Thomas ... an abushar
vyntler of London ...

... charlys ... as ...
to by ... A At the ...
... full fyldo / the ... of my
executors / ... do mak end of
... the will of me as within
all the man of london ... and
... of them / and more / ... ...
... v ... a ... to ... ...
... own margate ...
... dud / distance my ...
my last wyll ... full fyldo ...
all my ... to ... ...
... my ... Thomas